BODIES IN THE MIDDLE

MAYA HISLOP

BODIES
IN THE
MIDDLE

Black Women, Sexual Violence, and
Complex Imaginings of Justice

THE UNIVERSITY OF
SOUTH CAROLINA PRESS

© 2024 University of South Carolina

Published by the University of South Carolina Press
Columbia, South Carolina 29208

uscpress.com

Printed in the United States of America

Library of Congress Cataloging-in-Publication Data
can be found at https://lccn.loc.gov/2024005170

ISBN: 978-1-64336-488-9 (hardcover)
ISBN: 978-1-64336-489-6 (paperback)
ISBN: 978-1-64336-490-2 (ebook)

This book will be made open access within three years of publication thanks to
Path to Open, a program developed in partnership between JSTOR, the American
Council of Learned Societies (ACLS), University of Michigan Press, and The University
of North Carolina Press to bring about equitable access and impact for the entire
scholarly community, including authors, researchers, libraries, and university
presses around the world. Learn more at https://about.jstor.org/path-to-open/.

CONTENTS

LIST OF ILLUSTRATIONS

ACKNOWLEDGMENTS

This project began in the fall of 2012, the beginning of my second year of graduate study as a PhD student in the English department, University of Virginia. Up until then, I had not given my dissertation much thought. I knew that my project would center Black women in some way. That was as far as I had gotten. I will be forever grateful to the Commonwealth Professor of American Studies and History, Grace Hale, for teaching a life-changing course that term titled "The South Since 1900" and, specifically, for including historian Danielle McGuire's book, *At the Dark End of the Street: Black Women, Rape, and Resistance—a New History of the Civil Rights Movement from Rosa Parks to the Rise of Black Power*. Throughout my academic career as a student of English, the connection between rape and racism was a constant, but Black women were rarely at the center of the discourse, and if they were the issue began and ended with enslavement. McGuire's book was a revelation—not only did it center Black women in a critical rape-race discourse it also brought that conversation into the twentieth century. Most important to note, however, McGuire introduced (or reintroduced) me to key figures in the movements against rape and racism—Recy Taylor, Rosa Parks, Joan Little, Jerry Paul, Karen Galloway, as well as other figures not centered in my own book but key to my understanding of the historical scope of the work Black women have been doing concerning their own bodies. Thank you, Dr. Grace Hale, for guiding me through my initial thoughts on McGuire's work, serving as the outside reader on my dissertation committee, and believing in this project at a very early stage. Thank you, Danielle McGuire, for writing a history that is so desperately needed and has altered the course of my own life as a scholar.

Bodies is a development of my dissertation, which I would have never completed without the intellectual generosity and unbelievably supportive energy of my dissertation committee: Marlon B. Ross, Victoria Olwell, Lisa

Woolfork, and Anna Brickhouse. A very special thanks to the committee cochairs, Marlon B. Ross and Victoria Olwell. There are barely words to describe my enormous thanks to Marlon B. Ross, without whom I do not believe I would have completed my graduate studies. Your warm and spirited guidance as a teacher, scholar, and professional mentor has provided reference points throughout my career, and this book would not have been possible without you—a special thank you for introducing me to the work of Gayl Jones! A hearty and bombastic thank you to Victoria Olwell, the first professor to make me feel safe and smart at UVa and who was a huge supporter and guiderail for this project from inception to completion. Thank you, Lisa Woolfork, for your thoughtful chapter notes as well as your continued inspiration as a scholar, activist, and teacher. Thank you, Anna Brickhouse, for being one of the kindest and most patient persons in the profession I've ever met. There are countless other professors at the University of Virginia who shepherded this project to completion directly or indirectly, but I'd like to name them here: Deborah McDowell, Susan Fraiman, Jennifer Greeson, Claudrena Harold, Sylvia Chong, Njelle Hamilton, Clare Kinney, and Lisa Russ Spaar.

The institutional support that I received to complete the research necessary to bring this book to fruition was invaluable. Thank you to the University of Virginia Arts, Humanities and Social Sciences Summer Research Award; the UVa Buckner W. Clay Endowment for the Humanities; the UVa Graduate Fellowship from the Americas Center/Centro de las Américas; the UVa Society of Fellows; the UVa Power, Violence, and Inequality Initiative Fellow; the Clemson University Humanities Hub; and the Clemson Strategic University Challenge for Competitive Excellence and Expertise in Discovery and Scholarship (SUCCEEDS) Project Completion Grant. The last of these allowed me to afford to pay for the most compassionate and thorough developmental editor, Amy Brown. All these awards gave me the time and money I needed to travel to requisite archives as well as to get all of my writing done. A special thank you to all of the librarians and archivists who held my hand through their valuable collections, namely the Alabama Department of Archives & History; the Southern Historical Collection of the University of North Carolina Chapel Hill Wilson Library Special Collections; and Boston University's Howard Gotlieb Archival Research Center.

My final set of thanks goes to friends, artists, and family who provided an enormous amount of emotional and spiritual support that helped me to finish this book. Thank you to the best graduate school comrades I could ask for: Sophie Abramowitz, Alyssa Collins, Aaron Colton, Anastatia Curley, Shermaine Jones, Eva Latterner, and Esther Yu. Words cannot even begin to express how much I have learned from each-and-every one of you about what it means to form a community of friendship and love around our interests as writers, thinkers, and teachers. Thank you to my colleagues and friends at Clemson University who provided professional models and templates around which I was able to write this book with as little fear as possible: Erin Goss, Angela Naimou, Gabriel Hankins (thank you for introducing me to Amy!), Mike Lemahieu, Elizabeth Rivlin, David Coombs, Nic Brown, Jonathan Beecher Field, Walt Hunter, Jillian Weise, Aga Skrodzka, Emily Boyter, and Keri Crist-Wagner. I give a very special thank you to Rhondda Thomas for showing me, in your own astounding work as a scholar and community activist, what the academy makes possible. And I give an extra special thank you to Maziyar Faridi, Tareva Johnson, Clare Mullaney, and Jumah Taweh for always making me feel like I not only had something to say but also that it was absolutely worth saying.

I did not expect writing a book to be a happy experience, but much of the art, especially music, that I consumed altered my brain chemistry to make the experience far more ecstatic than it would have been otherwise. Thank you for blessing me with music to write, think, groove, and exist to: SZA, Rihanna, Taylor Swift, Phoebe Bridgers, Doja Cat, Olivia Rodrigo, Fiona Apple, James Blake, Childish Gambino, Dorothy Ashby, Toumani Diabate, Frank Ocean, Megan Thee Stallion, and Drake. Thank you for making art that inspired me: Mickalene Thomas, Kara Walker, Carrie Mae Weems, Kehinde Wiley, Nick Cave, Claudia Rankine, Gayl Jones, Raven Leilani, Brandon Taylor, Sally Rooney, Brit Bennett, Chimamanda Ngozi Adichie, Toni Morrison, Kathleen Collins, Ann Petry, Nella Larsen, Richard Wright, James Baldwin, Barry Jenkins, Jordan Peele, Dee Rees, Nia DaCosta, Ari Aster, Sydnee Washington, Marie Faustin, Dwayne Perkins, Larry Owens, Jerrod Carmichael, Jay Jurden, Pat Regan, Cat Cohen, Ramy Youssef, Leslie Jones, Joel Kim Booster, John Early, Kate Berlant, Sam Jay, Zack Fox, Hannibal Buress, Eric Andre, Neal Brennan, Moshe Kasher, Chelsea Peretti, Liza Treyger, Kara Klenk, Brian Safi, Erin Gibson, Langston Kerman, and David Gborie.

There is no *Bodies* without the spirits of the real-life women moving through this project. To Recy Taylor, Joan Little, and Nafissatou Diallo, I am in awe of you and will spend my life trying to match your courage, benevolence, and rage at injustice.

The only reason I have made it this far is because of my family—some of the most supportive people on the planet. Thank you for sharing with me the abundance and love that made this book possible, Francis Hislop, Julie May, Rasheed Hislop, and Gerald Palubniak. I love you all.

INTRODUCTION

Black Women Use–Resist Justice as a Weapon

On November 14, 2014, Sabrina Erdley published her now retracted and de-famatory story, "A Rape on Campus," in *Rolling Stone* on November 14, 2014. Erdley's article reported on the sexual assault of an anonymous University of Virginia (UVa) student named "Jackie" by a group of fraternity brothers at an on-campus party. The article's core message was that the university had grossly mishandled the reporting of the rape and that this was a systemic issue plaguing universities across the country. During this time, I was a graduate student at the university in question. Almost immediately after the publication of the *Rolling Stone* article, undergraduate students, mostly white women, faculty, and staff members began organizing protests, meet-ings, and teach-ins around campus; there was a palpable sense of anger in the air. I was one of these organizers. At the time, I remember being some-what shocked to see how quickly galvanized the UVa undergraduates could be. It was my third year at UVa, and no protests had taken place in my entire time of being there. In fact, I had heard that UVa students were relatively apathetic politically. Suddenly, the massive anti-rape protests were proving that stereotype wrong. Not only were students engaged, that engagement was effective. They had the attention of the president of the university at the time, Theresa Sullivan, who was taking meetings with student organiz-ers regularly. In fact, all kinds of institutional officials were compelled to make adjustments, however slight, to satisfy the demands of the protestors. I was astonished and proud to see the university community—some of them my own students and professors—so engaged and invested in holding the institution accountable. However, I was quickly reminded of some of the systemic reasons why the anti-rape protests had been so successful.

Only a week or so after the *Rolling Stone* article and the anti-rape pro-tests, another national (albeit less localized) event occurred. The decision came down from a Missouri grand jury not to indict Darren Wilson, the police officer responsible for the murder of Michael Brown, a young Black unarmed man whose body was left in the street for hours before paramedics were called. Black UVa students on campus led a small and silent protest, part of which went through two campus libraries carrying signs that spoke to their feelings of frustration and anguish at yet another failure of the justice system to protect and value Black life. The campus responses to these two national events were starkly different. Black protestors were met with an inordinately strong police presence for such a small protest, and the majority of students, particularly non-Black students, were completely disinterested in the plight of Black students as signified most heinously by the anonymous app Yik Yak. Previously used for social groups on college campuses to highlight their events or for students to gossip about the best food spots, Yik Yak was like Snapchat for text, allowing anyone to anonymously post anything. The app blew up after the Black Lives Matter (BLM) protest in defense of Mike Brown. Yik Yak users were spouting all kinds of racist rhetoric about the Black protestors, comparing them to farming equipment and animals. The responses that weren't explicitly racist were, perhaps, even more disturbing in their apathy and judgment. I distinctly remember one Yik Yak user commenting on the pointlessness of the protest and how it was distracting students from their studying. Furthermore, in contrast to the anti-rape protests, it took weeks, if not months, for anyone from the administration to agree to speak with Black organizers about the painful mistreatment that they received from other students and, ultimately, nothing was really done to make those Black students feel safer on campus.

The gap in reactions to these two protests aligned closely with historic trends. One of the protests was majority white-women-led and the other was mostly Black-led. On this particular predominantly white campus in the Mid-Atlantic Southeast, the distinction in the responses was informative, letting us all know whose pain mattered and what were viewed as "appropriate" ways to express that pain. The anti-rape and BLM protests that occurred on the campus of UVa in 2014 were perfect examples of the placelessness that Black women experience when confronted with the largely white women's movements and the largely Black-men-focused pro-Black movements. Given the centrality of the college campus in my own experiences with this placelessness, I began to think of ways that I may use a book project to address this in-betweenness that Black women experience, specifically when they are victims of sexual violence. How do Black women define justice for sexual violence? How do/how have Black women redefined justice for themselves?

Bodies in the Middle argues that Black women of the twentieth century depart from their predecessors by defining justice for sexual violence around failure, self-destruction, and the destruction of others. This project works both in collaboration with and as a departure from previous scholarship, which claims that Black women get justice from sexual violence solely through healing, community, and storytelling. Evidence of these positivist forms of justice work exist in our history, literature, and anti-oppression pedagogies. These have been the positive kinds of stories we are familiar with. But we have overlooked and left unheard the other ways Black women have been defining justice for themselves. When we closely examine specific moments in history, literature, and pedagogy, we see how Black women define justice for sexual violence around failure, self-destruction, and the destruction of others. *Bodies in the Middle* seeks to make a place out of no place for Black women who have developed harmful ways of coping with trauma. In keeping with the work of other Black Studies scholars, this book acknowledges the ways in which Black life functions amidst anti-Black oppression. That anti-Black oppression will be captured more specifically for the purposes of this project by the scholar Moya Bailey's term, "misogynoir," which combines "misogyny" with the French word *noir,* meaning Black, to refer to the specific kinds of discrimination and neglect that Black women and femmes experience.[1]

Though it was a contemporary moment of protest at my alma mater that partially spurred the idea for this project, it was my introduction to stories of the past that firmly grounded the beginning of *Bodies* in 1940s Alabama. Brilliant Black Studies scholars like Saidiya Hartman and Hortense Spillers have made vital and groundbreaking inroads into scholarship around race and (sexual) violence, largely explaining the psychological and affective registers of white supremacy through careful close readings of the archives of enslavement: the papers of enslavers, slave narratives, and the documents surrounding what few legal cases exist around the enslaved. In her foundational text, *Scenes of Subjection,* Hartman sets the template for my own work by insisting upon the law as a key text for underscoring and understanding not only the hateful violence of white supremacy but also the bizarre form of love that enslavers purported to feel toward their slaves. Spillers's essential essay "Mama's Baby, Papa's Maybe" inspired me to consider what story the violated bodies of enslaved women tell even when they themselves are not given an opportunity to speak. However, their work and much of the work that places Black women at the center of critical rape and critical race studies stages that inquiry in the period of enslavement.

Bodies in the Middle recognizes the necessity of early American studies but pushes the research around rape and race forward into the twentieth and twenty-first centuries. From a Black Studies perspective, it is understood that enslaved women had little to no legal recourse and were therefore subject to the will of their enslavers, particularly regarding sexual violence. There is a sense from the slave narratives of Frederick Douglass and Harriet Jacobs that not only was the institution of enslavement a vehicle for profiting off of the sexual denigration and degradation of enslaved women, but also that the inability for enslaved women (or any enslaved people) to "get justice" for the heinous crimes committed on their bodies acted as a double violence. The first violation upon enslaved women was a physical one and the second violation was a psychological one that was completely determined by the United States legal system—thus this study's focus on law as well as literature. This double violation of enslaved women has left most scholars—like Hartman and Spillers—with the sense that when Black women are at the center of rape–race discourse, they are completely abject not only in their brutalization but also in their voicelessness. However, the notion of Black women as totally abject shifts radically in the mid-twentieth century.[2]

In her book *At the Dark End of the Street: Black Women, Rape, and Resistance–a New History of the Civil Rights Movement from Rosa Parks to the Rise of Black Power,* historian Danielle McGuire details the stories of several Black women from the 1940s to the 1970s. The most central figures in McGuire's book are Recy Taylor and Joan Little as each of their cases are such pivotal illustrations of the time and place in which they occurred. Both Taylor and Little were raped or sexually assaulted in the South in the mid- to mid-late twentieth century, and both sought justice for these violations from the legal system. When I encountered the stories of Recy Taylor and Joan Little, they were brand new historical figures to me. It was astonishing. I could not believe that I had never heard the stories of these women before, though, as McGuire argues, it makes sense that stories of violated Black women did not enter our mainstream understanding of the civil rights movement because of the movement's need to sanitize itself, especially with regards to sex. In fact, as Evelyn Brooks Higginbotham details, many Black rights struggles have felt the need to desexualize themselves or repress sexuality in order to appeal to white, middle class, Christian mores.[3] The relative suppression of the stories of Recy Taylor and Joan Little showcases the misogyny of the civil rights movement, but their stories themselves also defy the myth that Black women who experience sexual violence have and always will suffer in silence and utter abjection. The cases of Taylor and Little establish the need to make a distinction between the period of enslavement and the twentieth century when we are talking about Black women, sexual violence, and justice precisely because of the central role that the justice system suddenly begins to play in that discourse.

Given the pivotal role that Taylor and Little play, their cases sit at the center of *Bodies in the Middle,* and honoring their legacies is a key objective for the book. Aside from these key historical figures, the ideological basis for the argument that Black women of the twentieth century define justice for sexual violence around failure, self-destruction, and destruction of others is rooted in the three central pieces of African American literature in the book.

Literature plays a vital role in the civil rights movement and its aftermath (in which we are still living, as evinced by the Black Lives Matter Movement). Nonfictional literary works like Malcolm X's *Autobiography* and Martin Luther King Jr.'s "Letter from Birmingham Jail" established the ways in which writing and the struggle for Black rights are intimately intertwined, and fictional works are equally important. African American literature is key to understanding a Black past as it actually occurred, but also a Black past, present, and future that circulates the possibilities that exist within and beyond fact. Lorraine Hansberry's *A Raisin in the Sun*, Langston Hughes's "A Dream Deferred," Ann Petry's *The Street*, Gwendolyn Brooks's "A Bronzeville Mother," Audre Lorde's "Afterimages," and Toni Morrison's *Beloved* are just a few of the works in which Black writers have taken a directive from the Black rights struggle to uplift the stories of Black life as it was lived either in their own moment or in an imagined past.

The literature at the center of *Bodies in the Middle* is *Native Son* by Richard Wright, *Corregidora* by Gayl Jones, and *Americanah* by Chimamanda Ngozi Adichie. There are satellite texts circulating this book, which are *The Street* by Ann Petry, *The Color Purple* by Alice Walker, and *Beloved* by Toni Morrison. The selection of Wright, Jones, and Adichie was primarily due to an underlying common denominator: each of them shows some level of investment in a system—be it the US legal system, the general idea of criminal justice systems outside national bounds, or the US immigration system. *Bodies in the Middle* answers the questions: How do Black writers of the twentieth and twenty-first centuries, through their depictions of various kinds of legal systems, enter the discourse of rape and race with Black women at the center? What roles do these Black writers, who show such systemic investment or divestment, believe that these systems play in the lives of the Black female characters who have been sexually assaulted? How do these systems help or hurt the ways in which these Black female characters define justice for the sexual violence that they've experienced? Because the literature at the center of *Bodies* is more systems-focused, the outlook and tone of each text tends to exist on a spectrum between hope and hopelessness. My close readings of the literature works in conjunction with close readings of the legal case materials of Recy Taylor, Joan Little, and Nafissatou Diallo to showcase the ways in which both the real-life Black women, the fictional Black women, as well as their allies/defenders formulate a new kind of justice that has not yet been explored in Black studies: "Afro-pessimistic justice."

Afro-pessimism existed long before it had a name. The work of Black Studies luminaries like Orlando Patterson, Sylvia Wynter, and Fred Moten are works of Afro-pessimism even though they are not labeled as such. Revolutionary scholar and activist Frank B. Wilderson coined the term in his autobiographical book *Icognegro*, which details his experiences as an American activist in apartheid South Africa; but it is only recently that scholars have taken their own work in the direction of Afro-pessimism (again, with or without that explicit label) with such varieties of faces that the ideological basis for the realm of study is somewhat unclear. Some scholars define "Afro-pessimism" as the cultural representation of Africa as a single country in which only corruption, neglect, and poverty thrive (Evans and Glenn). Other scholars think of Afro-pessimism as a way of framing a post-civil rights era in US history. Rather than remain stuck in the ideology that rights are equivalent to freedom or liberation, scholars of Afro-pessimism consider what kinds of alternatives to "rights" exist, and what possibilities are open to Black folks and people of other marginalized groups.

For Wilderson, Afro-pessimism is a much more strictly defined ideology that is not only theoretical, but also a practical way to move through the world. Afro-pessimism asks theoreticians and practitioners to acknowledge that Black life in American society was, is, and always will be constrained by the enslaver–enslaved dynamic. Following Wilderson, enslavement is a condition that Black people cannot escape so long as they are in the United States and white people cannot escape their status as enforcers of white supremacy and anti-Black violence. It is also key to Wilderson's formulation that Black people are the only people who suffer this particular constraint and that the violation impressed upon Black people is significantly distinct from the ways in which non-Black and non-white marginalized people are oppressed in the United States. While there is value in all of the schools of thought circulating the hub of Afro-pessimism, I use a much broader definition that allows for both Wilderson and others to co-exist.

The definition of Afro-pessimism that I use throughout *Bodies in the Middle* is conjured by a passage from Jared Sexton's 2016 introduction to an issue of *Rhizomes: Cultural Studies in Emerging Knowledge,* where the writer states: "It is suggested that one can see readily the need to foreground Black rage, but we must ask after the nature of an equally pressing emphasis on Black hope. What would one hope for in a scenario where one's murder is required for others' peace of mind?" I interpret this as opening up the possibility of thinking of Afro-pessimism not necessarily as a dialectical battle in which anti-Blackness is inescapable and locked into our hearts and minds forever (though this is also true), but also a space in which we are suspicious of hope rather than accepting it wholeheartedly as the default. I also think that scholars like Claudrena Harold, Brittany Cooper, and others are right to bring up the much more complex rhetoric around Black hope and love that Martin Luther King Jr. and others espoused. Afro-pessimism is key to the journey that *Bodies in the Middle* brings us all on. I use Afro-pessimism to examine each of the stories because each story at the center of *Bodies* puts a dubious eye on hope. It is nothing new to see Black women who experience sexual violence as dubious of hope, but it is new to center the stories of those who have been hopeless and yet still attempt to use the justice system or a justice structure. To not only contribute to the field of Afro-pessimism, but also to portray the common thread between all of the stories I'm examining in *Bodies,* I've come up with the term "Afro-pessimistic justice." Afro-pessimistic justice encompasses the host of strategies that the Black women at the center of *Bodies* use to access some kind of healing and/or to punish the perpetrators of sexual crimes against them.

I have used the word "justice" many times throughout this introduction so far, and I want to clarify this layered and confusing term. When I discuss "justice," I am, on the one hand, referencing the most general and traditional view of legal justice in the context of criminal law: the punishment of a perpetrator for the crime against a victim. However, "justice" also refers to a much more expansive and liberatory set of things that, as many scholars and revolutionaries have elucidated over the decades, lies outside of the US legal system in community organizing, political activism, and abolitionist work.[4] *Bodies* sits in a complex and uncomfortable position as I want to both honor the Black women who have sought justice from the US legal system and also acknowledge that this system continuously fails them and that abolishing this and other oppressive systems built on anti-Black violence is the only way to true liberation for all oppressed people. The Black women at the center of this book exist along a spectrum of justice work, some of which are situated on the more conservative side of a rights-based Black struggle in which the machine of the US legal system is at the center and others exist so far outside of the legal system that they must create their own justice systems to heal the wounds of the violent trauma that their assailants have inflicted. At the same time, what draws all of these stories together is that they exhibit Afro-pessimistic justice tendencies, a set of strategies toward healing from sexual violation that circulate around failure, self-destruction, and the destruction of others. Each part of the book is geared toward illuminating this set of strategies. Part 1 focuses on historical cases in which Black women have sought justice from the law; part 2 focuses on key texts of African American literature that point to the specifics of Afro-pessimistic justice.

Chapter 1, "Justice in the Abstract: The (Un)intelligibility of Sexual Violence Against Black Women in the Case of Recy Taylor," offers an overview and analysis of the case of Recy Taylor. Taylor was a 26-year-old Black woman who was gang raped by six white men, ranging in ages from 16 to 21, in Abbeville, Alabama, in 1944. The men were never indicted for their crimes, but a massive national movement, in both the North and South, led by Rosa Parks, the NAACP, and white allies in labor movements, rallied to defend Taylor at a time when Black women were often invisible as victims of all kinds of assault, but especially sexual assault. This chapter points to Taylor's case as forming the building block of Afro-pessimistic justice, which requires failure to function. I argue here that without the failure to indict, Taylor's case becomes unintelligible.

In chapter 2, "Manipulating Bodies: Versions of Justice in *State of North Carolina v. Little*," another facet of Afro-pessimistic justice emerges: a triumphant form steeped in doom and the inescapable cycle of incarceration for poor, Black women living in the rural South. Little, a young Black incarcerated woman in Beaufort County, North Carolina, is assaulted by her white jail guard. She kills her rapist in self-defense and, after a year of massive protests and fundraising, she is acquitted of the murder charge. The historic and joyous triumph of Little's acquittal is, however, overshadowed by her continued presence in the carceral system. Though her murder charge was dropped, Little still had to return to jail to finish the rest of her sentence for the initial larceny charge, and she continued to go in and out of jail for much of her life. Despite their relative triumphs, both Taylor and Little's cases capture the core of Afro-pessimism as defined by Frank B. Wilderson, which is that there are no safe or effective forms of liberation for the Black body in America. Neither the progressive movement to defend Joan Little nor the supposed justice system truly works to liberate her; rather, the system works to defend itself. These cases confirm that the US justice system only protects the Black femme body insofar as it is convenient for the white supremacist system to continue to function. However, the abjection of Black women and their bodies is not total: not only because Taylor and Little believe that the justice system may offer them actual justice, but also because of the millions of people of all races and genders around the world who stand up to defend the right of Black women to equal protection under the law.

The absence of a totalizing victory for Little follows us as we arrive at the final case examined in chapter 3, *State of New York v. Dominique Strauss-Kahn*. In May 2011, Dominique Strauss-Kahn, the French former director of the International Monetary Fund (IMF) assaults his maid, Nafissatou Diallo, in an upscale New York City hotel. Diallo does everything "right." She reports it immediately, gets a rape kit, and does not have a criminal record. She is what Lisa Lowe and Mae Ngai might call a "good immigrant" and what sociologist Nils Christie would call an "ideal victim."[5] Diallo's fatal flaw, however, is that she is a Guinean refugee who, on her asylum application, lied about a previous rape in her home country. This lie leads to the dismissal of the state's criminal case against Strauss-Kahn, but Diallo's civil case settles, allowing her to receive financial compensation for damages. This twenty-first century case illustrates another way in which failure is central to Black femme forms of justice. In some ways, Diallo's defense team knew that a criminal case would be difficult to prosecute and, in fact, the dismissal of the case gave them fire to blame the District Attorney for systemic inadequacy, which lead to a kind of triumph through the civil courts. Diallo also shows the ways in which consent-based definitions of sexual assault or rape make power-based forms of sexual abuse impossible to criminally prosecute. All three of the historic cases in part 1 mark justice as apparently "real" in the sense that the court system exists, juries exist, and prosecutors exist to either right historical wrongs or not. But, time and again, these systems prove to be hypothetical for Black women, incapable of functioning in any way that provides traditional or transformative forms of justice. And yet these women yield to the machinations of these systems anyway, because what choice do they have? The depressing resignation to opt into the criminal justice system as a Black rape victim is one of the starting points that the stories of Taylor, Little, and Diallo offer.

The literary cases, to which this study turns in part 2, display some wildly different and some markedly similar versions of justice, but the literature accomplishes what the cases cannot: imagining a justice system or a set of systems that does not yet exist. In part 2, chapter 4 ("Bessie's Song"), the Black female victim of rape, Bessie, in Wright's *Native Son,* speaks to abjection, one of the many sides of Afro-pessimistic justice. This is the side that cites all justice for Black women as impossible, foreclosed, and nonexistent. Yet Wright makes Bessie's mutilation legible for the reader, presenting Bessie as a participant in her own public rape while also removing her completely from the narrative. In this way, *Native Son* becomes a corollary for the Recy Taylor case. Once again, Afro-pessimistic justice is depicted through the revelation that no liberation exists for the Black body. In fact something less than liberation exists for the Black woman's raped body: unintelligibility. *Native Son* plays a slightly different role in this book. Rather than offer a vision for justice for Black women that lies outside of reality, the novel communicates the brutalist vision for what is possible in 1940 for a poor, raped Black woman with no family and no defenders. Bessie's song prepares us for the superreality (that is also deeply historical) that Gayl Jones draws for us, thirty-five years later, in her novel, *Corregidora.*

Chapter 5, "Ursa's Song," considers the ways in which justice systems created by the Corregidora women of Jones's *Corregidora*—a justice system by Black women for Black women—can still perpetuate toxic forms of abuse and violence. The novel centers on Ursa Corregidora, a blues singer in 1940s Kentucky, the descendent of a grandmother and great grandmother who were born enslaved in Brazil and coerced into sex work by their forefather and enslaver, Old Man Corregidora. The Corregidora women use their own bodies and voices to build a justice system that circulates around failure, self-destruction, and the destruction of others. In chapter 6, "Ifemelu's Song," I turn to Adichie's novel *Americanah,* whose protagonist, Ifemelu, a Nigerian immigrant living in 1990s America, experiences a form of assault that cannot be named when she "chooses" to perform a sexual favor for money at a desperate financial time in her life. What happens afterward is nothing. Adichie's Ifemelu exemplifies the boredom, restlessness, depression, and self-loathing of the Black femme immigrant rape victim who has absolutely no interest in formal systems of justice. Out of this "nothing," this lull, this quiet, Ifemelu creates a new digital world, a blog, in which her rape is both invisible and hypervisible. The stories of Black women turning to justice systems or creating their own in parts 1 and 2 are vital, but they form an incomplete picture of the ways in which Black women define justice for themselves. The conclusion of *Bodies* considers abolition as a perfect frame for understanding what the future of justice is through the lens of Afro-pessimism.

Part 1

A HISTORY

Chapter 1

JUSTICE IN THE ABSTRACT

The (Un)intelligibility of Sexual Violence against Black Women in the Case of Recy Taylor

It is the evening of January 7, 2018. The 75th Annual Golden Globes ceremony is in full swing, and Oprah Winfrey is on stage to accept the Cecil B. DeMille Award for outstanding contributions to the world of entertainment. She gives an invigorating speech about diversity, representation, and equity in the industry. But the bulk of Winfrey's speech, and the parts which went viral on social media the following day, was the part she devoted to the #MeToo and #TimesUp movements. The #MeToo movement is a broad online conversation about sexual violence, while #TimesUp is a specific movement around the issues of sexual assault in the workplace, particularly the film industry of Hollywood.[1] Rather than speak narrowly about these contemporary movements, Winfrey established how far-reaching the problem of sexual violence is not only historically, but also geographically. Most significant is that the story that Winfrey used to express the gravity of this point was the story of Recy Taylor. After triumphantly expressing gratitude to the long list of women in occupations and fields of labor—from domestic workers to academics—who have come forward, Winfrey introduces the world to Recy Taylor:

> And there's someone else. Recy Taylor. A name I know and I think you should know too. In 1944 Recy Taylor was a young wife and a mother. She was just walking home from church service when she was abducted by six, armed white men, raped and left blindfolded by the side of the road coming home from church. They threatened to kill her if she ever told anyone. But her story was reported to the NAACP where a young worker by the name of Rosa Parks [applause] became the lead investigator on her case and together they sought justice. But justice wasn't an option in the

era of Jim Crow. The men who tried to destroy her were never persecuted [*sic*].[2] Recy Taylor died 10 days ago, just shy of her 98th birthday. She lived as we all have lived, too many years in a culture broken by brutally powerful men. For too long, women have not been heard or believed if they dared to speak their truth to the power of those men. But their time is up. Their time is UP! [applause] (Winfrey, 00:05:19-00:06:55)

As this excerpt demonstrates, Winfrey tells Taylor's story in graphic detail. But it is vital to note that Winfrey never mentions that Taylor was a Black woman. Instead, Winfrey allows the majority white and wealthy audience in the room to infer Taylor's racial identity: they are given clues like the whiteness of the assailants, the intervention of Rosa Parks, the NAACP, and the historical context of the Jim Crow South. She relies on the audience knowing, without being told, that Black women are the ones who suffer such deprivation of rights in US history. It almost seems unnecessary to mention Taylor's Blackness given this historical truth. Nevertheless, it is the explicit omission of Taylor's Blackness that allows for Winfrey to further abstract her in the latter half of the quote: "She lived, as we all have lived, too many years in a culture broken by brutally powerful men." By omitting any mention of Taylor's Blackness and thus inviting Taylor into a royal "we," Winfrey transforms Taylor from one who is particularly embodied into a disembodied symbol at the center of a neat, universal story about sexual violence.

In beginning this chapter with her Cecil B. DeMille acceptance speech, I do not mean to overemphasize the significance of either Oprah Winfrey or her speech; clearly an awards show speech is not exactly the appropriate format for nuanced and complex discourse. Yet this speech is a useful and contemporary container for some of the most vital aspects of Taylor's case, as well as of this chapter: abstraction and intelligibility. Winfrey, in fact, uses Taylor and her story in much the same way that Taylor's committee of defenders used her. In the first part of this chapter, I show the layered and complex nature of the discourse around Taylor's defense through an analysis of select documents from the Alabama Department of Archives and History. Integral to following the logic of this chapter is some engagement with this term "abstraction" and my usage of it.

When I use the word "abstract" as a verb, I am contributing to volumes of scholarship concerning Black erasure, the dangers of whiteness as a universal default, and the notion of abstraction as a form of cultural smudging a la Orlando Patterson, Fred Moten, and Marlon B. Ross.[3] In the context of

Taylor's case, as well as other stories in this book, to be abstracted specifically refers to being abstracted from aspects of one's embodiment, be that
raced, gendered, or sexually traumatized. In this chapter I argue that Taylor's
case is instructive, helping us to see that the role of the law is not only one of
the villain who coerces Black women into abjection, into a space of neglect
where their sexual violations are never made intelligible to the state nor to
its inhabitants.[4] As mentioned in the introduction, however, this is not a
legal analysis of the Taylor case, but rather an historical analysis of the case
and the movement to defend a Black female victim of rape. This analysis will
set the stage for the Afro-pessimistic justice that Black women who have
experienced sexual violence create for themselves in the literary works I will
unpack in part 2. Using the work of Frank B. Wilderson, Jared Sexton, Toni
Morrison, and Suzan Lori Parks, I discover an Afro-pessimistic analysis of
the case under consideration. From this perspective, the law is not always a
branch of naked oppression; in fact, the law can both combat the abstraction
of Black women at the very same time that it weaponizes that abstraction to
maintain the unintelligibility of those women. In order to engage with the
complex layers of critical rape studies and critical race studies that are at
play in the case of Recy Taylor, we must first understand exactly what happened to her.

On September 3, 1944, in Abbeville, Alabama, Recy Taylor, 24, was walking home from church with her friend, Fannie Daniel and Daniel's teenage
son West. Suddenly, a group of seven young white men pulled up in a car;
a few of them emerged. One had a rifle trained on the three Black people.
These young white men were Hugo Wilson, 16; US Army Private Herbert
Lovett, 18; Dillard York, 17; Billy Howerton, 14; Luther Lee, 17; Joe Culpep-
per, 15; and Robert Gamble Jr., 17.[5] One of the men threatened Taylor, warning her that she was accused of stabbing a young white boy in a neighboring
town and that if she did not go with them (presumably to be taken into the
custody of the Sheriff) they would have no choice but to hurt her. Once in
the car, they continued to taunt and threaten Taylor, driving her deep into
the woods a few miles from Abbeville, then raping her one by one. The rapists then drove Taylor a few miles away and threw her out of the car. Left
totally alone and violated in the middle of nowhere at night, Taylor thought
she had been left for dead.

Taylor wandered around, her clothing torn and soiled, until she found a
general store, Four Corners, where she was able to get the store owner to call
Sheriff Gamble. Her brother and father had already been alerted by Fannie

Figure 1. This portrait photo of Recy Taylor; her daughter, Jayce Lee Taylor;
and her husband, Willie Guy Taylor appeared in the *Chicago Defender* sometime
after the first grand jury convening and case dismissal on October 9, 1944. The
article by Fred Atwater recounts the horrific crime and the local mishandling of
the case. The photo caption in the newspaper claims this to be the first published
photo of Recy, demonstrating the danger she felt in revealing herself too publicly
due to the death threats she was receiving for reporting the rape. The photo has
been cropped with approval of the Alabama Department of Archives and History.

and West Daniel, so they were driving around and doing their own patrolling
to see if they could find her. Eventually they arrived at the same Four Corners to get Taylor and bring her back home. For the next few days, Taylor's
father called Sheriff Gamble, attempting to get the rapists apprehended. Only
one of the rapists was ever apprehended, and even then was probably in custody for only a few hours before having his low bail paid and released. None
of the white men who raped Taylor was ever charged with any crime.

Thanks to pressure that Rosa Parks and the NAACP put on state and
county officials, a grand jury was held on October 3, a full month after the
crime was committed, but the all-white, all-male jury chose not to indict.
Months later, as a result of a national movement to defend Taylor and all

Black women from being raped with impunity, Governor Chauncey Sparks of Alabama assigned state officials to conduct a reinvestigation of the case, which managed to get the grand jury to reconvene. Danielle L. McGuire rightly points out that this second meeting of the grand jury was a huge triumph in its own right, signaling that there was a global audience of mostly liberal white women, industrial labor union leaders, and Black churches with enough social and financial capital to prompt even a Deep South government to action. However, upon meeting for a second time, the grand jury failed to indict again. Throughout all of this, Taylor received death threats. An attempt to set fire to her house prompted her to move with her husband and child to Florida.

Six decades later, in 2011, the Alabama Senate joined the House in passing Resolution 194 that expressed "deepest sympathy and solemn regrets" to Taylor for the cover-up of the crime, a cover-up which was committed by local and state officials (Resolution 194, 2). The case of Taylor is a story of an injustice so enormous that it warranted a statewide apology. But this statewide apology obscures the full picture of what occurred. As the summary above demonstrates, Taylor's individual story in fact contains many complex stories. Her story is that of a Black female rape victim, a story of rape survival; a story of the modern expansion of the civil rights movement; a story of the failure of a justice movement; a story of World War II; a story of conservative views of democracy and of the legal justice system and of liberal feminism and of the politics of respectability. The stories contained in this single case are nearly too numerous to list.

It is not within the purview of this project to address each of these narratives. My project engages with the problem that Black women who are sexually violated pose to the very legal systems from which they are trying to get justice. Due to a long history of sexual violence under slavery, as well as the stereotypes about Black female sexuality that haunted Black women throughout the postbellum period, literary scholars and historians such as bell hooks, Crystal N. Feimster, Darlene Clark Hine, and Saidiya Hartman often argue that Black women lack access to justice for sexual crimes committed against them. Taylor's case proves that this argument about access is incomplete. True, Taylor did not receive justice. But we cannot pretend that she utterly lacked access to justice either. Taylor was the first Black woman whose report of her rape sparks a national movement called the Committee for Equal Justice for Mrs. Recy Taylor. Our story begins in 1944. Although her case receives widespread attention, it fails to bring Taylor any justice in the traditional sense. As mentioned in the introduction, traditional justice is when those accused and convicted of a crime are told that they must pay for that crime through prison time or by incurring other kinds of damages to the self.

The primary concern of this chapter is, how is the raped Black female body made intelligible as having had a crime committed against her? I define "intelligible" as a state of being that satisfies a few requirements: (a) the state and the public recognize that the Black woman has been sexually violated; (b) the state and the public act in defense of the Black female victim either to compensate her, punish her assailants, or both; and (c) the state and the public explicitly assert all of the victim's identities when declaring her right to be defended from harm. Intelligibility is distinct from legibility. For a person to be legible either socially or by an official body (one which has the power to determine who has or does not have access to rights—what I am broadly calling the state), the public and the state can satisfy only one of the requirements of intelligibility—acknowledging the victim's race or gender— but not both at once. In other words, a Black woman who has experienced sexual violence can either be made to feel that parts of her identity grant her the right to being defended on paper (legible) or that she has a right to all parts of her identity being embraced and understood as those that make her defendable as the victim of a crime.[6]

Kimberlé Crenshaw's concept of intersectionality, outlined in her groundbreaking work of critical race theory, "Mapping the Margins," under-girds the distinction I'm trying to draw between Taylor as legible or intel-ligible to the state and public. Intersectionality is an analytical frame meant to uncover modes of power used to oppress Black women in particular. Crenshaw points out the ways in which the US legal system framed dis-crimination as a single-identity issue: a Black woman could either claim, in an employment discrimination case, for example, that she was being racially discriminated against or sexually discriminated against, but not both. The discourse around Taylor's case proves Crenshaw's point: in 1940s Alabama there is little or no space in which Black women can simultaneously be fully embodied and understood as victims of crimes (be it of employment discrimination or sexual violence). In this chapter I use close readings of material from the Recy Taylor Committee archives to demonstrate the ways in which both Taylor's liberal (mostly white) defenders and her white su-premacist violators (grand jury, assailants, Alabama officials) refuse to see her Blackness and her womanness as aligning with the status of victim of a sexual crime.

I want the reader to understand that in the story of Black women and sexual violence, the law is not always the villain while the activist is the rescuer. And vice versa. The law does not always function to objectify and exclude Black women. In the realm of humanities scholarship that centers Black women, it is not difficult to observe a divide between research that illuminates an area of Black life that is much more full of liberation or resistance than previously thought and scholarship that articulates the devastation or horror of living in the Black body. I refer to this as a divide between recovery work and acknowledgment work.[7]

Recovery work about Black women often involves special attention to recovering or reframing racist stereotypes of Black womanhood that were popularized as fact in the nineteenth century, such as notions of Black women as so hypersexual that they were always consenting to sex and therefore unrapeable. Scholar Evelyn Brooks Higginbotham counters white supremacist myths around Black female sexuality, drawing attention to the extreme emphasis on modesty in certain nineteenth-century Black women's clubs, social groups, and church groups. Black women, especially of certain classes, were perpetually working to defy the eugenicist notions that their race was inherently linked to a lack of control over bodily desire. Farrah Jasmin Griffin points to these white supremacist ideas around Black female sexuality when she quotes the very real, very racist words of some of the nation's most esteemed figures, including Thomas Jefferson and Benjamin Franklin. Griffin's quotation of Frederick Law Olmstead is perhaps the most distinctly and succinctly disgusting, capturing the mundanity of misogynoir in the nineteenth century: "[The slave women were] clumsy, awkward, gross, elephantine in all their movements, pouting, grinning, and leering at us; sly, sensual, and shameless in all their expressions and demeanor; I never before had witnessed anything more revolting than the whole scene" (519). Such nineteenth-century misogynoirist notions continue to leave their traces, not only in the ways people treat Black women and Black girls, but also on a number of systems, such as education, employment, and legal. The 1970s Black feminist group the Combahee River Collective is one of many examples that makes a case for the perpetuation of the hypersexual sapphire trope in the twentieth century. Taylor's case is yet another example of how this trope continued in the white imaginary and had devastating consequences for Black women. McGuire is certainly in the recovery work camp: she attempts to claim that the liberal activism around Taylor's case is evidence that although misogynoir certainly persisted, even in 1944 there was resistance to such thinking among a politically active and, for the most part, staunchly Democratic segment of the population.

In her 2010 book, *At the Dark End of the Street: Black Women, Rape, and Resistance—a New History of the Civil Rights Movement from Rosa Parks to the Rise of Black Power*, McGuire situates a number of rape cases in which Black women were victimized at the center of a civil rights discourse. She opens her book with the story of Taylor, whose rape case had gone unrecognized since it occurred in 1944. Though Taylor passed away on December 29, 2017, she and her brother spoke with McGuire several times before her death. These exchanges are the crucial strengths of the book, which was the basis for Nancy Buirski's 2018 documentary, *The Rape of Recy Taylor*. Buirski's documentary, which heavily features interviews with McGuire, reveals that it was McGuire's work that motivated Taylor's brother, Robert Corbett—eight years old at the time of the rape—to bring the case to the Alabama Senate when he was in his sixties. Corbett fought hard to have his sister's violation be acknowledged as a crime for which there should be compensation, either through punishment of the assailants or financial compensation, for the damages that Taylor and her family incurred.

Thanks to McGuire's book and the state of Alabama's public apology to Taylor in 2011, her case gained more widespread attention from news and online media outlets. That same year, Taylor spoke with Cynthia Gordy of *The Root*, an online Black news outlet. In an interview with Gordy, Taylor mentioned her support of Robert's actions, saying, "It was a long time ago. But I still think something should have been done about it." Her words are vague. What could she mean by "something"? This vagueness encapsulates the disregard with which society treated the rape of a Black woman in 1944. It makes sense that Taylor could not articulate precisely what "should have been done" because she had no "thing" to refer to. There is only "something." "Something should have been done" implies that nothing was done, that no action was taken. McGuire, however, in keeping with the tone of recovery work, would say that something was indeed done in the form of a national network of activists publicly standing up to defend Taylor and acknowledge her as a Black female victim of a sexual crime (figure 2). Despite the ultimate failure of a very public year-long campaign, the Committee for Equal Justice for Mrs. Recy Taylor (which I will refer to as the Committee throughout this

Figure 2. The illustrated cover of one of several pamphlets produced by the Committee for Equal Justice for Mrs. Recy Taylor (CEJMRT) visually showcases her abstraction.

chapter) set an important precedent for anti-rape and anti-racist activism that eventually spread around the country.

Taylor is right to say what she says in her interview with *The Root*. Ultimately, she received no justice. Taylor's words echo loudly in this chapter because they prove the unintelligibility of the raped Black female, even today. It seems that nothing can be done for the woman who society has deemed unrapeable and constantly sexually available. But it is not so simple. The actions and rhetoric of the Committee confuse the tautology of the Black female as totally unintelligible. After all, the Committee's year-long campaign attempted, very earnestly and sincerely, to make Taylor's rape intelligible. Even if they were unsuccessful, their attempt is proof of a change in cultural attitudes toward Black women which deserves specific attention.[8] Her case is essential to our understanding of the raped Black woman not simply because it documents the dismissal of bodily suffering (there are likely many stories of this nature), but also because Taylor's rape was made *temporarily legible*—not intelligible, as I will explain—through the more than year-long campaign by the Committee for the Equal Justice for Mrs. Recy Taylor.

The Committee for Equal Justice for
Mrs. Recy Taylor and Legible vs. Intelligible

Upon going through "The Case of Recy Taylor" files in the Alabama Department of Archives and History, I found hundreds of letters, postcards, telegrams, and petitions to Governor Chauncey Sparks asking him to bring justice for the young Negro woman in Abbeville, Alabama (Alabama Governor (1943–47: Sparks). In this section, I'll look closely at a few of these artifacts to reveal the ways in which both sides, the white supremacist legal system and the liberal white defenders of equality, are unable to make Taylor intelligible as the Black female victim of a crime. It is crucial to understand the several strategies-in-common that Committee leaders and concerned individual citizens used to make Taylor intelligible to Governor Sparks and the anti-Black state that he represented.

However, before delving into these strategies, I want to explain an important detail. The Committee makes Governor Sparks the target of all of their efforts. And this makes sense. It is within Governor Sparks's power to investigate the Taylor case and force another grand jury to convene in an attempt to indict. But it is worth noting that Governor Sparks's powers are limited.[9] He did, in fact, appoint officials to investigate the case and got another grand jury to convene in Abbeville. But once he did so, it was up to the individuals on that jury to indict Taylor's rapists. That the Committee chose to focus their criticism on state powers is one indication that the organization was not expecting systemic change—reform of the jury selection processes, consideration of race and gender as aspects of what make for a "fair" jury—but rather sought to use the case to point to broader systemic inequalities. Instead of aiming to fix the issues that were specific to Taylor's case, the Committee, the NAACP, and Rosa Parks saw her case as an opportunity to make public certain systemic injustices, such as the threats being posed to the equal rights protections in the constitution: this is the difference between "making legible" and "making intelligible." The Committee were able to make Taylor's rape legible to a wider public audience, meaning that they were able to convince those living and working outside of the Committee (even the Governor, Attorney Generals and other state officials) that a crime was committed against Taylor.[10] To make Taylor "intelligible" requires that not only is the crime made evident as a crime against a Black woman, but also that there is some level of action against the rapists.[11] At the same time that I want to commend the Committee for their efforts, it is essential to see

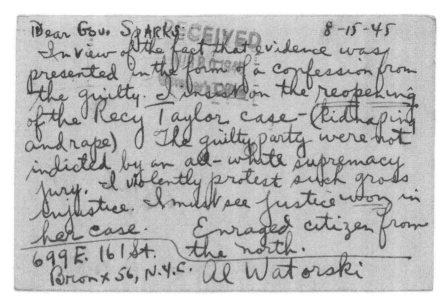

Figure 3. Postcard from concerned citizen, Al Watorski, from Bronx, NY, demonstrating the widespread movement in defense of Recy Taylor.

the limits of those efforts to provoke action against Taylor's rapists. It is clear that the Committee was aware of its goal to make Taylor legible as criminally raped to audiences with a range of receptiveness to this idea. What is most significant is that when communicating to a more conservative audience, the committee *abstracts* Taylor from her particular, embodied identity in the hopes of making her a defendable universal symbol. There are more specific things about their strategies that we can uncover by investigating a few of the most common rhetorical themes running through a selection of archival materials that the Committee produced.

As mentioned, the Committee left behind an impressive record of their work on Taylor's behalf; the archival material includes hundreds of letters, telegrams, and postcards. The writers of these documents are often from the kinds of politically active, left-leaning social justice organizations one might expect to be involved in civil rights work, such as colleges, Black churches, interracial labor unions, Black justice leagues, and white anti-racist organizations from the North and South (figure 3). There was special investment from women's rights organizations and individual supporters of such causes. Carrie Chapman Catt was one such individual. Catt, one of the establishing members of the suffrage movement and founder of the League of Women Voters, was one of several white, Northern letter-writers to make a connection between Taylor's case and the dissemination of democracy abroad through World War II (History.com). Catt makes this connection between domestic and international struggles in her letter to Governor Sparks dated January 19, 1945, four months after the crime:

> In the course of a lifetime I have received a good many letters from organizations, informing me of some terrible crime that has been committed and asking me to do something about it. I have always felt that this was not the responsibility of private citizens, but now that our indignation is whipped up daily by some kind of crime committed in the name of war by the Germans or the Japanese, I feel that our own reputation for decency and morality is at stake. (SG012505, folder 4)

In this excerpt, Catt uses one of the most common rhetorical strategies among letter-writers. In general, Catt's sentiments about "decency and morality" are wildly at odds with racist and sexist perceptions of Black women in 1940s America. As the signifiers of all things bodily and earthly—their bodies nearly synonymous with the earth—Black women were relegated to the past, a slave past, a primitive African past, that permitted and even mandated their sexual victimization as white men were granted open access to their bodies.[12] Black women are seen as unrapeable because one cannot coerce or force sex upon a body that is predisposed to be sexual, or so the misogynoirist logic goes. Though it is remarkable that Catt defies white supremacist illogics here in defense of a Black woman, there are also limits on this defense of Taylor as a defense of national morals. At the same time that these concerned citizens want to defend Taylor, they will only do so under the conservative view of equal protection that subsumes Taylor's racial identity to her gender identity. Catt is eager to incorporate the attack on Taylor as an attack on national ideals. Like Winfrey's abstraction of Taylor in the opening of this chapter, it is possible that Taylor's defenders lean so heavily on the concept of equal protection that it fails in its efforts to make intelligible the raped *Black* female. Liberal allies of Taylor like Catt and the Committee know that if they make Taylor's Blackness explicit, this will turn the cause into a Black rights issue when they really want to maintain its status as an equal rights or women's rights or human rights issue.

On the one hand, Catt's rhetoric is radical for her time, as she refers to what happened to Taylor as a "crime" and to the defense of Black women as on par with issues of national security. On the other hand, the language that Catt uses is also a helpful introduction to the relatively conservative rhetoric echoed by so many other concerned citizens who eagerly abstracted Taylor from her Blackness as a means of defending her from being overlooked as the victim of a crime. This conservative logic around the Black female body is found in the letters to the governor from individuals, but it is also present in the propaganda material circulated by the Committee.[13]

As the Committee chairwoman, Buckmaster writes several pieces of correspondence with Governor Sparks. Henrietta Buckmaster and others like author Earl Conrad and journalist Eugene Gordon also write documents that form the Committee propaganda. These documents were written with the intention of circulating Taylor's story quickly, to apply external pressure to the governor to act in her defense. Buckmaster writes a short preamble to a petition titled "A Plea for Equal Justice." Another version of the same kind of activist literature is called "A Story of Unequal Justice: The woman next door." A few of the documents that Buckmaster and other Committee leaders wrote evince the way the Committee used different rhetorics around Black women and intelligibility depending on the audience that they were trying to sway. Buckmaster sent a telegram to the Alabama governor that asserts conservative views—similar to those of Catt—toward rights and political subjectivity; this is one of the earliest pieces of correspondence received by Governor Sparks's office December 29, 1944, only three months after the first Grand Jury failed to indict on October 3, 1944. Buckmaster writes: "Our deep interest [in Taylor's case] is dictated by considerations of the protection of all American womanhood and equal application of the laws which protect women from brutality regardless of the race or color of any of the persons involved . . . " (1, SG012505, folder 4).

Buckmaster's phrasing "regardless of the race or color" is on the one hand radical for its time, and, on the other hand, is a phrase that abstracts Taylor from her racial identity and thus forming a paradox: Taylor needs to be portrayed as a Black woman to accurately tell her story, but her Blackness also contradicts access to intelligibility given the deeply embedded myths around Black women as unrapeable and the ways in which whiteness and femininity are the conjoined twins of fragility and ideal victimhood. Even the chairwoman of the very movement that was fighting for Taylor to receive justice could not do so without abstracting her Blackness from her "womanhood," her race from her gender. Buckmaster is aware that she must translate Taylor's defendability as a raceless one for an audience like the Governor of Alabama. Taylor must be positioned as deserving of rights not *because* she is a Black woman, but rather despite this fact. Her race, therefore, becomes not just an incidental trait, like a birthmark or a speech impediment, but also a stumbling block to political equality rather than a boon.

Such abstraction within the context of activism is far from surprising. The civil rights movement as a whole has received much retrospective criticism and was even criticized at the time for ignoring other identity-based issues that were perceived as possibly distracting from the focus of racial injustice. McGuire asserts that although the subjugation of Black women in slavery has been heavily theorized, the rape of Black women has never been addressed as historically relevant to the modern civil rights narrative. Her subtitle alone, "A *New* History of the Civil Rights Movement" (emphasis added), suggests that the old history excludes the stories of raped Black women because such stories were not conducive to formations of national identity. Buckmaster's strategy above is aligned with mainstream civil rights strategies: use cases in which Black women are violated as examples of broader human rights violations so as to make an argument for either racial equality and/or gender equality overall.

To represent Buckmaster and the Committee fairly, it is necessary to consider her audience. As any activist would, Buckmaster communicates a certain version of Taylor's story, one that she believes will best stir her audience. Buckmaster does not abstract Taylor from her Blackness to make her rape intelligible as a crime *unless* doing so would be beneficial to the fight for that intelligibility. In sum, one must consider Buckmaster's audience in a full analysis of the Committee's archival materials. In addition to letters to the governor, the Committee also produced a number of organizational propaganda to spread word of Taylor's plight to universities, left-leaning institutions, and other interested individuals. One such piece of propaganda is an informational pamphlet titled "Equal Justice Under Law" (Buckmaster). The pamphlet is a call to action. Aimed at an audience that would likely be sympathetic to Taylor's plight, the pamphlet tells the story of Taylor's violation, the subsequent governmental inaction to come to her defense, and what the pamphlet's readers can do to push those in power to defend Taylor. In this Committee propaganda, Buckmaster's rhetoric appears more radical, eager to use Taylor less as an abstracted symbol of rights denied and more as a specifically Black female symbol of the denial of a woman's right to protect her own body:

> When indignities occur, when humiliation is thrust upon any woman in
> Alabama, in New York, in California, it is an indignity which must strike

the nervecenter of everyone who deserves the name of human being. The sacred white-woman-cult of the South is a blood-sucking disease which affronts me as it affronts you. It robs the white woman of hope and self-respect, and it strips the Negro woman of dignity and confidence. Let us acknowledge then what Recy Taylor represents to us. She represents more than a woman who chances to be a Negro in Alabama. She represents all the past and the future—our hope of a free new world, our passionate conviction that the day has almost come when women everywhere may raise their children without fear, and love their husbands with assurance, and be the individuals to which their highest hopes and capacities entitle them. This is what we are fighting for. When we say "Equal Justice for Recy Taylor! we are also saying, "Equal Hope, Equal Joy, Equal Dignity for every woman, child and man the wide world over!" Is that too much to ask? Why, that is the very meaning of life itself. (2, SG012505, folder 4)

There are two ways to read this excerpt. A less generous reading sees Buckmaster's language as a repetition of the previous excerpt. Buckmaster pushes Taylor's Blackness aside when she states, "[Taylor] represents more than a woman who chances to be a Negro in Alabama." This dismissal could be read as demonstrative of the narrow line the Committee walked between Black rights as human rights and Black rights as Black rights. In other words, for the Committee, it is not Taylor's Blackness that makes her deserving of rights—it is not the centuries of disenfranchisement; it is not the particular conditions of poverty that the Jim Crow South enforces; it is not a mental system of intimidation and corruption that keeps white men in power protecting other white men in power who commit acts of sexual violence—it is her raceless humanity. Not only is Taylor not a mere representative of her race or her gender, but "[she] represents all the past and the future—our hope of a free new world, our passionate conviction that the day has almost come when women everywhere may raise their children without fear, and love their husbands with assurance." With her repeated emphasis on gender here, Buckmaster once again positions Taylor as a symbol, the crime done against her Black and gendered body is once more abstracted as a crime committed against the highest ideals of the country, such as hope, freedom, and egalitarianism.

But there is a second, more generous way to read this excerpt. Buckmaster is abstracting Taylor from her race, but she is simultaneously racializing her. Buckmaster invokes "[the] sacred white-woman-cult of the South" as a "blood-sucking disease . . . that strips the Negro woman of her dignity and confidence" (2, SG012505, folder 4). This graphically racial and violent language is completely absent from Buckmaster's direct message to Governor Sparks, precisely because it would not convince him of Taylor's humanity to hear of how the specific myths around white female purity put Black women in a specific kind of vulnerable, threatened, and physically brutalized position.[14] What Buckmaster's and other Committee leaders' various writings for the Committee make clear is that any defender of Taylor who was invested in speaking to a variety of audiences spanning the political spectrum had to talk out of two sides of their mouth: out of one side, defenders and allies had to defend Taylor, which meant to abstract her from the very thing that made her undefendable—her Blackness; out of the other side, they could defend Taylor *as* a raped *Black* woman and not ignore or smudge the very aspect of her identity that made the crime committed against her unintelligible to a grand jury not just once but twice.

Much like the Committee, I am pointing to Taylor as a universal symbol, her case as representative of larger problems that Black women seeking justice for their rapes had to confront at the time. So I am committing a similar act of abstraction. But there is in fact historical precedent for this. Unfortunately (or fortunately), Taylor's case quickly becomes representational for the raped Black woman. McGuire details how subsequent anti-rape/anti-racist protests that arose in the 1950s and beyond explicitly bore the legacy of Taylor's case. These protests used some of the strategies they learned from the Committee and other earlier civil rights movements to build defenses of other individual Black women like Melba Patillo, Betty Jean Owens, and Joan Little. Little's case will be discussed at length in chapter 2. Buckmaster and Catt are working within the slave abolitionist and suffragist frameworks of previous generations, so it is no wonder that abstraction is their key to intelligibility for the raped Black woman when communicating Taylor's defendability to certain audiences. However, this does not erase the fact that the various correspondence and propaganda of the Committee showcase how Taylor was abstracted from her Blackness in order to be made intelligible as a victim of a crime for specific audiences.

Conclusion

Language is a limited lens through which to view the past. I realize that in the above reading of some of the archival materials surrounding Taylor's defense, I place special emphasis on language, perhaps at the expense of other factors. However, in its limitations, the language that a writer does or does not use remains a vital tool through which to access history, especially the history of Black women and sexual violence. For the hundreds of years that Black women have lived in America, their access to written language was limited by law and so, when we talk about Black women from the seventeenth to even the nineteenth centuries, we are not always listening to the stories as they have written them, but rather reading in between the lines of white people who wrote about Black women, whether in sympathetic or violent ways. I recognize that I am committing a similar act above by centering the words of Taylor's white defenders and her violators rather than her own words, of which there is not much record.

But part of the process of determining how Black women who have been sexually violated define justice for themselves is to first determine the context in which that definition takes place. The most explicitly racist parts of that context are determined by the anti-Black violence that she received not only from her rapists, but also from the grand jury, and from the life-threatening violence she experienced during and after the investigation. These white supremacist and fascist forces that insist upon doubling down on Taylor's violent denigration are quite blatantly and boldly seeking to remove her, erase her, debase her. One would think that Taylor's mostly white defenders would work in the absolute opposite way, eager to uplift Taylor herself, embrace her fully and with careful attention to all aspects of her identity. However, the Committee evinces that the context of the United States in 1944 did not yet allow for a total embrace of Black femininity when drawing sympathy to that body as a victim of sexual violence. Instead, Taylor's allies and defenders feel compelled to abstract her from her body, particularly from her Blackness, in the language that they use to attract sympathy for her case from various audiences. This turn to abstraction must also be seen within its context as a triumph of some kind, as it occurs in a mid-century America that has a number of civil rights groups and activist movements lying in wait to charge against white supremacy *and* there is at least some level of hope within the NAACP, in Rosa Parks, in Henrietta Buckmaster, in Carrie Chatt that the US legal system is a place to turn to for justice.

The failure of Taylor's case, however, is vital to the study of how Black women who have been sexually violated define justice for themselves because it is one of the most stereotypical examples of the utter hopelessness that is the US legal system for Black women. A common refrain in Black communities across the United States is, "Why bother reporting? What good would it do? It takes the police an hour to get to our neighborhoods. They don't care about us." I wanted to use Taylor's case to establish the ways in which the same misogynoirist tropes continue to persist in 1944 Alabama. But I also wanted to demonstrate how Taylor's case proves that a fundamental shift takes place in the mid-twentieth century. The Committee for the Equal Justice for Mrs. Recy Taylor and the national movement in defense of Taylor create this shift. This shift is made seismic by the national outcry against Taylor's assailants and Taylor's treatment by the white supremacist state of Alabama as a whole. The work of Taylor's allies showcases that, at least in some politicized circles, the law is no longer viewed as a completely stagnant and unchanging representative of the state. The work of Taylor's allies proves that many Americans had enough faith in the law to believe that, with enough force, it can overcome its anti-Black baggage and bring about justice for sexually violated Black women. Even though the result of both grand juries would indicate the continued racism and sexism inherent in the law, the attempt to use the law to bring about justice for a Black woman who has been raped is a huge step forward, from the perspective of many historians.

In this book I argue that Black women define justice for themselves in ways that center failure, self-destruction, and the destruction of others. I call these strategies Afro-pessimistic justice. Taylor's case sets the stage on which the Afro-pessimistic strategies play out. We cannot get the "triumph" of Joan Little's case of 1975, the subject of the next chapter, without Taylor's case proving not only that the legal system is racist and sexist, but also that the terms around which largely white justice movements define justice for Black women are failing those women both bodily and spiritually because they insist upon their abstraction.

Chapter 2

MANIPULATING BODIES

Versions of Justice in *State of North Carolina v. Joan Little*

Black women and other women of color have fought for centuries to have the crimes committed against them, sexual or otherwise, recognized as crimes. As Saidiya Hartman so compellingly argues in her book *Scenes of Subjection*, many of the ways in which Black people are considered guilty before proven innocent is rooted in the era of enslavement when Black enslaved people were quite literally only ever allowed in a courtroom when they were accused of a crime; they were not permitted to testify as victims of crimes. In chapter 1, I argued that although the state and individuals of the Jim Crow era were prepared to make a Black woman legible as raped, they were not yet ready to make her rape as a Black woman intelligible as a crime. For her rape to be deemed a crime, it must not only be declared unlawful; it must also be an act for which the law breakers are punished. However, in the 1970s this fight for intelligibility evolves. This chapter demonstrates how failures of justice stemmed from the insistence on Black women's abstraction and set the stage for another development that is in a way the other side of the coin of abstraction—identity politics.

This chapter moves forward in time, examining a legal case that takes place in the era of the Black Power and the women's movements: *State of North Carolina v. Joan Little* (1974–75), tracing the ways intelligibility begins to become more accessible for Black women.[1] This does not mean that such access is easy. In this chapter, I focus on Joan Little's legal case as it continues to reveal the ways in which a functional white supremacist legal system works to exclude, malign, and denigrate Black women and their allies. These victims and their allies, Black and white, therefore work hard to manipulate a white supremacist system so as to coerce it to function for Black women rather than against them.

Abstraction and manipulation are both strategies for creating justice. Abstraction was the tool for getting justice that fails in many ways, as was argued in the last chapter. Manipulation, in the case of Joan Little, means the deployment of all legal maneuvers at one's disposal to impact the context in which the legal procedures are happening so as to change the outcome. In other words, no one expects justice for Joan Little. As Christina Greene mentions in her 2015 article on the case, Little is regarded by her opponents as an "impoverished, disreputable young woman" and even seen by her defenders as someone who must work excessively hard to prove her victimization (440). What has changed from abstraction to manipulation are two things: (a) there are by now enough people on the side of justice who see the necessity of speaking frankly about race, class, and gender to defend the Black woman who has experienced sexual violence, and (b) there are additional tools within the legal system that are now at the disposal of activists and other civil rights advocates. In Little's case, her defenders manipulate the system by realigning the meaning of terms that in misogynoirist imaginary would lead to utter abjection to signify differently. According to white supremacy, Little's class, race, and gender are precisely the things that ought to place her completely outside the realm of victimhood. The Free Joan Little movement and the rhetoric of her legal team publicly insist upon Little's full identity being precisely the reasons behind her victimization rather than the obstacles to it.

The term "manipulate" is an important one for this project overall, as its title, *Bodies in the Middle*, implies. Much of the most influential Black feminist criticism has worked to rescue Black women who have experienced sexual violence from the margins of society in and around which their bodies, emotional labor, and freedoms are manipulated. I want to maintain the focus on being manipulated while acknowledging the spaces in which Black women are the manipulators.[2] Each of the cases in this book offer such spaces, ones in which the manipulated bodies become manipulators of not only their own bodies, but also the very definitions of justice that have historically made it impossible for them to access justice. Of utmost importance is that these sites of manipulation tend to circle failure, self-destruction, and the destruction of others, forming a group of strategies I call "Afro-pessimistic justice." In this chapter, I will explore the various areas of manipulation in which Black women and their allies operate. For *State v.*

Little, there are many areas of manipulation, but I'll be focusing on geography and voice. Because each of these areas of manipulation in *State v. Little* are distinct, I will analyze them individually.[3]

Geography as a Tool for Justice in State v. Little

On the night of August 4, 1974, Joan Little, a twenty-one-year-old Black woman jailed for larceny, breaking and entering, and receiving stolen property in Beaufort County, North Carolina, was visited by Clarence Alligood, a sixty-two-year-old white prison guard. As guard of the prisoner for many months, Alligood was often inappropriate with Little, making sexual comments, entering her cell at his leisure, and giving her sandwiches. But on that August night, Alligood made those implied gestures physical when he forced Little to perform fellatio, using an ice pick to threaten her life if she did not comply. During the sexual assault, Little struggled to retrieve the icepick from Alligood, and, once successful, struck at him several times. She then fled the jail using Alligood's keys and went into hiding. By her account, Little left Alligood alive behind her though he died within a few hours. The whole county and even state was abuzz with the scandal of having a known fugitive on the loose, no less a Black woman wanted for murdering a white prison guard. While Little hid in the house of a friend (often placing herself between a mattress and a bed frame when the police were searching for her), the news alerted Golden Frinks, a well-known local Black civil rights lawyer with connections to the famed activist group the Southern Christian Leadership Conference. A friend of Little's, Margie Wright, who knew where Little was hiding, called Frinks. Frinks himself had just been released from jail with the help of his friend, local white civil rights lawyer Jerry Paul.

Given Frinks's recent run-ins with the law, Paul was asked to offer his assistance by covertly moving Little, with the help of Margie Wright, from her hiding place in Beaufort County, which was under constant police surveillance, to Chapel Hill.[4] Paul immediately began to negotiate her surrender to the head of the State Bureau of Investigation, Charles Dunn. Little was arrested for first-degree murder on September 7, 1974, and two days later was indicted by an all-white grand jury in Beaufort County. Almost exactly a year after her assault, an entirely different jury in an entirely different county acquitted Little of murder and found her not guilty on the grounds that she acted in self-defense against her rapist. It is the move of the trial from Beaufort County, NC, to Raleigh, NC (Wake County), that proves pivotal to Little's triumph. Her defense attorney Jerry Paul's strategy to liberate Little

Figure 4. This image of Joan Little pictured here in a knitted, pink hat is from her 1975 interview with CBS after her acquittal. CBS re-released the short interview and coverage of the case to YouTube in 2015 to recognize the 40th anniversary of her historic acquittal. To my knowledge this is the only televised footage of Joan Little from that time that has been released to the public.

from geographic constraints marks an essential shift in the discourse around Black women and sexual violence that *State v. Little* helped to push forward.

In the 1970s, North Carolina was undergoing an enormous amount of upheaval due to school desegregation, Black rights activism, and white supremacist violence.[5] At the same time, the nation as a whole was beginning to respond to mostly white women's rights organizations, such as the National Organization for Women (NOW), founded in 1966, which called for awareness and legal action around a host of issues, including reproductive rights, job discrimination, domestic violence, and rape.[6] *State v. Little* arrived into this perfect storm around sexual and racial discourses. Little's defense team, consisting of Paul and Karen Galloway, wished to prove that Little was raped and was innocent of murder, and they were also determined to place very public pressure on the criminal justice system. Because Little was a poor, Black woman with a criminal record, the social structures of race, gender, class, and regionalism worked against her. An all-white jury in Beaufort County immediately indicted Little of murder. Conscious or not, long-standing myths about Black female sexuality and Black women as un-rapeable lead the jury to question the veracity of her claim that she had been sexually violated. Paul and Galloway intended to use the racism displayed by the grand jury in Beaufort County to get the case moved to a different county, which had never been done on the grounds of racial and gender demographics.[7] Crucially, the defense could never have proved the racial bias that existed in Beaufort County without the $300,000 raised through the social activism of an interracial and gender diverse coalition called the Joan Little Defense Fund (aka the Free Joan Little movement), which bears some resemblance to the Committee for the Equal Justice for Mrs. Recy Taylor mentioned in the previous chapter. Unlike the Committee defending Taylor, the Free Joan Little movement was successful in achieving its goal of getting Little acquitted. But it is important to mention just how much effort was put into this success. In particular, the money and labor invested in Free Joan Little was instrumental in establishing the need for trial relocation; this difficult collective labor was required to make Little intelligible as the victim of a sex crime.

The funds that were raised through the Joan Little Defense Fund were used to cover several expenses, but perhaps the most important was the commission of sociological research about racially biased jury selection strategies and an attitudinal survey which determined significant racial bias among white Beaufort County residents. Although Little's defense was successful in their efforts to relocate the trial from Beaufort County—a majority white, rural county—to Wake County, a more urban, diverse one, Judge Henry A. McKinnon refused to acknowledge that the trial relocation was based on race. So although the official record says otherwise, it is clear from the archive that Little's defense team was able to make a convincing case for relocation because of the research on racial bias. This research was conducted by Courtney Mullin, a graduate student in social psychology at North Carolina State University, when she heard about *State v. Little*. Mullin became aware of Little's case from the local newspaper, which announced that the defense had petitioned the court for money to hire a criminolo-gist to conduct a survey, though they were not yet sure what kind of survey. When the judge denied this motion, Mullin called Paul and Galloway and offered to conduct research on racial bias in both counties, volunteering her training and experience conducting surveys. When Mullin met with Gal-loway, the two women were trying to figure out a way to present reasons to move the trial; Mullin states in her interview with James Reston, "neither of us had a clear idea of how to do that at all" (James Reston Collection of Joan Little Trial Materials, 00:05:13).

Eventually, Mullin worked with her adviser at North Carolina State University to develop a questionnaire and an area survey. Some of the money in the defense fund was used to pay a sample size of 100 participants who were interviewed either over the phone or in person. Funds were also used to pay research assistants for their labor. Again, I am describing this in detail because I want to communicate all of the work that went into guaranteeing trial relocation, one of the more successful attempts to manipulate the legal system to benefit Little. The primary goal of the area study that Mullin and others conducted was to determine "attitudes" of participants. However, the researchers were also interested in the jury selection process. If they could prove that white residents of Beaufort, NC, held biases and were consistently taking up all of the slots on juries due to partial jury selection processes, then they could argue for the need to relocate the trial. Mullin concluded that more white residents than Black residents of Beaufort County saw Black women as having "lower moral standards than white women" and that "a black woman who is raped by a white man has probably tempted him into it" (Reston, 184). In other words, Mullin used sociological research to prove that white people held onto the white supremacist, psychosexual myths surrounding Black female sexuality. Another aspect of Mullin's work was finding evidence that the courts were conducting jury selection in such a way as to purposely exclude Black jurors, but she was unable to do so because of how closed that process was. Though Mullin could not prove with total certainty that the jury selection itself was biased, she found damning evidence that there was a widespread bias against Little among Beaufort's white residents, which was enough to get the trial relocated.

Instead of acknowledging Mullin's impact, McKinnon granted relocation on the grounds of the bias he cited against Joan Little in Beaufort County. The small county, McKinnon explained, was poisoned against the case as a whole due to overexposure to details through high levels of local and national media coverage.[8] And this was true. Not only were white residents of Beaufort biased against Little, as Greene discusses at length in her article, much of the white population in the region was increasingly anti-Black in both their attitudes as well as in their policies. In fact, North Carolina had no formal sentencing guidelines up until the Fair Sentencing Act of 1979, which did not go into effect until 1981. The absence of sentencing guidelines granted judges even more power than they already had so that sentences were completely indeterminate, which explains why, in January 1974 (and prior to the rape-murder case), Joan Little receives up to twenty years in prison for nonviolent theft charges which were treated as felonies for her and misdemeanors for her brother (Greene "She Ain't No Rosa Parks", 434). McKinnon could blame the high publicity of the case because many Beaufort County residents did resent that their town was suddenly under the nation's microscope as a stand-in for all that was racist, southern, and backward. But once the survey findings are reviewed, it is difficult to ignore racial and gender bias.

The results of Mullin's survey regarding the opinions of Beaufort County residents (Black and white) about justice, Black women, sex and sexuality are quite pertinent. Indeed, Mullin's work even set a precedent for future arguments around jury reform.[9] She used her attitudinal survey to argue that the large differences in opinions between Black and white residents in Beaufort proved that the race of an individual juror has an impact on how that individual makes decisions as a juror. The survey posed a variety of questions about race, justice, and the Little case specifically, but some of the most alarming results concerned Black women (figure 5).

As defense expert witness, Dr. Robin Williams, a sociologist from Cornell University, said of the results, "With the question, 'Do you believe Joan Little killed Clarence Alligood in self defense?' the differences there are very, very great, with almost no Black people saying no. I would take that to mean they are withholding judgment on that matter, whereas fifty-eight percent of whites said no, creating the presumption in my mind that they have already made up their minds" (Reston, 185).

The relocation of Little's trial demonstrated a shift around Black women and sexual violence. Prior to this case, the general strategy of civil rights lawyers and activists, when faced with the rare case of a Black woman reporting her rape to authorities, was to either hope that the system would work to protect her or that the very public failure to do so would prompt activism in her defense.[10] Though Little's defense team incorporated the latter strategy by creating the movement Free Joan Little, they also integrated strategies made possible by a slightly more progressive national context than the preceding generations. In the case of Recy Taylor only thirty years previous, it seemed unfathomable that any jury in any southern state would acknowledge that a white man had raped a Black woman, let alone follow through that acknowledgment with some form of public action. The state acquitted Joan Little, but not because the 1970s criminal justice system

The Innocence of Joan Little   *184*

RACE *(cont'd)*

	Whites	Blacks	Percentage Difference Between Blacks and Whites
Attitudes relevant to rape victims			
1. A black woman who is raped by a white man has probably tempted him into it.	58%=No	81%=No	23%
2. If a woman says she's been raped, that should be enough evidence that the rape has actually occurred.	15%=Yes	29%=Yes	14%
3. Black women have lower moral standards than white women.	49%=No	72%=No	23%
Attitudes about the Joan Little case			
1. Do you believe Joan Little killed Clarence Alligood in self-defense?	58%=No	1%=No	57%
2. From your knowledge of this area, do you believe Joan Little can get a fair trial in Beaufort County?	34%=No	86%=No	52%
Other attitudes			
1. Policemen spend too much time arresting kids for smoking marijuana.	17%=Yes	41%=Yes	24%
2. Police should not hesitate to use force to maintain order.	71%=Yes	59%=Yes	12%
3. People should support state authorities even when they feel they are wrong.	29%=Yes	43%=Yes	23%
4. White people are more greedy than black people.	27%=Yes	83%=Yes	56%

Figure 5. This is one of the charts that Courtney Mullin—graduate social psychology researcher working on behalf of the defense—used to show her findings about misogynoir in Beaufort to Judge Henry A. McKinnon.

suddenly needed to protect Black women. On the contrary, *State v. Little* marks the beginning of a new rhetoric around Black women and sexual violence in which the manipulation of the law can in fact function to gain state acknowledgment of the crime and subsequent action by the law. As seen in the trial relocation strategy, the system must be manipulated for it to function for Black women who have been raped.[11] The necessity of manipulation still means that Little triumphs in spite of her Blackness, not because of it. *State v. Little* acts as a precursor of the fictional Corregidora women in Gayl Jones's novel (discussed in chapter 5), who must manipulate the context of systems of justice—both within and without the American legal system—to achieve what I call Afro-pessimistic justice.

Only a few months after the end of the trial, Paul made a telling comment to Wayne King of *The Charlotte Observer*, confirming that justice for Little was compelled from the system rather than a natural product of its functioning. "[Paul] says . . . that the whole trial process had nothing to do with justice . . . He says that he simply 'bought' Joan Little's acquittal . . . This system doesn't want justice. It wants convictions. That's why, given enough money, I can buy justice. By saying that, I point out the defects of the system. You hold it up to ridicule" (King, 1). When Paul claimed to have "bought" Little's freedom, he was not resorting to false histrionics. On the one hand, as a white man, Paul has access to manipulating the system in ways that Little and (more broadly, women of color) do not. On the other hand, Black women were also working behind the scenes to quite literally "buy" the system. Before the trial began, Paul, Rosa Parks, Karen Galloway, Paul's co-defense attorney, the Student Nonviolent Coordinating Committee, Southern Christian Leadership Conference, and other civil rights organizations donated to the Joan Little Legal Defense fund, which raised over $300,000. This money paid for Mullin's research as well as "the best counsel, to mount an extensive jury selection process, to hire investigators, to fly in expert witnesses, to spend thousands on 'counseling'" (King, 1). The extensive jury selection was perhaps one of the most important costs. Paul's motion to have the trial relocated from a smaller, whiter county in North Carolina to a larger, more diverse one was central to what made *State v. Little* historic. Little's defense team proved that in order for Little to have a fair trial, fair access to even the *possibility* of her rape being intelligible as a crime, they had to work on her behalf to manipulate the system to the fullest extent available.

It is important to mention, however, that not everyone praised Paul for laying bare systemic inequality. Louis Randolph, famed Black city councilman of Little's hometown of Washington, North Carolina, lamented Paul's comments as a foolish "mockery of the criminal justice system" and implied that Little was in fact guilty. Paul's comments indeed almost cost him his license to practice law (Greene, "'She ain't no Rose Parks,'" 435). Despite perhaps committing a public *faux pas*, Paul's comment makes explicit the shift that occurred for raped Black women seeking justice. This shift is most starkly characterized by the misogynoir that Black women face from ordinary people, state officials, and systemic mechanisms, which render legal justice accessible only through manipulation, a forcing of the system to work to make the Black woman intelligible as a victim of rape without abstracting her from her race and gender identity. Little's acquittal is a great triumph because of how it exposed the system as malleable, but her liberation is also bittersweet because she could not expose the system without also exposing herself as a formerly incarcerated person in the process.

While Paul and Galloway worked to convince Judge McKinnon to acquit Little of murder charges, they also argued that her felony charges for theft should be thrown out due to the fourteen trial errors they found, including a "serious question of effective representation." Furthermore, they discovered that during this previous trial, the jury was not informed of the reasons behind the sudden confession against Little's brother, Jerome. That the defense was unable to fully liberate Little from prison points to the continued limitations around Black women as those who cannot expect much of anything from any and all systems let alone justice from the law. As a formerly incarcerated woman, Little was in an especially fragile position when she exposed herself to not only additional prison time, but even the death penalty in her willingness to stand trial for murder so as to attempt to get justice for the sexual violence she experienced. Such exposure required her to not only attempt to manipulate (and have her lawyers manipulate) her own voice but to remain vulnerable to the manipulations of others who would use her voice against her.

The Role of Voice in State v. Little

Every trial relies on voice as evidence in one way or another, be it through witness testimony, phone records, or confessions. However, the voice is an especially contested aspect of a rape trial given the centrality of consent. This is conceptually paradoxical because victims must use their voice on the witness stand to try to convince a jury that they were incapable of using their voices to "resist" coerced sex.[12] Consent was especially frightening territory for a rape victim seeking legal justice in 1974. In the 1990s, there was a sizeable rape reform movement and, abstractly, the focus was largely on the voice. Two of the achievements of this movement were the advent of rape shield laws and the decentering of verbal and physical resistance from the definition of rape in rape law. Rape shield laws are (albeit non-binding) guidelines that certain attorneys, judges, and other legal officials voluntarily incorporate into their approaches to specific cases. Over time, this practice had a major impact, particularly regarding the treatment of rape victims in the courtroom. One of the successes of rape shield laws was to keep victims' sexual histories out of the trial so that victims would feel safer reporting their rapes to the authorities. Reformers also hoped that by broadening the definition of consent and resistance, this would also make more women feel safer reporting their sexual violations. Little's case occurs almost two decades prior to the advent of rape shield laws, so none of these official protections were available to her.

But because juries, no matter their makeup or location, are always already mapping a certain set of stereotypical sexual histories onto Black women's bodies—as the results of the Mullin's surveys demonstrate—Little's defense team was acutely aware of the issue of sexual history and how to frame Little's resistance to Alligood's sexual advances so that the jury leaned more on the truth of Alligood's attack, rather than relying on their potential biases against Black women. The prosecution, comprised of William Griffin and John A. Wilkinson, were similarly aware, however, of the issues of race, gender, and sexual history and how they could use misogynoirist myths about Black women's hypersexuality to leverage the jury's prejudices. Just as the defense manipulated the legal system, the prosecution manipulated Little herself, hoping to obscure her intelligibility as a Black woman whose rape could be seen as a crime. The trial transcripts reveal in detail the constraints placed on Little's voice in the courtroom as the prosecution attempts not only to goad Little into revealing herself to be the lascivious Black woman stereotype that some of the jurors already believed her to be, but also to squash her voice into something insignificant, not deserving of being valued, protected, heard. Lead prosecutor Griffin forms a case centered on voice using two crucial strategies: limiting the testimony of the victim and (re)inscribing myths of Black female sexuality.

In his book *Rape and the Culture of the Courtroom*, Andrew E. Taslitz describes the multiple strategies that defense lawyers in rape trials use to place a rape victim's testimony under severe suspicion. One such tactic is the use of "forced-choice" questions. As Taslitz asserts, "[research] indeed shows that 'forced-choice' questions—those requiring a yes or no answer—are quite effective in limiting the witness's independent voice" (90). Throughout his cross-examination, Griffin asks Little forced-choice questions. One of the most representative examples occurs when Little describes her sighting of the "murder" weapon and affirms her utter lack of consent to Alligood's assault that fateful night in her cell:

Q: You had known he wasn't supposed to be [in your cell] on previous occasions, hadn't you?
A: Yes.

Q: But there he was, fully dressed at that time, did you see an ice pick in
    his hand at that time?
A: No.
Q: What did he say to you?
A: He came in and stood at the door and he said it's time that you be
    nice to me because I been nice to you.
Q: What did you say?
A: I told him no that I wasn't gonna be nice to him.
Q: Is that the words, is that the exact words that he used?
A: That he used?
Q: Yes?
A: Yes.
Q: Is that the exact words that you used?
A: Yes. (225–26)

Griffin tries to confuse Little here, to see if the barrage of yes or no questions will cause her to make a mistake. Though the forced-choice questioning strategy fails here, closer examination evinces the goal of the tactic:
Griffin uses a yes or no line of questioning to limit the amount of time that
Little speaks and that the jury hears Little speaking. As the prosecutor, it
is Griffin's job to poke holes in the testimony of the accused, but Griffin's
tactics are so clearly accusatory that at the very end of this exchange, Paul
objects "to him arguing with her" (226). This exchange restricts Little's
voice on a meta level. Not only is Griffin limiting Little's voice, but he also
limits her voice while she narrates her own resistance to Alligood's sexual
advances: "I told him no that I wasn't gonna be nice to him." He attacks the
possibility that Alligood lacked consent by immediately questioning Little
about the precise language of their exchange: "Is that the exact words that he
used?" Griffin uses these and other strategies throughout the examination
and cross-examination, attempting to manipulate Little's voice and how it is
perceived. Little resists such manipulation as often as she can. Throughout
the testimony, her replies are often "I don't know" or "I don't remember," one
of the few forms of resistance that Taslitz mentions is at the disposal of the
victim (95). But the "choice" between silence or assertiveness that victims
of rape face on the witness stand is racialized and gendered. We see that,
for Little, being silent or resisting can be both a weapon to wield against
misogynoirist tactics to trip her up, or it can be held against her to make her
seem like an uncooperative Black woman.

The final aspect of voice in *State v. Little* that I want to cover is how Griffin exploits misogynoirist stereotypes to denigrate Little's character thusly attempting to block her access to being intelligible as the victim of a sexual crime.

Taslitz's overall argument is that the culture of the courtroom is patriarchal, adversarial, and capitalist and therefore anathema to the kind of culture that would support rather than demonize rape victims. Given that *Rape and the Culture of the Courtroom* is part of a series called Critical America edited by two of the founders of critical race theory, Richard Delgado and Jean Stefancic, and that it is published in 1999, near the time of the inception of critical race theory as a field, some of Taslitz's claims on race and gender are overly general and verge on essentialist. But this does not discredit all of the arguments that Taslitz makes. One of Taslitz's most compelling assertions supports the aforementioned double-edged sword that Black women confront in the courtroom: "Black women . . . face a race-based catch-22. If they speak 'women's language,' they will be less credible, as is true of white women adopting the same style. But if Black women adopt a more assertive style, white jurors will perceive them as rude, hostile, out-of-control, and hence less credible" (79). By "women's language," Taslitz refers to overtly feminine forms of speech, such as speaking softly, behaving with shyness and, to some extent, embarrassment.[13] But, Taslitz adds, Black women are just as distrusted when they are performing in stereotypically feminine or quiet ways as when they are vocal. The Black woman's voice is therefore under enormous scrutiny. Griffin intensifies this scrutiny by attempting to solidify misogynoirist stereotypes around Black female sexuality and thus, as Taslitz says, discredit Little.[14] Griffin uses many aspects of Little's life to denigrate her character and undermine her, including her home life, her romantic relationship with Julius Rodgers, and her criminal history.

The "Black Jezebel" myth is perhaps the most harmful in Griffin's arsenal. A Jezebel, in the simplest sense, is a sexually promiscuous woman, but it is a term weaponized specifically against Black women, a means of marking them as inherently inferior to white women due to a lack of morality. Drawing on the work of Kali Gross, Greene outlines this important historical connection between race, sexual transgression, and criminality:

Marked by their race as "born thieves," African American women accused of criminal activity were portrayed in the press as "colored amazons," an image that cast aspersions on offenders and non-offenders alike. As historian Kali Gross has noted, while the vast majority of African American women (and men) did not break the law, "the image of the colored amazon cast long shadows." The caricature portrayed African American women not only as criminals, but as sexual aggressors too, a re-configuring of the age-old Jezebel image. (433)

During his cross-examination, Griffin conjures the Jezebel trope when he makes a disrespectful reference to Little's sexual history and criminality. His formulation of the following questions triggers an immediate objection from defense attorney Jerry Paul.

> Q: You were in love with Julius Rogers were you not?
> A: Yes, I cared about him . . .
> Q: Now at the time that Mr. Freeman turned you in, did you tell him that you would have sex with him if he signed your bond for no fee?
> MR. PAUL: Object to that . . . this type of character assassination has nothing to do with this trial and what they are trying to do with this girl. (126)

When Paul objects here to Griffin's insinuation that Little was a prostitute, willing to exchange sex for financial favors, he foreshadows aspects of rape law reform that will arrive in a little under twenty years. Paul understands that Black women's experiences with "character assassination" are rooted not only in sexist myths about female sexuality, but also in racist myths surrounding Black female sexuality. Even so, Griffin pulls a cruel maneuver. By getting Little to confess genuine care for an ex-lover and then immediately imply sexual impropriety, Griffin attempts to convince the jury to distrust Little based on reductive stereotypes about class, criminality, and Black female sexuality. In other words, if she is willing to be in a sexual relationship with a man she does not love, what else might she be willing to do? Griffin exploits the power of his own voice's whiteness and maleness over Little's to try to convince the jury of pejorative stereotypes of her race, sex, and sexuality.[15]

To conclude this analysis of voice in the trial, I must acknowledge that there is no such thing as "Little's voice" in the sense that we do not have access to an unmediated and unrehearsed version of Joan Little speaking. Almost all of her statements on the witness stand had been worked on with the defense team tirelessly. McGuire mentions the months of coaching and training that Little undertook to ensure that she would be able to withstand the pressure of testifying to an audience—who, apart from a racially diverse group of jurors, was mostly comprised of aged white men, from the judges and lawyers to the news reporters on the case—that she had been raped by an aged white male. Little's resistance to Griffin's attempts to trap her on the stand was likely the result of this training. But there is an especially salient moment in her testimony when Little's preparedness is not just a smart defense move, but also a potentially vital source of empowerment for a rape survivor. Where once her refusal to have sex with someone was completely and utterly ignored, where once her voice was powerless to keep her violation from happening, now her voice has the power to not only captivate an entire room, but also manipulate the audience in that room to regard her as the victim of a crime. Griffin tries to catch Little in a lie, but she uses her voice to completely take control and question the very system of "voice as evidence" with which he is attempting to manipulate her:

> Q: So, and you didn't let the other jailers know that he was coming back there bringing sandwiches, is that right?
> A: If I had they wouldn't ever have believed me anyway.
> Q: Well you had the evidence right there to show them didn't you?
> A: Mr Griffin sometimes you have evidence and you tell people the truth, but then they twist it in a way that it makes it seem that you're not telling the truth and in Washington, North Carolina, coming up as a black woman it's different in saying what you did and having your word to go against a white person's. It is not acceptable. (151–52)

As seen here, Little and her defense team never let the jury forget about race or the larger issues at stake in this case. And I would argue that this was one of the keys to their victory. As discussed at length in chapter 1, Recy Taylor was unable to make herself intelligible as a *Black* woman who had been the victim of a sexual crime. In this chapter, Little is a Black woman who *is* able to convince the public, a jury, and state officials, that she has been sexually assaulted. This achievement cannot be understated. Though there are major circumstantial differences in their cases, it is remarkable that, as discussed in the previous chapter, only thirty-five years prior an Alabama jury could not even charge Recy Taylor's rapists with a crime let alone compensate her for that crime. Joan Little and her defense team prove that Black women can use justice systems to make themselves intelligible as victims of sexual violence.

However, just looking at the preceding excerpt, it is clear that this intelligibility is still mired in historical baggage: as Little says, "sometimes you have evidence and you tell people the truth, but then they twist it in a way that it makes it seem that you're not telling the truth and in Washington, North Carolina, coming up as a black woman it's different in saying what you did and having your word to go against a white person's. It is not acceptable." When Little says "people," she is not only referring to the white residents of her hometown or the other white police jailers; she is also referring to the local and state police, the county sheriff, the attorney general, the judges, the prosecutors, and the jury. She is marking a clear distinction between telling the truth and being believed. Her acquittal in 1975 works to shorten the distance between telling and being heard for Black women, but it is not a clean victory. There is almost no way that Joan Little would have been acquitted without the massive resources that she and her allies worked to gather in her defense, resources that could be used to not only "have the evidence" but also to coerce the system to see this evidence as legitimate proof that a crime occurred. Joan Little and her allies are able to manipulate geography so that not only can Little's voice be manipulated to resist manipulation by the opposing side, but also the audience of that voice can be manipulated to believe that voice using trial relocation.

Little's defense team manipulated areas of the law to which they had access through funding and educational resources. It was the goal of Paul and Galloway to show the public that the system could be manipulated to both protect and punish American citizens. They particularly wanted to demonstrate that, if you are a Black American woman who has been raped, history shows that it is far more likely that the system will be manipulated to punish you rather than to protect you.[16] Their strategies revealed specific injustices within the system (i.e., the potential harm of racially and sexually homogeneous juries) to shift the conversation around Black women and sexual violence which had, in earlier cases like Taylor's, placed passive trust in the system, hoping that exposing its failures would awaken enough public sympathy to provoke change. This perspective is common and can be seen in civil rights-era legal strategies which took a "long view" of justice, often hoping to achieve some kind of precedent rather than justice in the moment. The success of Little's case from the perspective of mainstream civil rights movements would not necessarily be her release on murder charges, but that the success of her case acts as precedent for the next legal strategy to defend the next Black woman who is raped. Does Little's case set such a precedent?

Some would argue that it absolutely does, as the first time in US history that a victim was able to use a self-defense defense to avoid a murder conviction. But I would argue that the case does not set a precedent. If anything, Little's case presents an exception to the rule not only because of the ways her defense was resourced, but also because of the circumstances (e.g., it is a murder trial not a rape trial) surrounding the sexual violence itself.

Conclusion

Upon her acquittal in September 1975, Joan Little was able to briefly revel in and enjoy her victory, but this came to an abrupt end when she had to return to prison to complete the remainder of her original sentence on three felony charges for breaking into Black-owned trailers and stealing about $1,300 worth of property. The fact that Little had to return to jail even after a year of being maligned by the media, at risk of a death sentence, and her character questioned throughout the trial, is the final nail in the coffin of this case as a prime example of Afro-pessimistic justice.

Afro-pessimistic justice consists of a host of strategies that Black women use to either depart from the traditional criminal justice system or use its own mechanics against itself in an attempt to get some form of compensation for the crimes committed against them. As I've shown in this chapter, Little's case is an example of the latter as she, her defense team, and the Free Joan Little movement behind her worked within the hopeless understanding that justice is not possible for raped Black women unless the mechanics of the system can be used against itself for the desired outcome. Paul and Galloway used mechanics like trial location and funding to move the needle as many inches as they could in Little's favor. But, ultimately, the very fact that it took so much effort to prove the innocence of a Black woman who was so clearly raped and without the resources to commit premeditated murder, the fact that she and the movements behind her were required raise such an enormous amount of money for her defense, and the fact that she returned to jail immediately after her acquittal are signs of deep failure. The failure is not Joan Little's, but rather a legal justice system incapable of taking an entire person and her context into account when judging the case.

When Little returns to jail, it is the most obvious moment in which the criminal justice system seems to have absolutely no sense of what has occurred during this case or how to prevent things like this from happening again. Little returns to jail where she could be in danger of being assaulted again. Little returns to jail rather than given any resources or guidance that could actually benefit her life and the lives of so many other Black women who may see that reporting the sexual violations they experience would not lead to their own destruction but could lead to their own thriving and enrichment. In other words, Little's case can be considered a micro-success, as it keeps one more Black woman from being murdered by the state for protecting herself against violence; but it is also a macro-failure due to its reliance on the destruction of Little—of her self-image, of a perpetuation of myths around Black women through the prosecution and media spin, of her return to jail after the trial—and the destruction of any possible way for Black women to feel holistically redeemed by a precedent being set for them. A Black woman of Little's status, who has been raped and is considering reporting, may see this case and still think it is not worth it; that there is too much risk here and too much counting on a grassroots movement that may never come together as it did for Little. Of course, years later Black women do continue to take the enormous risk of reporting their rapes to authorities. No case is more exemplary of the continuation of the issues Little faced, while also demonstrating the very new challenges that the twenty-four-hour news cycle poses in the twenty-first century, than the case of Nafissatou Diallo, which I analyze in chapter 3.

Chapter 3

"I LOVE THIS COUNTRY, BUT SOMETIMES I'M NOT SURE WHERE I AM"

Black Immigrant Women, Sexual Violence, and Afro-pessimistic Justice in *New York v. Dominique Strauss-Kahn*

This chapter extends the arguments of chapters 1 and 2 about the (un)intelligibility of raped Black women into new territory.[1] Black immigrant women face new challenges to being intelligible to the law and simultaneously have access to new avenues for finding community and modes of expression around those challenges. Despite these new possibilities, Afro-pessimistic justice is still very much present here and offers brand new ways for Black women and the systems from which they seek justice to fail. A key component of Afro-pessimistic justice for Black immigrant women is the immigration system and how it works in conjunction with the criminal justice system to misinterpret Black women and their specific needs. For Nafissatou Diallo, the victim at the center of *New York v. Dominique Strauss-Kahn*, the need for a justice system that understands the ways in which she was discriminated against by the immigration system cannot stand beside her need for justice as victim of sexual assault. As I'll show through a careful dissection of the case, almost all of the concerns about Diallo's "reliability," as Manhattan district attorney Cyrus R. Vance put it, are rooted, directly or indirectly, in her immigrant status. In other words, Diallo's intelligibility as a victim of rape is inextricable from the story of her path to US citizenship. Diallo's case helps us to explore the problem of complex social identities that many immigrant women of color pose to legal systems.

Chapters 1 and 2 cover historic cases in which a Black woman is raped and seeks justice for that violation. However, this chapter is a departure from the first two because it focuses on a Black immigrant woman, Guinean-born Nafissatou Diallo. Her story maintains the thread that ties all of these women and their experiences with the legal justice system: Taylor, Little, and Diallo are simultaneously invested in, distrustful of, and divested from the legal system. Diallo's case poses a departure from the first two because the victim is a non-citizen and her case occurred in the twenty-first century.

Consequently, these shifts in temporality and identity impact the victim's engagement in and with Afro-pessimistic justice, a result of new technologies as well as minor changes in norms around rape trials. In this chapter, I will demonstrate the extent to which the context of Diallo's case impacts her, while centering how her own savvy and learned behavior allow her to maneuver through the law in ways that neither Little nor Taylor ever could have dreamed. Ultimately, the case of Diallo contributes yet another example of how Black women have developed strategies to pursue legal justice for rape, strategies that are wrapped up in failure and self-destruction. A major part of this failure is rooted in Diallo's identity as a Black immigrant woman. The relationship between failure and immigration status is borne out in the criminal trial that never occurs. Though there was a successful civil suit against Strauss-Kahn by Diallo, there was no criminal trial against Strauss-Kahn. This chapter extends the arguments of chapters 1 and 2 about the (un) intelligibility of raped Black women into new territory.

To fully understand *New York v. Strauss-Kahn*, it is worth reaching back a decade prior to the case, returning to the 1990s when identity politics, feminist theory, and political movements around gender began to have a real impact on overarching policy rather than one-off, case-by-case effects as in the story of Joan Little. In her 1991 essay, "Mapping the Margins," Kimberlé Crenshaw uses the analytic framework of intersectionality—first introduced by Crenshaw in 1989—to consider how legal systems and political institutions perpetuate violence against Black women and other women of color. One population Crenshaw focuses on are undocumented immigrant women of color who come to the United States to marry permanent residents, citizens, or undocumented workers. If such a woman is in an abusive relationship, her access to services that may be of assistance (such as police or social service agencies) is limited, not only because she fears deportation, but also because of possible cultural or linguistic barriers (1248). At the time Crenshaw wrote this essay, women who had obtained visas through marriage could not apply for permanent residence status without their spouse present in many states, a requirement that put these women at great risk. Furthermore, because communities of color and immigrant communities of color are more heavily policed, the police are considered a threat to, not a potential advocate for, immigrant women suffering from domestic violence. Though there have been attempts to reform immigration laws since then, immigrant women of color remain extremely vulnerable. *New York v. Strauss-Kahn* exemplifies this persistent vulnerability, as do hundreds of cases of immigrant women struggling to survive in the xenophobic Trump era.

Taken as a whole, contemporary discourse around immigration is so toxic that Crenshaw's call for more significant policy changes to protect the most vulnerable has gone largely unheard; politically violent attacks on immigrant women of color have continued, if not increased. There are reports of women being arrested by Immigration and Customs Enforcement (ICE) agents at the courthouse before or after their hearings against their domestic abusers; stories of white nationalists committing hate crimes against women in hijabs or those that they presume to be immigrant women of color from Muslim countries; and a general stoking of fear of immigrant women as invasive reproducers, seen most notably in the "anchor baby" uproar of 2006.[2] Fear of immigrants, especially dark-skinned immigrants, has been a consistent presence in the United States since the nation's founding, and both federal and state law have served as critical enforcers of such xenophobia. However, what is especially frightening about the current moment are the laws that empower enforcement agencies like ICE and the Department of Homeland Security to use technology to track, incarcerate, and deport immigrants.[3] Yet at the same time that law enforcement agencies have weaponized relaxed digital privacy laws against immigrants, everyone, whether documented or undocumented, can also use some of the same technology as a mode of creative expression, community formation, political organizing, and healing.

All of these currents—a rise in the use of intersectionality as a framework, the current resurgence of xenophobia, and the rise in political organizing among activist groups like the DREAMers—lead to the question: how have these concerns also been expressed through the voices of Black immigrant victims of sexual violence? And in what ways does Nafissatou Diallo's struggle for justice resemble or depart from the other avenues toward Afropessimistic justice seen in the cases of Recy Taylor and Joan Little?

New York v. Strauss-Kahn *and Afro-pessimistic*
Justice for Black Immigrant Women

On May 14, 2011, Nafissatou "Nafi" Diallo, a 32-year-old Guinean maid
working at the Hotel Sofitel in New York City, entered the room of a guest
who, she later learned, was Dominique Strauss-Kahn, the head of the International Monetary Fund (IMF). Diallo, believing that the guest had checked
out and the room was empty, began to clean it. Upon entering the bedroom
of the large suite, she found a naked man.

The man, who proceeded to attack her, pushed her into a corner, groped
her vagina, and forced Diallo to her knees to perform fellatio, then eventually released Diallo from his grip. Diallo exited the hotel room and stood in
the main hallway. She saw her attacker, now clothed, exit the room and get in
the elevator. Diallo immediately told her supervisor, Jessica, what happened.
The police were notified, and Diallo submitted to a rape kit at a nearby hospital. The rape kit revealed that the redness of Diallo's genitalia, as well as her
hurt shoulder, were consistent with her account of sexual assault. Diallo's
clothing was also swabbed and eventually tested positive for Strauss-Kahn's
semen. There was, in other words, significant physical evidence to suggest that a sexual assault occurred. Police apprehended Strauss-Kahn that
same day at the airport, moments before his flight from New York to Paris.

On May 19, 2011, a Manhattan grand jury indicted Strauss-Kahn on two
counts of a criminal sexual act in the first degree, forcible touching, unlawful
imprisonment in the second degree, sexual abuse in the first degree, third-
degree sexual abuse, and first-degree attempted rape. Such a high number
of criminal charges left Strauss-Kahn facing up to seventy-four years of jail
time. Later, Strauss-Kahn's lawyers convinced the judge to release him on $1
million bail so long as he remained under house arrest and surrendered his
passport.[4]

But only a few months later, on August 22, 2011, the Manhattan District
Attorney's office dropped the criminal case. After months of investigation
and mass media frenzy around the case, prosecutors filed a motion to have
the case dismissed and all of the criminal charges against Strauss-Kahn
dropped. The primary reason that the prosecution offered for dropping
the criminal case was its assessment of Diallo as a witness. The DA's office
conducted at least five separate interviews of Diallo after the grand jury
indicted Strauss-Kahn and every interview revealed a new inconsistency in

her story about the assault as well as her personal history. District Attorney Cyrus R. Vance, who was slated to represent the state of New York against Strauss-Kahn, wrote in his motion to dismiss that "our post-indictment investigation severely undermined her reliability as a witness in this case" (The People of the State of New York, 2).

It is not exactly the fault of Vance—though, interestingly, he has come under fire recently as the same lawyer who dismissed a case against Harvey Weinstein in 2009—that the case against another powerful white man accused of rape was dropped. It is a symptom of the wider failure of a criminal justice system whose standard for conviction is "beyond a reasonable doubt" and which defines reasonable doubt in ways that disadvantage immigrant women who came to the United States fleeing violence and deprivation. In the words of Kristie Dotson and Marita Gilbert, who write about Diallo in their essay "Curious Disappearances: Affectability Imbalances and Process-Based Invisibility," the failure of the case is the fault of a system that is incapable of reading "complex social identities" (875).[5] Vance, by virtue of his job title, is incapable of reading Diallo complexly because of the questions he is required to ask. The criminal case against Strauss-Kahn failed not because of a single district attorney, but rather because of a legal system that asks, "Is this victim's testimony reliable?" instead of "How can we understand the systemic underpinnings of this victim's 'unreliability'?" Before engaging more decisively with what it means for Vance to find Diallo "unreliable," I want to lay out some significant details about the case and its representation in the media.

Amidst all the activity at the DA's office, many high-profile news outlets were meanwhile reporting on the case, but none with as much fervor as the *New York Post*, a well-known conservative-leaning daily tabloid newspaper. I will offer close readings of some of the *Post* cover stories about the case later in this chapter, but it is important to understand that as soon as Diallo decided to come out in public as the victim of Strauss-Kahn, the *Post* almost immediately deemed her a hooker, a lying prostitute, and a (Black) whore in their coverage. Diallo later won a libel suit against the *Post*.

Unreliable Narrator or Immigrant Playing the System's Game?

The details of Diallo's journey to America and her application for asylum cannot be examined because those records are confidential. However, here is what we do know. When Diallo was around twenty-seven years old, she was

*(**NOTE:** Use Form I-589 Supplement B, or attach additional sheets of paper as needed to complete your responses to the questions contained in Part B.)*

When answering the following questions about your asylum or other protection claim (withholding of removal under 241(b)(3) of the INA or withholding of removal under the Convention Against Torture), you must provide a detailed and specific account of the basis of your claim to asylum or other protection. To the best of your ability, provide specific dates, places, and descriptions about each event or action described. You must attach documents evidencing the general conditions in the country from which you are seeking asylum or other protection and the specific facts on which you are relying to support your claim. If this documentation is unavailable or you are not providing this documentation with your application, explain why in your responses to the following questions.

Refer to Instructions, Part 1: Filing Instructions, Section II, "Basis of Eligibility," Parts A - D, Section V, Completing the Form," Part B, and Section VII, "Additional Evidence That You Should Submit," for more information on completing this section of the form.

1. Why are you applying for asylum or withholding of removal under section 241(b)(3) of the INA, or for withholding of removal under the Convention Against Torture? Check the appropriate box(es) below and then provide detailed answers to questions A and B below.

I am seeking asylum or withholding of removal based on:

☐ Race   ☐ Political opinion

☐ Religion   ☐ Membership in a particular social group

☐ Nationality   ☐ Torture Convention

A. Have you, your family, or close friends or colleagues ever experienced harm or mistreatment or threats in the past by anyone?

☐ No   ☐ Yes

If "Yes," explain in detail:
1. What happened;
2. When the harm or mistreatment or threats occurred;
3. Who caused the harm or mistreatment or threats; and
4. Why you believe the harm or mistreatment or threats occurred.

B. Do you fear harm or mistreatment if you return to your home country?

☐ No   ☐ Yes

If "Yes," explain in detail:
1. What harm or mistreatment you fear;
2. Who you believe would harm or mistreat you; and
3. Why you believe you would or could be harmed or mistreated.

Figure 6. Page 5 of Form I-589, Application for Asylum and Withholding of Removal shows the limited and overly simplistic ways the US immigration system forces asylum-seekers into boxes they may not necessarily fit.

already in the United States, living apart from her seven-year-old daughter, who remained in her home country of Guinea.[6] It was then that Diallo began the process of applying for asylum.

To apply for asylum, one must fill out an I-589 form and pass an interview (figure 6). Both the form and interview act as extensive checks on the applicant's background, residence history, current and former relationships, family, and children. But the most important question posed by both the form and the interview concerns why the applicant is applying for asylum: "I am applying for asylum . . . based on: [check the appropriate box] race, religion, nationality, political opinion, membership in a particular social group, torture convention" (US Citizenship and Immigration Services, 5).

In none of her interviews with the DA's office does Diallo reveal her answers to this or any other questions on the form, but she does admit to the DA that she "made a mistake" on the application. Her refusal to say exactly where she made a mistake makes it likely that she lied on this part of the form, the part that asks why she is seeking asylum. According to her interviews with the DA, Diallo admitted that she lied on her application and that she even lied to the DA about the lie. Two days after Strauss-Kahn was accused, the DA asked Diallo if she had been the victim of any other assaults in her past. Diallo responded with an account of a gang-rape by soldiers in Guinea with great emotion and conviction. She also mentioned to the DA that this was the story she told in the interview portion of her application for asylum. Later, her attorney Ken Thompson urged her to admit that not only was the story of the gang-rape by soldiers false, but also that she did not use this story in her asylum application. In a footnote of the motion to dismiss, there is a significant detail: "In her interviews of June 9 and June 28, the complainant stated that she had indeed been raped in the past in her native country, but in a completely different incident than the one that she had described in her earlier interviews. Our interviews of the complainant yielded no independent means of investigating or verifying this incident" (15). These lines reveal that, according to the DA, Diallo claimed to have been raped in Guinea, but in a "completely different incident."

Before the case was dismissed, Diallo revealed the story of this rape in her televised interview with ABC News in 2011 (Katersky, "Dominic Strauss-Kahn's Accuser Speaks Out").[7] She explained that she was gang-raped by a group of men while closing up her brother's cafe where she worked in Conakry, the capital of Guinea. In the latter half of this section, I will touch more on the emotional aspects of such telling and retelling for Diallo in her ABC News interview, but for now it is most important to recognize this pattern of lying. First, Diallo tells a story to the DA about a gang of soldiers raping her in her brother's café. Then, after additional interviewing, this story changes, leading Diallo—according to the DA and even her own lawyer, Ken Thompson —to admit that this story was a lie. Furthermore, in the nationally televised interview with ABC News, which is at the center of my analysis of this case, Diallo re-tells a story about a gang rape that she insists is true. There are key details that change between tellings of this story that reveal a pattern of lying. This pattern demonstrates the ways that systems, as well as cultural norms around immigrant narratives, condition such lies.

The work of scholars Lisa Lowe and Mae Ngai regarding the dangers of restrictive immigrant narratives helps situate Diallo's lies within a wider American socio-historical context. In her book *Impossible Subjects*, Mae Ngai argues that narratives about illegal immigration both inside and outside of the law have been used to racialize citizenship in the United States, particularly for Asian immigrants. Ngai builds on Lisa Lowe's foundational work, *Immigrant Acts*, which asserts that the story of Asian immigration in the United States is the story of legal, racial, cultural, and linguistic exclusion often disguised as economic and political inclusion. Both Ngai and Lowe are also interested in the issue of narratives and norms. The United States tells its own stories about "foreigners" and those stories deeply infect the cultural memory in ways that influence legal, cultural, and racial definitions of citizenship. As we will see, Diallo's case is embedded in the history of what has been called the "good immigrant" narrative because of the ways in which her case relies heavily upon the standards by which someone is judged as worthy of asylum (or not). When Black immigrant women try to use strategies of assimilation to make themselves legible to the state as citizens, the outcome has similarities to the Black American women discussed in the previous chapters. Joan Little and Recy Taylor also sought to utilize the trappings of white middle class respectability to make their right to being seen as victims of crimes (the right of a citizen) visible. Taylor, Little, and Diallo (and their defenders) all, to varying degrees, assimilate to make themselves legible to a system, dismantling their identities in an attempt to access justice. This is just one of the Afro-pessimistic strategies on display in Diallo's case. There is a long history of various groups using whiteness (and all of its supposedly moral attachments) as a means by which to legally apply for citizenship.

Landmark Supreme Court cases such as *Ozawa v. U.S.* (1922) and *U.S. v. Thind* (1923), in which men of Asian descent attempted to become legally white, were essential to cultivating scripts for a group now called Asians as not white and not of African descent and therefore ineligible for citizenship (Ngai, *Impossible Subjects*, 38). The decisions in *Ozawa* and *Thind* not only define whiteness against a specific racialized otherness but also demonstrate an early instance of the "good immigrant" narrative, a narrative that the plaintiffs, Takao Ozawa and Bhagat Singh Thind, attempted to use as evidence of their assimilability. This narrative commonly stresses the immigrant's hard work and devotion to family as key to their ability to assimilate. Thind emphasized his time served in the US Army, while Ozawa asserted his "honesty and industriousness" to the court. These and other characteristics designate a good immigrant in the eyes of official systems. The narrative of the hardworking immigrant who contributes to society, lacks a criminal record, and is family-oriented did not work for Ozawa and Thind, but their arguments reveal the standards by which immigrants are judged as assimilable, and those standards are highly racialized.

If Thind and Ozawa were unable to use their white-passing (in terms of both skin-color levels and class) as a guarantor of citizenship, it follows that assimilation would be even more of a struggle for dark-skinned immigrants from Africa, who face all of the same assumptions that white supremacy thrusts upon Black Americans except with the added suspicion of their fitness as citizens and the resulting danger of deportation. In particular, immigrants from Africa carry the burden of white supremacist stereotypes (held by white Americans as well as many Americans of color) created to maintain the status of Africa as backwards, poor, disenfranchised, and as politically and socially primitive.[8] It is important to recognize here that several scholars use "Afro-pessimism" to contain precisely this racist, western perspective of Africa as one country unified in its inability to join the "civilized" and progressive world, hindered by internal violence, illness, malnourishment, and other ills. The definition of Afro-pessimism that I use and as outlined in the introduction of this book differs from this one: I use the term to denote skepticism toward hope rather than (according to Frank B. Wilderson's definition) a complete and totalizing rejection of the possibility for Black people to be whole in the American political and social landscape. To repeat Jared Sexton's definition phrased as a question (sort of), "It is suggested that one can see readily the need to foreground black rage, but we must ask after the nature of an equally pressing emphasis on black hope" (Sexton, 8). In other words, I use Sexton's definition to see Afro-pessimism as a way of doubting rather than rejecting hope.

Though the criteria for asylum and naturalization differ, both act as gateways to citizenship. Those who are granted asylum can work, they pay taxes, and they can apply for a green card (what can be a very long and expensive process). But there is another standard of the "good immigrant" that Diallo had to fit: the violence she faced in her country had to be political, in other words, a kind of violence she could only escape by physically escaping her country. This is probably why Diallo did not merely lie about being gang-raped by soldiers; she also admitted to the DA that a male friend gave her a recording of someone else telling this story and she memorized it in preparation for her asylum interview. According to the checklist portion of the application for asylum, Diallo's story of being a target of political violence would qualify her for asylum in two categories: "political opinion" and "member of a particular social group" (figure 6), the latter because she could argue that she was a victim of gender-based violence. The DA gained access to her asylum application and verified that she used the story of the gang-rape on her application. The story involves not only being gang-raped by soldiers, but also that this rape was an act of retribution against Diallo's husband, a political dissident. This story makes Diallo legible to an asylum application review board as a victim of "political" violence, a kind of violence that, presumably, her country cannot protect her from because the government is sanctioning it. Diallo shows that new immigrant bodies and new avenues to citizenship and migration require the "good immigrant" to engage in what Lowe calls "immigrant acts": the maneuvers that immigrants of color must make to either disappear into the US cultural lexicon or to be legible as one who has suffered in the right way—in other words, one whose suffering marks a need for asylum.[9]

The lies on Diallo's asylum application and in her interviews with the DA are understandable given the various assumptions and scripts that exist for Black women, immigrants, and immigrant women of color in particular. And, in fact, the lies that Diallo tells on her asylum application are a large part of her Afro-pessimistic justice strategy. Prior to her attempts at making herself visible as a victim of rape, Diallo, like many asylum seekers, is well-trained in the art of making herself visible as a victim in need of a path to US citizenship, in need of safety from violence in her home country of Guinea. As both an asylum seeker and a seeker of legal justice, Diallo's lying is a strategy that, whether she knows it or not, has the capacity to both save and destroy her; and, in this way, Diallo replicates the Afro-pessimistic justice strategies that, as we have seen in the previous chapters, circle failure, self-destruction, and the destruction of others. The ability or inability of Black women to live up to or fail to embody certain scripts about race, gender, and sexuality continues to affect how they go about accessing justice for themselves.

The lie on Diallo's application appears as an attempt to simultaneously confirm and deny the script that Black women from socially conservative African countries are in desperate situations as a result of the political ineptitude, legal misogyny, or despotism in those countries. In *Terrorist Assemblages*, Jasbir Puar observes how misogyny can act as a scapegoat for American geopolitical warfare and intervention (6–7). In other words, Puar argues that US foreign policy often hinges upon a kind of white-male-savior-coming-to-save-poor-brown-women-from-oppression-complex. Diallo's asylum narrative confirms the myth that the United States is a savior of women and so, perhaps, her story is more compelling within a framework of America's self-fashioning as a safe haven for darker skinned women. The United States has a vested interest in maintaining an image of itself as a champion of women's rights, despite, as Puar would say, not only perpetuating its own racist-misogynistic rhetoric and principles on its own citizens, but also economically benefiting from international alliances with countries in which such systemic misogyny exists. Furthermore, in true hypocritical fashion, the United States turns back and villainizes enemy states who do the same thing.[10] Puar helps us to see that the DA's decision to dismiss the case also reflects the ways in which both the legal system and the immigration system folds Diallo into stereotypical notions of Blackness, low socioeconomic status, and femininity in both foreign policy and domestic US contexts.

Diallo is a single mother living in government-subsidized housing with her 15-year-old daughter, working as a hotel maid. These details not only place Diallo into a pathological understanding of Black women as promoted by Daniel Patrick Moynihan but also add to her unreliability (Battle and Ashley, 6).[11] In the motion to dismiss the case, the DA mentions Diallo's "additional falsehoods," one of which is that she failed to mention income on her application for low-income housing (16). Another falsehood was that she received money from a man who was now in jail for drug trafficking, which Diallo claimed to believe was money that he made selling handbags. Obviously, being a poor, Black single mother does not automatically discredit Diallo. But it is striking that the systems can initially recognize her as a victim because of these narrow stereotypical subjectivities and then those same subjectivities work to discredit her when they reveal her negative interactions with other historically racist systems: the housing system, the prison industrial complex, and the immigration system. Diallo lies about the facets of her life to make herself legible as a victim which fits into the Afro-pessimistic justice strategy evident in Little's case (see chapter 2). Lying as a way of manipulating a system you anticipate will not work for you is a form of Afro-pessimistic justice because, even in its attempts to make a racist-sexist system center Black women, there is a recognition that all such attempts are doomed.

Though Diallo lied on her asylum application to the grand jury and to the DA, she did so under enormous systemic pressure. One can only speculate about her reasons for lying to the DA, but I suspect this may have been an Afro-pessimistic justice strategy: while it maintained the story of her migration, lying also put Diallo in a position to be vulnerable to harm and therefore has a doomed-to-fail quality. Perhaps Diallo recognized that, since the case was going to trial, any previous assault she mentioned to the DA would have to be politically charged in some way in order for her to be legible to the jury as a political asylee. Or perhaps she recognized that the story of a previous assault would have to be dramatic and compelling enough to convince any public audience of her status as a credible victim. Whatever the reason that Diallo lied to the DA, it is crucial to see that the system through which people migrate to the United States conditions these kinds of lies. Was Diallo safer in Guinea because she was raped by citizens instead of soldiers? In other words, is someone more or less in danger because the danger that they face is "political"? The US immigration system would have us believe that only politically or socially motivated violence make one's desire to flee their homeland legitimate. Diallo's case forces us to reconsider not only the means by which human beings become intelligible as needing "asylum," but also the limited modes of expression at the disposal of immigrant women of color who have experienced sexual violence to use Afro-pessimistic justice strategies to attempt.

Such limited modes of expression are evident in the civil cases that Diallo won against Strauss-Kahn and the *New York Post*. Let us begin with the civil case against Strauss-Kahn. The files of this case are closed, so there is no way of knowing precisely how Diallo was able to make herself a compelling victim to the jury.[12] The one document at our disposal is the civil court filing that Diallo's lawyer Ken Thompson made against Strauss-Kahn on August 8, 2011. The standards of proof for a civil case are much lower than those of a criminal case; the civil cases overseen by the Supreme Court of the State of New York, Bronx County must be for settlements above $50,000. The case was settled for an undisclosed amount on December 10, 2012. Diallo's win should be marked as a triumph but also understood within the lower standards of civil cases. Whereas in the criminal case Diallo had to prove beyond a reasonable doubt that Strauss-Kahn sexually violated her, in the civil case she had to prove that she suffered damages during their encounter and in the mass media aftermath. She also had to prove that these damages put a significant financial strain on her and her family. The civil court filing encompasses the official charges of battery, assault, intentional infliction of emotional distress, and false imprisonment. The definition of justice also differs between civil and criminal court. For criminal court, justice typically means the imprisonment of the criminal for a certain amount of time. In civil court, justice is considered monetary compensation for damages incurred by the plaintiff. In the "prayer for relief" portion of the filing, Thompson argued that Diallo is owed an "award . . . to compensate Plaintiff for all monetary and/or economic harm; for harm to her professional and personal reputations and loss of career fulfillment . . . compensation for mental anguish; all other monetary and/or non-monetary losses suffered by Plaintiff" (Thompson, 15). The civil court filing is clearly acting in lieu of the criminal case because so many of the charges regarding the physical assault are the same, but the form of justice is distinct. After the criminal case, Diallo and her defense team sought other ways to substitute and/or supplement legal justice. Having failed with criminal law—in other words, after criminal law failed to ask the appropriate questions to capture what happened to her in Guinea and therefore find her story about Strauss-Kahn credible—Diallo looked for other avenues through which she might be able to use her own language to not only express her story, but also make it legible to a new audience, the audience of prime time evening news. The ABC News interview aired July 25, 2011, before Diallo and her defense team knew for sure that her criminal case against the former IMF director would fail.

Diallo never wanted to "be in public," as she says in her ABC News interview. Instead, she felt compelled to reveal herself only to clear her name and reputation after several media outlets falsely reported that she was a prostitute in an attempt to, supposedly, discredit her claims that Strauss-Kahn assaulted her.[13] *New York v. Strauss-Kahn* was an extremely high profile case during the summer of 2011, garnering frequent coverage from reputable news outlets like *The New York Times*, *Slate*, *The Nation*, and *The Atlantic*.

Figure 7. This first *New York Post* cover features a defeated Strauss-Kahn under the headline "He Did Have Sex with the Maid." Both the image and the headline reflect that both public and legal support were more or less with Diallo prior to the leaking of information about her application for asylum.

However, no local news outlet covered this case more than the *New York Post,* which devoted nineteen front-page headlines to the scandal.[14] The extensive coverage in the *Post,* known as a sensationalist and punny rag, captures the evolution of Diallo's story as it was portrayed in the mass media. There is a clear evolution in public perception of Diallo as the following front page covers demonstrate.

Figure 7 is from the May 17, 2011, issue of the *Post,* published less than a week after Strauss-Kahn was accused of assault. It represents much of the coverage at this early stage, when little to nothing was known about Diallo (because she initially requested to remain anonymous) and the case seemed like a straightforward example of a powerful white man abusing that power to exploit someone innocent and powerless. The *Post* seemed to revel in watching the downfall of this powerful man. However, the headline makes no judgments about the sex as consensual or not—which ends up setting the stage for the news outlet's absolute flip from seeing Strauss-Kahn as a powerful abuser of an innocent maid to the vilification of Diallo as a money-hungry prostitute. The next cover, published less than two months after the first, speaks to how swiftly the public narrative around the case changed once she was no longer anonymous and it became public that the prosecution was having doubts about Diallo's credibility.

Figure 8. This second *New York Post* cover is almost a complete reversal of the one above as it portrays a smiling Strauss-Kahn under the headline, "DSK Maid a Hooker." Though the *Post* is not the most credible of sources and is quite conservative, the cover reflects the ways in which both legal and public support for Diallo ran dry after the leaking of information about her asylum application. (Source: Gobry.)

In this July 2 issue, reporter Brad Hamilton uses both image and word to express a complete reversal in perspective. In the span of two months, we see Strauss-Kahn go from slumped, disheveled, and guilty of assault to a smarmy yet charming, refined womanizer. In this July issue, Hamilton makes the unsubstantiated assertion that Diallo worked as a prostitute in various hotels around the city. This headline is a mass media reflection of a leaked letter that Vance sent on to Strauss-Kahn's legal counsel on June 30, 2011, which expressed the doubts that the prosecution was having.[15] The front page then takes that prosecutorial doubt about Diallo's credibility to its most racist and sexist conclusion: if Diallo was lying about Strauss-Kahn forcing her to perform a sexual act, what else might a Black woman of a certain class have been doing in the hotel room of a powerful white man? The reporter borrows from long-held myths about Black female sexuality as excessive and boundaryless as well as myths about domestic workers and immigrant women of color as desperate, money-hungry victims or as perpetrators of sex trafficking in its many forms (2).[16] These *Post* headlines are offensive and hurtful. Fortunately for Diallo, that offense and hurt was recognized when the *Post* settled her civil libel lawsuit against them.[17] But the headlines retell Diallo's story in terms that are familiar to the immigration-processing systems in the United States. The "hooker" rumor about Diallo is just one manifestation of precisely the problem that Diallo poses to the legal system and to the immigration system discussed earlier. In effect, Diallo reveals the US binaristic view of immigrant women: an immigrant woman of color can either be the victim of political abuses (whether those are the abuses of Strauss-Kahn, a wealthy banker and former IMF director, or the abuses of soldiers in her home country) or a lying whore.

In an attempt to challenge these media rumors, Diallo took her story to the public stage. Around the same time as rumors circulated that the case would be dropped, she decided to reveal herself as the victim of Strauss-Kahn and tell her side of the story on national television. Diallo's interview with ABC News reveals both the openings for and limits on immigrant women of color who opt to use public forms of expression to narrate their traumas. The full interview is over an hour long (and available online) but is cut down into a three-and-a-half-minute segment of sound bites for air. In addition to editing, Diallo had no say over other production details, the questions she was being asked, lighting, audio, or special effects. As much as Diallo tried to take control of her story, the means of mass media production made such control nearly impossible. Mass media thus replicates the machinations of a legal system that cannot recognize Diallo as someone who is on a sliding scale of danger that does not reach the level of intelligibility for a criminal case nor satisfies the requirements of federal agencies such as Homeland Security and Immigration and Customs Enforcement. As limited as the televised news interview is as a platform, at the very least it provided Diallo an opportunity to express herself.

On July 25, 2011, Diallo's interview with anchor Robin Roberts aired on ABC News. The interview reached national airwaves at a critical point during the New York Defense Attorney's (NYDA) criminal case against Dominique Strauss-Kahn. The interview aired before the NYDA officially announced the dismissal of the case on August 11, but after June 30, the date that the NYDA had leaked a letter to the defense about Diallo's lack of credibility (Osborn and McConnell). The prosecution expressed doubts about the strength of her testimony in a criminal trial after several interviews with Diallo that revealed gaps in her account of the assault as well as lies about her past.

The actual content of the TV news interview is vital, but so is its very existence. Diallo's apparent decision to sit down for an interview with a major news media outlet is an active choice to defy her right to remain anonymous under rape shield law, made federal under the Violence Against Women Act of 1994.[18] Rape shield laws give rape victims the right to remain anonymous throughout criminal proceedings, which primarily means that news media are banned from releasing their names. Whether she knew about such protective laws or not, Diallo expresses in her interview with Roberts that she feels safe coming forward as Strauss-Kahn's victim because she is doing so in America.[19] She elaborates that she believes America to be different from Guinea, not necessarily in terms of how sexual violence is reported, but rather in broader terms of equality: "I know if that was my country, he's a powerful man like that? They gonna kill me before someone know what happened to me. This country? America? They do the right things. They take everybody like the same . . . Doesn't matter if you poor or you rich . . . But that day—I don't know that . . . I think they gonna kill me" (Diallo, 00:02:06). Diallo explains here that she is aware that the context of Guinea is different from that of America and that this benefits her. There are multiple times throughout the interview that Diallo calls upon American ideals as motivators for her asylum application, for her feeling safe enough to report her rape, and for her feeling safe enough to go on national television to talk about her rape. This not only reveals the ways in which scripts of the "good immigrant" determine how systems digest the stories of sexual violence from immigrant women of color, but also how narratives of the US as a fair and equal country hold shared weight over which modes of expression immigrant women of color seek to tell their stories of assault.

Diallo demonstrates the extent to which an understanding—or, at the very least, an awareness—of the racialized and nationalized nature of several systems, combined with access to media (digital or televisual), is a particularly good recipe for an Afro-pessimistic justice strategy for immigrant women wishing to supplement or seek alternatives to legal justice. In her turn to televised news—as troubled a system as it is—Diallo's story is a statement about the legal justice system's failure to offer a comparable platform for her voice, her story, and her pain to be heard. This turn is an Afro-pessimistic justice effort to generate enough public good will in defense of her case and to defiantly reject xenophobic and misogynoirist myths about her life and her body because she is unable to do so in the setting of a criminal trial.

In Jordi Xifra's article about the role of media coverage in *New York v. Strauss-Kahn*, the author pays little to no attention to Diallo and is much more interested in Strauss-Kahn's media strategy as he went on an apology tour on French news outlets after the criminal charges were dropped.[20] Xifra, a communications studies scholar, uses image repair theory to conduct an analysis of Strauss-Kahn as an example of how the politically powerful course-correct after scandals.[21] Yet Xifra's analysis overlooks the fact that Diallo (and Thompson, no doubt) also used the media as a mode of expression.[22] Diallo and her defense team likely saw the televised interview as an opportunity to pull public opinion back in her favor despite signs that the criminal case would not proceed. In the ABC News interview, Roberts asks Diallo why she has chosen to come forward now, and Diallo states that she was motivated to come forward by the lies of outlets like the *Post*:

> I never want to be in public. Now I have to be in public. Like my daughter tell me, like two weeks ago, I was so crying I don't know what to do. I hear people call me many names now. I just don't know . . . One day my daughter tell me, "Look, stop crying . . . this guy, everybody say he's a— I don't know how to call that in English—he's a powerful man. He's— everybody knows him. But you? . . . People don't know you. That's why they say bad things about you . . . Any place you used to live or any place you used to work, and the people knows you back home, all of them they say good things about you because they know you . . . And I know you mom. You are a good mother." (00:2:30)

Though Diallo does not mention here the specific "lies" that prompted her to come forward with her story, it is difficult to ignore that the *Post* headlines calling her a "hooker maid" were some of the most splashy and sensational. This excerpt from Diallo's interview is notable because she directly states that her desire to reveal her name and identity as the victim of Strauss-Kahn is an effort to change a false narrative about her, her sexuality, and the general deviancy of immigrant women of color. Diallo is adamant that the prostitute narrative is false and must be replaced with (for example) the "good mother" narrative; this is just one of several narratives that Diallo lays out to transform the conversation around her from one about her unassimilability to one about her assimilability.[23]

Later on, when Roberts asks Diallo, "Are you a prostitute?" Diallo responds in the negative but also names Strauss-Kahn himself as benefiting from this invalidating account of her sexuality before posing a significant question: "That's why I have to show myself. I want everybody to see me. They gotta know that I'm not [a prostitute] because everybody [who] knows me, they know that I'm not . . . They call me that because of *him*! Because he want to make me look the—Because I'm poor? Because I'm what?" (00:49:30). In these last two questions, Diallo opens the door to a broader question about why this particular label of "prostitute" gets attached to her.

Diallo recognizes that it is one thing to be called a liar but wonders why the notion that she receives money from guests for sexual favors would feed that lie. She wonders, logically, if prostitution is linked to her because of her socioeconomic status. But in this line of questioning, she does not mention race as a possible factor. The exclusion of race from her questioning here could be a result of having lived outside of an US context, outside of a context in which, in the presence of a Black minority, white supremacy breeds certain sexualized racial stereotypes.

Race would not serve the new narrative that Diallo offers in this interview. One of Diallo's Afro-pessimistic justice strategies is to present counternarratives that denounce the false, misogynoirist narratives. In other words, she asserts her counternarrative through negatives: I am *not* a liar, I am *not* a prostitute. These are Afro-pessimistic statements because they almost certainly are doomed to fail or, at the very least, not function to exonerate Diallo fully from racist-sexist tropes that her body, voice, and skin color are always already telegraphing. Another strategy is her attempt to replace those negative narratives with positive ones, such as being a hard worker and a good mother. But what is important to note is that Diallo is squeezed into a defensive position as she states that her reason for going public is to combat lies about her and to tell her side of the assault. Underlying this reasoning, however, is the fact that the televised interview offers Diallo an opportunity to present counternarratives to the racist-sexist-classist scripts that mark Black women as prostitutes and Black immigrant women as gold diggers. As discussed earlier, both the DA's motion to dismiss and the asylum application process put immigrant women of color who have experienced sexual violence into a binary that resembles these misogynoirist tropes: either the trauma they have experienced is political and makes them worthy of asylum, or the trauma is personal and makes them unworthy; either they are a credible witness beyond a reasonable doubt or they utterly lack credibility and cannot be made intelligible as the victim of a crime. Diallo speaks to a more complex story of an immigrant woman of color who lies about some things but is not a "liar," who has suffered both political and personal violence and the distinction between those things should have no bearing on her access to asylum, but it does.

But why do Diallo and her lawyer, Thompson, choose the televised interview as the mode of expressing this counternarrative? What are the limits and openings of this medium for immigrant women of color who have experienced sexual violence? I have excerpted a number of quotes from Diallo's

ABC News interview not only to portray the content of what Diallo says to defend herself against media accusations, but also to capture the way in which she says it. Diallo uses the television news format so that she may put herself on display sonically and visually. Her aesthetic presentation personalizes her side of the story as the story of an immigrant woman of color.

These aesthetic aspects of the interview are key to concluding how Diallo manipulates a media system as a means of supplementing legal justice. As mentioned, though the criminal case against Strauss-Kahn was dismissed, the accused settled with Diallo in civil court; this is the legal justice to which I am referring. In the above quote, Diallo says, "That's why I have to show myself. I want everybody to see me. They call me [a prostitute] because of *him*! Because he want to make me look—." During the interview, Diallo stops at the word "look" because she is searching, trying to imagine what category she fits into that is most beneficial to Strauss-Kahn's defense. Given the medium of television, it is telling how often Diallo emphasizes the visual here, using the words "show," "see," and "look." Diallo touches on an important disadvantage to rape shield law: if a victim of sexual violence uses rape shield law to protect their identity, they are also, in some ways, foreclosing visual and sonic avenues through which to present themselves as victims of crimes. This is especially limiting for immigrant women of color whose skin color, bodies, accents, and voices contribute to the audience's sense of them as whole humans with particular identities.[24] Up until her interview, there were no images of Diallo in the newspaper, and no one had heard her voice. One way to view this absence of self-presentation is that it provides the press with a vacuum and thereby with an opportunity. If the victim does not present themselves to the press, the news media is free to fabricate an image of the victim that aligns with the most sellable version of their character. Clearly newspapers, social media, and televised news can conjure stories about personalities in a criminal case whether the defendant or plaintiff offer their own narrative or not. However, for rape victims who are immigrant women of color, anonymity is unique in the way that it restricts their ability to let their bodies speak for them both visually and sonically.

As discussed earlier, Diallo's decision to "show" herself, as she says, is not one that all immigrant women of color can pursue. Her refugee status, proclaimed love of hard work, and relatively assimilable appearance grant her some of the security to reveal herself to the world. Through dress, hair style, skin color, and gesture, Diallo's image doubles down on her defendability, the defendability that the *New York Post* rejects (figure 9).

Figure 9. Nafissatou Diallo attempts to make the case for her respectability which is, subtextually, a case for her right to being seen as a credible victim of sexual violence. (Source: National Organization for Women.)

During her ABC News interview, Diallo is dressed relatively conservatively in a half-sleeve peach cardigan, white scoop-neck blouse, and Black slacks (not pictured). She wears little to no makeup on her face and her hair is straightened into a not-quite shoulder-length bob that frames her face. Diallo's attire offers visual confirmation of her own verbal counternarrative to the *Post*'s "hooker maid" narrative. Conservative dress has the ability to speak volumes about one's character, implying that a person is decent, trustworthy, and financially independent. We do not know whether Diallo dressed herself, ABC News gave her a specific wardrobe, or her lawyer provided her with suitable clothing. In any case, the fact remains that her dress is useful and contributes to her agenda of appearing assimilable and trustworthy. Everyone who appears on national television can attempt to use dress to influence the audience's perspective of them, but Black women, especially non-American Black women with accented English, bear the pressure of attempting to use dress as a form of defiance against those misogynoirist scripts that their skin color, voices, and gender identities may be writing for them. Whether appealing to Judith Butler's language of performativity or Evelyn Brooks Higginbotham's politics of respectability, Diallo's strategy remains the same: using conservative dress to reject the rumor that she was paid for sex and promote her truth as the victim of an act of sexual assault.[25] Though dress is an important part of Diallo's effort to perform "white middle-class propriety," this strategy is not specific to her as an immigrant woman of color.

The sonics of her interview with ABC News tell a marginally different story about her status as a defendable citizen than her attire. As mentioned, there are two versions of Diallo's ABC News interview. There is a full, unedited version of the televised interview that was made available on the network's website on August 18, 2011, nearly a month after the edited version, which was broadcast on July 25, 2011. The full version is over an hour long, while the edited version is just under four minutes. I will be examining both versions because they share a great deal in common with regard to links between sonics and identity. From the outset of the full interview, after Robin Roberts asks her one of the first questions, "Why have you decided to come forward now?" Diallo responds, "Ok—I decided to come—Sorry, my English, you know, is difficult for me. I don't speak that much but I'm gonna try. " (00:03:17). The moment in which Diallo hesitates to apologize for her English is the moment that her identity as an immigrant woman of color becomes known, somewhat on her own terms. In the edited version, this moment is excluded. Robin Roberts's voiceover frames the edited interview with Diallo, but she does not mention that Diallo is from another country, only mentioning the most pertinent facts of the case: maid, Dominique Strauss-Kahn, hotel where she worked, trying to clean his room, IMF. After Roberts's in-studio framing, the video cuts to Diallo at the moment during her interview when she is at her most animated, the moment when she is using expressive hand gestures and pantomiming as well as her words in accented English to describe the act of sexual assault that Strauss-Kahn committed against her. There is then a cut to footage of Diallo walking alone on a New York City street and into a building while Roberts's voiceover explains that she is from Guinea, West Africa. This is quite powerful. ABC News allows Diallo's embodied voice to inform the viewer of her status as someone born outside of the United States. In this way, Diallo's accented English takes on a great deal of performative and interpretive weight, attempting to explain the parts of her identity that are, as Ifemelu would say, "wrapped in gauze": in other words, the parts of identity that make immigrant women of color both hypervisible and invisible.[26] Her accent, her apologies about her inability to express herself in her second language as fully as she would like—these sonic aspects of the interview mark it and its subject as an immigrant woman.

Diallo's accent is the most prominent aspect of the sonics of the interview that clearly present her as an immigrant woman of color, but there are other aspects of Diallo's voice that work to portray her not only as a non-American woman, but also as a victim of sexual assault. As I have tried to portray through the stitched image of Diallo above, over the course of the unedited interview (and even the shorter edited broadcast interview), Diallo expresses many versions of herself. She achieves this through facial gestures as the image indicates (figure 9), but also explores a range of emotions vocally. She begins the interview with a soft voice. Her voice has a raspy quality that could be her regular speaking voice, a tone that occurs when she speaks in English, or the result of a harrowing two-month period over the course of which, as she describes it, she has been crying, contemplating suicide, fearing for her life, and anxiously awaiting justice. Through the combined soft strength of her voice, Diallo is able to convey an image of herself as shy and yet also as entitled to justice, someone who experienced fear when being sexually assaulted in her workplace by a stranger. Her voice also seems to register shame when she must actually respond on national television to Roberts's question, "Are you a prostitute?" The soft, raspy quality of Diallo's voice never goes away, but rather is heightened when she becomes less meek and more passionate, less uncertain and more enraged, less fearful and more demanding of her assailant's punishment. Even as Diallo's voice reads as "soft" and thus fits a certain "ideal victim" profile, there are moments when the softness combines with expressed innocence or ignorance to represent the "ideal immigrant woman of color victim" more specifically.[27]

One of the most impactful moments of Diallo as an ideal immigrant woman of color victim is when she details the moment she just happened to bump into her supervisor, Jessica, immediately after the attack and was deciding whether to tell her what happened.

> I see her I say, "Oh, thank god, Jessica, I was gonna call you!" . . . I say "I was gonna call you! I wanna tell you something." And she say, "What do you wanna tell me?" I say, "Let's go inside" because, you know, that was a lot of rooms 'do not disturb,' I don't wanna like, you know—but I was so sad. I go in. I was spitting, I want to throw up. I don't know what to do, I feel so—I say, "Jessica—" but I was so *afraid* to lose my job. I don't know

the *law*! I don't know if someone do this to you, what you *have* to do? I don't know nothing about that in that job I don't know because I never had that happen there. (00:28:09; emphasis added where Diallo drags vowels)

Throughout this part of the interview, Diallo's voice vacillates between its lowest and highest volumes. Of special interest is when Diallo says, "I don't know the *law*!" She says this loudly and drags the "a" vowel of the word so that "law" gets the most emphasis in the phrase. Her statement here denotes a seeming lack of awareness that may be unique to immigrants. Even though Diallo does not say, "I do not know the law *in this country*!" the statement of a lack of knowledge combined with her accented English implies this interpretation. Diallo expresses a lack of knowledge in other moments as well, such as when she tells Roberts that she is aware of the difficulty of getting work without any formal education, when she makes it clear that she did not know who Dominique Strauss-Kahn was, and when she goes on to tell Roberts after this excerpt that she had no idea that reporting the assault would invite such chaos into her life.

However, behind her declaration that she does not know the law is a deeper admission about the scripts around immigrants. There are a variety of ways to view this statement as it relates to her identity. On the one hand, for Diallo to express ignorance of how the US legal system works is to position herself as an innocent, someone who does not lie, someone who could be easily manipulated and taken advantage of, someone who could be sexually assaulted rather than someone who manipulates a situation with a wealthy man for a payday. On the other hand, Diallo's expression of legal ignorance risks placing her in a category of "undeserving immigrant," someone whose ignorance is reflective of their inability to assimilate and therefore proof that they should be excluded from the country altogether.

This misogynoirist interpretation of Diallo's ignorance works in conjunction with standard asylum criteria to confound the immigrant subject, making her incoherent no matter what she does to try to make herself coherent. As we have seen before, any attempts by Black women victims of rape to make themselves coherent to a system or audience are doomed to fail and form one key element of Afro-pessimistic justice. The typical xenophobic standard maintains that to qualify for US citizenship, one must embed oneself in a certain version of American history, know the law, know English, and reject one's country of origin. Asylum standards require the immigrant's suffering to take on a certain form, one that is legible as political rather than personal violence. These standards are so incomparable that they are not even competing, yet Diallo seems caught between them and others, caught between a constant stream of binaristic expectations—knowledgeable/too knowledgeable, liar/victim, victim of personal violence/victim of political violence—with which her actual story (of assault and rape), body, and life cannot align.

The televised newsscape is a system Diallo is using—through visual and sonic cues—to craft a more complex version of the immigrant woman archetype for which the law does not have language: one who is sexually modest, religious, maternal, too ignorant to know "the law" but not so ignorant that she does not feel entitled to justice.[28] Diallo demonstrates how an immigrant woman of color might use her refusal of anonymity through televised news to pose her own counternarrative to the narratives that systems use to identify her as one thing or another.

Conclusion

In chapters 1 and 2, the cases of Recy Taylor and Joan Little are instructive in the way that they allow us to think about justice beyond the binary of justice–injustice. Taylor, Little, and their defenders utilize Afro-pessimistic justice strategies in an effort to make themselves intelligible to the legal system as victims of sexual violence. To reiterate this study's earlier definition of the term, when I use the word "intelligible," I refer to Blackness and womanness being included in how her status as a victim is communicated to a wide audience, whether it is a jury or a global social justice movement. For Diallo, the ways in which race, gender, intelligibility, and justice work together (and how Diallo moves through these categories as a victim) become more complicated because she is no longer only working within and against the criminal legal system; she is now operating within and against multiple systems all at once. Diallo's case demonstrates the significance of two other systems for Black female victims of sexual violence: the immigration system and the civil legal system. These systems place an added burden on the Black female immigrant victim of rape and her allies to make her intelligible as not only a victim of violence, but also as a person worthy of asylum, worthy of access to a path to citizenship. As we have seen, though one's "worthiness" or assimilability is certainly connected to the same kinds of standards set for Black women around "ideal victimhood," the lengths that Diallo has to go to attempt to be intelligible as a victim of a crime set her somewhat apart from

Taylor and Little. Despite their differences, however, all of the women fail in one way or another to be made intelligible as Black female victims of sexual crimes, and their awareness of the probable inevitability of this failure is at the center of their Afro-pessimistic justice strategies.

Part 2

LITERATURE

Chapter 4

BESSIE'S SONG

As mentioned in chapter 1, the case of Recy Taylor indicates that the rape of Black women cannot be both abstracted *and* intelligible. This assertion persists in each case study in part 1, where I argue that, in order for her rape to be validated, both the Black woman's racial and gender identities must be recognized when the state acknowledges the crime against her. This recognition of her full self as a victim of a crime is what I call "intelligibility." In part 2 of this book, I pair such legal cases with examples of literary representations of Black women who have been raped in order to investigate whether literature offers Black women a language for or definition of justice that the law does not, or whether justice—as an imagined concept—has different boundaries in literary worlds than in historical worlds. This chapter argues that the character of Bessie from *Native Son* offers an example of such recognition unavailable to women like Recy Taylor. Bessie is the raped Black woman who stands in partial defiance of Giorgio Agamben's state of exception; it is in fact her death, the very thing that is supposed to exclude her from society and the state, that begins to make her intelligible as a raped Black woman.

The work of Abdul JanMohamed is useful in locating Bessie's place in a biopolitical frame. Biopolitics argues that power is largely understood and theorized around various visions of "life"—which lives matter or do not matter to the state, whose life is valued and whose is not. Out of this framework, "bare life" emerges as an important concept to describe the lives that are of least value to the state. Both Agamben and Hannah Arendt, two foundational philosophers and theoreticians, grounded their understanding of biopolitics in the Holocaust of World War II. Many people have employed the biopolitical theories of Agamben in literature, but none quite so electrically and with such a Black studies lens as JanMohamed in his study of the works of Richard Wright, *The Death-Bound-Subject: Richard Wright's Archaeology of Death*.[1] Drawing upon the work of JanMohamed and Sondra Guttman, I will highlight the ways in which Bessie, one of the central characters of *Native Son* who is raped and murdered by protagonist Bigger Thomas, signals death as a potential Afro-pessimistic justice strategy.

It may appear unnecessary to remark on the centrality of rape in a novel like *Native Son*. Sexual violence, after all, plays such a major role in the plot: a young Black male protagonist who is accused of murdering and raping a young, rich white woman, actually rapes and murders his young, poor Black girlfriend, and, generally, has a difficult time separating pain from desire, pleasure from violence, throughout the novel. Here I place sexual violence at the center of a reading of *Native Son* because my project investigates the extent to which this crime can be intelligible as a crime when Black women are the victims.

Native Son *and the Shifting Metonyms of Racism, Death, and Rape*

Bessie and the crimes committed against her are abstracted in *Native Son* in a variety of ways. First, the way that Bessie is abstracted in both the novel and in scholarly criticism of the novel portrays the sexual violence that she experiences in a way that erases the act or subsumes it under seemingly all-encompassing terminology, namely that of death. JanMohamed, for example, categorizes the act of rape as just one of many abuses to which "bare life" is made vulnerable. I argue that JanMohamed mimics Wright and the character of Bigger Thomas in *Native Son* by eliminating all gender-specific boundaries that exist between rape, death, and other forms of physical and psychological abuse (9). In other words, when talking about sexual violence, gender is not discussed. This is key, because by not naming the raping of Black women in *Native Son,* the specific history of unintelligibility that this sexual crime holds is obscured, and so is the particular way that the law racializes and genders consent and rape law.[2]

Though JanMohamed blurs the lines between rape and death, he at least recognizes the role of gender in this blurring. However, even this acknowledgment of gender maintains a focus on Bigger Thomas while ignoring Bessie (81–82). In JanMohamed's estimation, whereas white supremacy utilizes forces of sexualization and racialization to "feminize" the Black male, Wright employs them to destroy, actually and metaphorically, the very objects his protagonist, Bigger Thomas, supposedly cannot own: the bodies of white and Black women. Though JanMohamed puts a great deal of emphasis on sex as an aspect of his theorizing, he elaborates upon his understanding of the specific role that he sees rape playing in Wright's work when he takes a close look at the author's introduction to *Native Son*, "How 'Bigger' Was Born":

> In the prefacing essay [Wright] argues: "the reason for the lynching is usually called 'rape,' that catchword which has garnered such vile connotations that it can raise a mob anywhere in the South pretty quickly, even today." "Rape" thus becomes the metonymic sign for all violations of the racial border. Wright's primary focus in *Native Son*, however, is, not on this injunction, or on racialized sexuality, but on the dialectics of death . . . Wright thus articulates the conjunction of eros and thanatos in such a way that he is able to enhance dramatically our understanding of how the slave or the Jim Crow racial economy deploys death to bifurcate life into two, into one portion that has use-value, which the slave is allowed to keep in exchange for the other portion, the exchange-value of life, which the master appropriates for his own use. (83–84)

Before exploring his inattention to sexual violence, it is important to note that JanMohamed is working within Frank B. Wilderson's definition of Afro-pessimism without labeling it as such. JanMohamed's consideration of the modern extension of "slave or the Jim Crow racial economy" implies its inescapability, which is a central tenet of Afro-pessimism. This inescapability from the master/slave bind is visible when JanMohamed replaces Wright's metonym for rape with his own metonym for death when he asserts, "'Rape' thus becomes the metonymic sign for all violations of the racial border." Both metonyms abstract Bessie, causing the act of sexual violence that Bigger Thomas commits against his girlfriend, Bessie, to lose its gendered and racial specificities. Let me be clear: Because JanMohamed's focus is on the entire body of Richard Wright's work through the lens of death, he is not wrong to place the abstracted violence, rather than the particular rape, at the center of his study. In other words, it makes sense that JanMohamed places Bigger rather than Bessie at the heart of his interrogation of the novel. However, for my purposes of centering Bessie so as to theorize the intelligibility of the raped Black woman, rape is not "the metonymic sign for all violations of the racial border" because this would require a hierarchical relationship between death and rape. This hierarchy is impossible for Bessie because Bigger both rapes and murders her. Yet the novel insists upon a hierarchy between these violent acts by constantly omitting the fact of this sexual violence. Even during the scene in which Bigger rapes Bessie, the fact of this rape is blurred for Bigger. The novel therefore insists upon a frustrated relationship between death and rape as well.

While JanMohamed mirrors Wright's text when he enacts an abstraction of rape under the guise of death in his theory of the death-bound subject, Wright himself seems to have created *Native Son* with this abstraction keenly on his mind, as "How Bigger Was Born" elucidates. In fact, *Native Son* is one of the most well-known contributors to the literary history of Black women, sexual violence, and the law. And it is possible that Wright himself consciously decided to contribute to such an entangled discourse.[3] Though sexual violence holds a privileged status in the novel, it is also continuously abstracted from the "real" crime that the protagonist commits. One such moment of abstraction occurs at a pivotal moment when Bigger Thomas has just confessed to "his girl," Bessie, that he murdered a white woman, Mary Dalton. In the following scene, Bigger's confession is bound to a proclamation of a troubling rape theory that allows him to maintain his status as an uncomplicated victim of white supremacy, a status that is highly gendered and sexualized:

> Bessie cried again. He caught her face in his hands. He was concerned; he wanted to see this thing through her eyes at that moment.
> "What?"
> "They'll . . . They'll say you raped her."
> Bigger stared. He had entirely forgotten the moment when he had carried Mary up the stairs. So deeply had he pushed it all back down into him that it was not until now that its real meaning came back. They would say he had raped her and there would be no way to prove that he had not. That fact had not assumed importance in his eyes until now. He stood up, his jaws hardening. Had he raped her? Yes, he had raped her. Every time he felt as he had felt that night, he raped. *But rape was not what one did to women. Rape was what one felt when one's back was against a wall and one had to strike out, whether one wanted to or not, to keep the pack from killing one.* He committed rape every time he looked into a white face. He was a long, taut piece of rubber which a thousand white hands had stretched to the snapping point, and when he snapped it was rape. But it was rape when he cried out in deep hate in his heart as he felt the strain of living day by day. That, too, was rape. (213–14; emphasis added)

Bigger's elucidation of his "rape theory" is one of the most famous scenes in the novel yet one from which scholars almost always exclude Bessie in their readings. However, Bessie is incredibly central to this scene. It is her knowledge of rape and race that (re)awakens Bigger to his own internalized confusion around rage, race, and rape when she says, "They'll say you raped her." Furthermore, the narrator uses language to abstract rape as just another form of violence in a larger cycle of violence: "Rape was what one did when one's back was against a wall and one had to strike out." The language of Bigger's rape theory is vague enough to remain open to several interpretations. On the one hand, I concede to JanMohamed's reading: Bigger abstracts rape here because it is a metonym for his own death-boundness. On the other hand, his theory is salient as much because of what it omits as what it declares: "Rape was what one felt when one's back was against a wall and one had to strike out, whether one wanted to or not, to keep the pack from killing one." This sentence erases the fact of rape as an act of sexual violence. Bigger's denial that rape is something done to people, usually women, is one of many times that Bigger will abstract Bessie. Sondra Guttman affirms this point in her essay "What Bigger Killed For: Rereading Violence Against Women in *Native Son*," in which she challenges the notion that Wright only uses rape as a metaphor for suppression of Black resistance. Guttman writes that in "*Native Son* the word 'rape' also means sexual violence against women—in particular black women" (170). At this point in the novel, Bigger has not yet raped and murdered his girlfriend, Bessie. She stands before him, confronting him with the reality he faces and he immediately removes her from his mind to focus instead on his own violation. It makes sense that Bigger is having difficulty focusing. After all, he is on the run for the murder and false rape of a white woman. But it is also true that even before physically brutalizing Bessie, Bigger repeatedly sacrifices her mentally so as to place himself at the center of a white supremacist world of violence.

The novel is a stunning work of Afro-pessimism as it argues that white supremacy makes it impossible for Bigger to see himself and Bessie (and an even larger collective of the poor, the Black, the oppressed) as bonded in their victimhood.[4] Within an Afro-pessimistic frame, there is no room for collective Black empowerment because the master-slave dialectic is unbreakable. Bigger can only see himself as a victim and Bessie as an obstacle. As violently disturbing as Bigger's rape and murder of Bessie is, his inability to even imagine himself as linked to Bessie or even see them both at the center of white supremacist violence together is perhaps the novel's darkest message. In the world that Wright creates, which is to say the real world, white supremacy completely truncates the possibility of a mixed gender, intraracial coalition against anti-Black violence.

Native Son *and the Courtroom*

As mentioned earlier, Bigger enacts an abstraction of rape (and therefore of Bessie) through his theorization of it. He goes on to abstract the sexual crime that he committed against Bessie in the courtroom scenes, which occur in the final section of the novel. In these scenes, Bigger continues to abstract Bessie in death just as he did in life. However, during the trial, Bessie is also made intelligible. Only now there are agents of Bessie's intelligibility (or lack of intelligibility) who are men other than Bigger. The trial scenes of the novel are key to establishing how the criminal justice system abstracts or makes intelligible Bessie as well as the sexual crime committed against her. In the courtroom, the white male state agents—the Deputy Coroner, the State Attorney, David Buckley, and Bigger's defense lawyer, Boris Max—enter the frame as arbiters of Bessie's access to victimhood as a raped Black woman.

It is clear that Bigger's incoherent theorizing of rape as an abstract concept is at odds with the trial scenes in the novel during which Boris Max, Bigger's defense lawyer, goes to great lengths to parse out the various crimes. For Max, the crime of rape is different from the crime of emotional trauma that Bigger suffers under white supremacy, which is different from the crime of murder. Even if the racism that Bigger experiences causes him to commit rape, Max treats them as separate. The spiritual murder of Bessie is a slow and painful process, one that Wright attempts to make the reader comprehend, but there is only so much that he can do to give Bessie her own voice when everything—every vision, dream, fight, fantasy, and nightmare—is focalized through Bigger Thomas.

A shift in this focalization occurs when the reader encounters the courtroom scenes. Like everything else in the narrative, these scenes are narrated from Bigger's perspective, but his typical narratorial diatribes are nearly absent from the proceedings, making way for pages and pages of dialogue between other characters who, unlike Bigger, sitting in silence, are endowed with the authority to speak in the courtroom. In other words, the chapter devoted to the trial provides a more neutral territory on which characters other than Bigger have an opportunity to become the focus of the reader's imagination. This is one of the many explanations for why much of the courtroom scene centers Bessie. Or, to state the matter more precisely, the courtroom scene centers Bessie's corpse. The revelation of Bessie's deceased body is not only the climax of the court case, but also the key to understanding the relationship between death and intelligibility for the raped Black woman and death as an Afro-pessimistic justice strategy. The requirements for intelligibility are different in the novel than they are in the case of Recy Taylor, for example. Taylor would have been intelligible if the state had recognized the crime committed against her as a crime (i.e., charged the assailants) and if those who committed the crime were punished. In the case of the novel, we already know that the criminal justice system will punish Bigger, Bessie's assailant, in some way, but it is not clear whether he will be punished for raping Bessie. For this reason, it is necessary to find clues of Bessie's intelligibility in the language that is used to describe her throughout the trial.

When the coroner presents Bessie's body as evidence, he makes an important intrusion into the world of the novel when he says: "As Deputy Coroner, I have decided, in the interests of justice, to offer in evidence the raped and mutilated body of one *Bessie Mears*, and the testimony of police officers and doctors relating to the cause and manner of her death" (306). This is one of the only moments when Bessie is made intelligible as a raped Black woman. It is in this small moment that Wright is once more commenting on the depressingly low status of Black women when he declares this marginal character's full name only after she has died. However, the simple detail of the Deputy Coroner, an appendage of state power, proclaiming Bessie's full name for the official court record proves that Wright is making another powerful statement. When Bessie is alive, she has a life full of "hard trouble" (215) largely because of the minimal role she is permitted to play in the world as well as the novel: Bessie exists as a vessel for Bigger's sexual energy; Bessie is domestic labor for white families; Bessie is "plain black trouble"; "Bessie is raped" (215–16). But who is "Bessie Mears"? Because the reader does not have access to Bessie's interiority, the novel does not offer meaningful answers to this question. However, the coroner's announcement at the very least makes the sexual crime against Bessie intelligible as such by publicly announcing it in a court of law.

As the scene continues, Wright uses Bigger to explain exactly who he thinks "Bessie Mears" is and, at the same time, emphasizes the necessity of death for the raped Black woman to become intelligible:

"Mr. Coroner," Max said. "This is outrageous! *Your indecent exhibition of that girl's body* serves no purpose but that of an incitement to mob violence . . ."

"It will enable the jury to determine the exact manner of the death of Mary Dalton, who was slain by the man who slew *Bessie Mears!*" the coroner said in a scream that was compounded of rage and vindictiveness.

"You are criminally appealing to mob emotion . . ."

"That's for the grand jury to determine!" the coroner said. "And you cannot interrupt these proceedings any longer! If you persist in this attitude, you'll be removed from this room! *I have the legal right to determine what evidence is necessary . . .*"

[Bigger] had completely forgotten Bessie during the inquest of Mary. He understood what was being done. To offer the dead body of Bessie as evidence and proof that he had murdered Mary would make him appear a monster; it would stir up more hate against him . . . They were bringing Bessie's body in now to make the white men and women feel that nothing short of a quick blotting out of his life would make the city safe again. *They were using his having killed Bessie to kill him for his having killed Mary, to cast him in a light that would sanction any action taken to destroy him. Though he had killed a black girl and a white girl, he knew that it would be for the death of the white girl that he would be punished. The black girl was merely "evidence." And under it all he knew that white people did not really care about Bessie's being killed* . . . His eyes rested wistfully on the still oblong white draped form under the sheet on the table and he felt a deeper sympathy for Bessie than at any time when she was alive. He knew that Bessie, too, though dead, though killed by him, would resent her dead body being used in this way . . .

The coroner rapped for order, then rose and stepped to the table and with one sweep of his arm flung the sheet back from Bessie's body. The sight, bloody and black, made Bigger flinch involuntarily and lift his hands to his eyes at the same instant he saw blinding flashes of the silver bulbs flicking through the air (306–9; emphasis added)

Bigger is right to be suspicious of the state's "use" of Bessie's body, which I will return to shortly. But for now, it is worth noting that the coroner's reference to the raped Black female body as "Bessie Mears" is an attempt to make her legible or, as Bigger's narration implies, to demonstrate that the Black female can be permitted entry into the cult of white womanhood, which was ostensibly the only way to access a kind of defended status, especially in Jim Crow America. That is to say, Bessie can gain access to her rightful place as a victim so long as she is dead, voiceless, mangled, and brutalized. In this moment, Bessie is intelligible as having had a crime committed against her. Pushing further into Bessie's portrayal reveals additional layers of raped Black female intelligibility.

As argued in chapter 1, there is a distinction between legibility and intelligibility. Recall that to make legible is to remove; to make intelligible is to add. Recy Taylor's case demonstrated that attempts to make the Black female legible require the removal of her gender from her Blackness, which can only happen temporarily. Once "Mrs. Recy Taylor" is absorbed into the realm of "All American womanhood," she becomes legible as a woman "regardless of race." To make the raped Black female intelligible in Jim Crow America is to recognize that a crime has been committed against the very body that has been socially scripted as unrapeable. In the realm of the novel, when the coroner uses Bessie's full legal name, he uses the trappings of middle-class mobility to make this poor, young, Black, female character into a full person with a past, an inheritor of familial history.

Bessie—like Topsy from *Uncle Tom's Cabin*, Queequeg from *Moby Dick,* or Dilsey from *The Sound and the Fury* and many other minor minority characters from American literary history—is not a fully realized character because she exists only in relation to the narrator or protagonist; she is a creature born from dependence and exists nowhere else.[5] Even so, when the coroner pronounces Bessie's legal name at the same time as he reveals her body, he is declaring that her Blackness, the fact of her rape, *and* her womanhood can be made citizen, that is, made legible—a stepping stone to intelligibility. This act of making Bessie intelligible, though, is not absent of violence. While this reading grants Bessie access to intelligibility, it is the kind of violent intelligibility that the state of exception enacts. Bigger narrates this violence as one that is in fact inflicted upon him: "They were using his having killed Bessie to kill him for his having killed Mary, to cast him in a light that would sanction any action taken to destroy him" (306). Bigger's ego forces him to maintain Bessie as a pawn, a tool of dependence, one who, even in death, solely exists in relation to him and his fate. Although Bigger is not exactly wrong, Wright's text implies that his protagonist's inability to privilege Bessie's pain above his own is yet another example of biopolitical maneuvering. The state is "using" Bessie to suspend the law—Bigger's execution for crimes to which he has confessed and for those that he has not seems justified.[6] Of course, the very "need" that Bigger felt to kill Bessie is a product of his abjection. Unfortunately, any attempt to center Bessie in a discussion about *Native Son* is somewhat doomed to fail. She cannot be a coherent subject because that is not her role in the economy of the novel. She exists only as a foil for Bigger Thomas. But Bessie resists simplification because, when her name is called out, her deceased body speaks for her and for the possibility of making Bessie intelligible as a Black female, raped and murdered by a Black male. Like Recy Taylor, Bessie Mears is neither coherent nor incoherent, neither subject nor object.

Now that we see that Bessie is made intelligible as a raped Black woman, what remains is an exploration of the other factors involved in this process of making the Black female victim intelligible as the victim of a sexual crime. Unfortunately, it is not sufficient to say that Bessie's death *made* her rape intelligible, because its intelligibility depends on a great many factors. One of those factors is the audience, which is receiving her corpse in the courtroom.

Race, Rape, Intelligibility, and Audience

I must retrace some steps to underscore the importance of audience and perception in Bessie's intelligibility. As Bigger explains it, Bessie is only intelligible as raped and Black so that she can be used as evidence that could lead to his execution for murdering and "raping" the white female Mary Dalton. Bigger is in fact making an argument about audience. Bessie's rape is intelligible because it is important for convincing a specific audience, the jury, of a certain verdict, a verdict of guilty with recommendation for the death penalty. Notice, however, that at the same time as Bigger makes a convincing argument about the role of audience in Bessie's intelligibility, he erases the fact that he raped her. Among many other literary strategies, Wright uses formal tactics to smudge out the fact of Bigger raping Bessie. Recall the excerpt examined earlier, so that we may look at in light of this strategy:

> They were using his having *killed* Bessie to *kill* him for his having *killed* Mary, to cast him in a light that would sanction any action taken to destroy him. Though he had *killed* a black girl and a white girl, he knew that it would be for the *death* of the white girl that he would be punished.

The black girl was merely "evidence." And under it all he knew that the white people never searched for Negroes who *killed* other Negroes. He had even heard it said that white people felt it was good when one Negro *killed another*; it meant that they had one Negro less to contend with . . . He knew that Bessie, too, though dead, though *killed* by him, would resent her *dead* body being used in this way. (307; emphasis added)

Nothing in the language above reminds the reader that Bigger rapes Bessie almost immediately before killing her. Her murder is the only crime that concerns him because it will be used as evidence against him. But I argue that this is not because Wright wants the reader to believe that Bessie is only intelligible as raped as a strategy to be used against Bigger. That is certainly true within the scheme of the plot, but it is also true that Bessie's intelligibility is dependent on factors separate from Mary and Bigger. While the narrator highlights the power of the white jury, his audience, the boundaries between rape and death soon blur, enabling Bigger to place himself and his own morality at the center of the trial. The number of times Bigger uses the word "kill" and "death" above showcases the tendency I highlighted earlier: the primacy of death over rape in the novel. Perhaps this emphasis on death is a result of Bigger's rape theory: everything is rape, so to mention the rape of Bessie is pointless. However, as we saw early in this chapter, such a verbal dismissal endangers Bessie's intelligibility as a raped Black female. In this short excerpt, Bigger refers seven times to his having *killed* Bessie. And not once does he mention raping her. On one hand, it is possible that Bigger does not admit that he raped Bessie because he actually does not believe that he did. According to Bigger's amorphous definition of rape, it is something that happens to him rather than an act of sexual violence he has committed against another. But, of course, Bigger Thomas is not the arbiter of what is just and unjust in the novel.

I do not think that Wright intends the reader to excuse Bigger's forgetfulness of Bessie or the fact that he raped her. In fact, this very forgetting, this inability to even remind himself of the fact that he raped her—at a moment in the novel when he expresses such deep sympathy for how she is "used" by the white supremacist court—acts as a special reminder to the close reader of her rape. Though Bigger mentions an external audience of white people who are clamoring to use Bessie's death against him, it is clear that he also sees himself as an audience for whom Bessie's death is nothing but a cog in the white supremacist machine that oppresses him. In other words, with

Bigger as audience, Bessie cannot be intelligible as raped. But there are other audiences to consider, namely that of the prosecutor, Buckley and that of Bigger's defense lawyer, Max.

No one in the novel acknowledges Bessie's Blackness—no one, that is, except for Bigger and Max. We have seen Bigger regard the corpse as "black and bloody," abstracting Bessie's race and gender. Bigger abstracts Bessie in this way because he is a particular audience and it suits his agenda for her to remain an abstracted symbol of his own oppression. Max is a different audience and therefore takes a different approach with regards to Bessie, attempting to revive her from obfuscation in his closing statement: "I have not explained the relationship of Bessie Mears to this boy. I have not forgotten her. I omitted to mention her until now because she was largely omitted from the consciousness of Bigger Thomas. His relationship to *the poor black girl* also reveals his relationship to the world" (367; emphasis added).

It is important that Max acknowledges Bessie's Blackness, class identity, and gender identity, as these are all of the things that, under so-called normal circumstances, render her rape invisible as a crime. However, there are some considerations to be made here when we review Max's words closely. On the one hand, Max acknowledges Bessie's Blackness, but only to advance his agenda to defend Bigger, as seen when he continues to remark upon Bessie. Again, this analysis is less a critique of wording or the character of Boris Max, but rather an indictment of the system that the novel sets up as one in which Bigger Thomas is centered to the exclusion of all others, except in the transitory moment of the many-voiced courtroom. Max's objective to defend Bigger from the death penalty leads him to assert Bessie's Blackness while eliding any explicit acknowledgment of her rape:

> But Bigger Thomas is not here on trial for having murdered Bessie Mears. And he knows that. What does this mean? Does not the life of a Negro girl mean as much in the eyes of the law as the life of a white girl? Yes, perhaps, in the abstract. But under the stress of fear and flight, Bigger Thomas did not think of Bessie. He could not. The attitude of America toward this boy regulated *his most intimate dealings with his own kind.* (367; emphasis added)

Setting aside for the moment Max's "abstract" illustration of equal protection for Black and white women, I want to focus on the direct acknowledgment of Bessie, "the poor black girl" and "a Negro girl." At this point in the novel, Max can directly use Bessie's Blackness, but he must evade the fact of her rape using vague rather than graphically violent language: "this boy regulated his most intimate dealings with his own kind."[7] In Max's estimation, the intimacy between Bessie and Bigger suffered at the hands of a white supremacist American system, rather than at Bigger's hands. As an attorney trying to keep Bigger from death row, Max must abstract Bessie's rape in order to also abstract the truth of Bigger-as-rapist.

Returning to the agenda of the opposition, represented by the prosecuting attorney, Buckley, as well as the state coroner, it is interesting to see where they diverge and converge with Max. It is of course in Buckley's interest to make Bessie intelligible as raped to the jury as a means of not only indicting Bigger, but also legally killing him. As state agents, Buckley and the coroner make her rape intelligible three different times: when her corpse is announced as "raped and mutilated" (306), when her corpse is brought into the courtroom as visual evidence of the crimes committed against her (306), and when they read the charges against Bigger (342). However, as Guttman reminds us, Bessie's is not the only name of a sexually violated woman that the prosecution announces. Buckley tries to pin several unsolved rapes on Bigger and Bessie acts as evidence of those rapes as much as she acts as false evidence of the falsely alleged rape of Mary Dalton. Guttman expounds upon this announcement of victims as another way that Wright makes the typically invisible sexual violation of Black women visible.

> While the women Buckley mentions are without a doubt white women, their numbers suggest the prevalence of sexual violence. Their whiteness coupled with the use of Bessie's body in Mary's trial make present uncounted numbers of raped black women—the women of whom Buckley will never speak unless their rapes give him some information about the violations of white women. (187)

I agree with Guttman that the prosecution tries to not only blame Bigger for the rape of a white woman, Mary (who he did not rape), but also for the rapes of other women who are named in the courtroom. The naming of those women (who are almost certainly white) speaks to this double standard around sexual violence and race for Black and white women. For example, white women are granted a certain amount of credibility that Black women are not. Guttman's insight reinforces the fact that the novel (and the systems of oppression it represents) cannot make room for Bessie or other Black female victims of violence unless they are pawns in a game that uplifts white women back to their rightful place as the truest victims, the true icons of defendable womanhood. The disparity between Bessie and Mary Dalton is clear.

In addition to acknowledging this disparity, I want to also assert that to take stock of the moments when Black women become intelligible to the state as sexually violated is historically and politically valuable because it defies the assumption that the law has only ever failed to acknowledge and act upon the violations of Black women as crimes. Though Buckley, the coroner, and Max have opposed motivations, they are united around their exploitation of Bessie in one way or another. Max must downplay Bessie's rape to save his client, while the prosecution makes Bessie intelligible as raped only to further his case against Bigger as a savage rapist of white women. I am not defending Buckley and the coroner, but even if they are motivated by the white supremacist desire to legally murder a Black man for the false rape of a white woman, the fact remains that they use the resources of the law to recognize Bessie's rape as a crime and one that deserves compensation.

Bessie's intelligibility—officially and simultaneously recognized as Black, woman, and raped—is therefore neither wholly positive nor wholly negative, but rather a neutral fact. But her intelligibility does open up the possibility of a fantastical optimistic reading of *Native Son*: perhaps if Max, Buckley, the coroner, and the judge were not so consumed by Bigger, if, in other words, this were another novel, perhaps Bessie's Blackness and gender could be made intelligible with less hesitation. However, just as the case of Recy Taylor evinces, we see two things here: although it is difficult (nearly impossible, in fact) to legitimize and make intelligible the raped Black female, perhaps she does not have to die for this intelligibility to occur.

Conclusion

In all of the other chapters in this book, I examine how sexually violated Black women and their defenders and allies define justice for themselves; I argue that Black women often define justice along far more self-destructive lines than current scholarship has observed, definitions that form a set of strategies I call Afro-pessimistic justice. This chapter on Wright's foundational novel is a departure from the others because of the confines of the literature under study here, *Native Son*, make it impossible to center the voice of the raped Black woman in question. Though the reader encounters Bessie Mears's voice a few times throughout the novel, it provides no access to her as a subject or as a participant in the legal system represented in the trial scenes at the end of the novel. Because Bessie Mears dies as a result of the enraged and psychopathic urges of Bigger Thomas, she does not get a chance to assert her own definitions of justice for her own violation. Would she want Bigger to suffer at the hands of the criminal justice system for the crimes committed against her? Would Bessie have alternative hopes for how she and Bigger could overcome his violation of her together—along the lines of transformative justice? Even if Bessie had survived Bigger's rape and testified against him, the economy of the novel forces her to remain a cipher for Mary Dalton; had Bessie lived, she would likely still lack access to her own voice, her own desires, her own strategies for healing from the wounds that Bigger caused.

Bessie is unable to define justice for herself; the definitions are formulated for her by the state, that is, agents of the criminal justice system. Despite their different subjectivities and motivations, the prosecution, the state coroner, and Bigger Thomas's defense still give us a sense of what kinds of intelligibility existed in the 1940s Black literary imagination. For Wright to assert that Black women primarily gain access to justice for their rapes by way of death is one of the most Afro-pessimistic readings imaginable. Bessie's death is the ultimate failure of justice. Although Bessie is acknowledged as a Black female victim of a sexual crime, it is precisely her death that conditions this acknowledgment. Bessie remains locked into a familiar pattern of abjection and degradation that an enslaved woman may have experienced. The difference here is that even in the mid-twentieth century white people, especially of the North, had some level of performative progressivism they wished to display, perhaps best demonstrated when the prosecution claims that the inclusion of Bessie's body is only meant to act as an example of Bigger's aggression. This is a lie, but the very fact that white representatives for the state feel that they must lie to cover up actions that under nineteenth-century rules would have been allowable in the out and open is indeed a sad but real step forward. And yet, still, the version of Afro-pessimistic justice that is given to Bessie (her rapist and murderer is punished but she is dead and therefore cannot feel whatever potential healing one might feel) happens in a court of law, something that no Black woman would experience in reality for at least another decade in 1959 when Betty Jean Owens triumphed over her four white rapists who were each given life sentences.

It is the beauty of literature that it can imagine whole worlds and universes that are beyond the realities of our own. In future chapters, I explore the ways in which Black authors offer some slightly more hopeful but still Afro-pessimistic readings of the relationship between the law, Black women, sexual violence, and justice, but *Native Son* offers no such hope. Instead, Richard Wright uses the constructs of literature to almost mimic, in the harshest and coldest shades of grey, the reality of life for Black Americans and, namely, the continued abjection of raped Black women in the twentieth century. I began this book under the notion that the twentieth century offered far more openings for raped Black women than wholly abjectifying theorizations of enslavement and its afterlives would have us believe, and that, given the cases before us, Black women who experienced sexual violence themselves were not always already assuming they were completely outside the realms of access to justice, were not always already assuming that to attempt justice for their violations was a lost cause, were not always already assuming that all hope was doomed to fail. The turn of the Afro-pessimistic screw comes in the form of all of the ways in which these cases *are* doomed to fail and how, in the case of Bessie, the apparent defenders of Black women like Bigger (in his mind) and Max, utilize failure, self-destruction, and death as ways of making the crimes against Black women intelligible.

But the very fact that *Native Son* requires its Black rape victim to die in order for her rape to be recognized as a crime is at the center of death as an Afro-pessimistic justice strategy: a strategy that is utterly doomed and puts the very idea of justice for raped Black women in doubt while at the very same time continuing to use the machinations of that system. It is this continued appeal to the halls of justice that is central to my reframing of the twentieth century as a new time for raped Black women and those interested in cultivating strategies to defend them and make them intelligible as victims of sexual crimes.

Chapter 5

URSA'S SONG

Native Son does not quite fit into the rubric I've established so far of how sexually violated Black women define justice for themselves. In previous chapters, we have become acquainted with Black women who at the very least express themselves or have social movements or allies working hard to make sure that their voices are heard. The latter is somewhat true for Bessie, but in a way that is ultimately still rooted in white supremacy and misogynoir. In other words, we do not get access to Bessie's definition of anything. By contrast, Gayl Jones's 1975 debut novel, *Corregidora*, investigates the interiorities of several generations of Black women. Though written in the 1970s, Jones's novel is set in the 1940s—close to the time Wright was thinking through justice for raped Black women in *Native Son*. Jones's work strongly resonates with its own contemporary moment: she is a young woman in the 1970s reflecting on the life of her mother, her mother's mother, her mother's mother's mother—as so many other Black feminist writers like Toni Morrison and Gwendolyn Brooks were doing at that time. However, *Corregidora* is also a marked departure from those works because of the way that she incorporates the justice system into her work rather than ignore it, imagine alternatives, or reject it completely.

Unlike Wright, Jones is a Black woman writing about Black women; as a result the reader gets far more access to an Afro-pessimistic justice system created by and for Black women. Bessie is doomed to be at the mercy of the criminal justice system rather than imagining herself in control of it. The transition from Bessie to Ursa, the protagonist of *Corregidora*, also marks the transition between pre and post–World War II America, in which Black Americans felt some figment of hope that they may be incorporated into the tangled block that is the American dream. By the 1970s of Jones's time, such hope has been completely dashed by a civil rights movement that ultimately failed to bring about the radical change it wanted. Jones writes in the midst of the Vietnam War, an economic depression, and the beginnings of brutal anti-Black violence perpetrated by the government and disguised as a "war on crime." Wright's novel invests enough hope in the criminal justice system that he imagines a world in which hearing a Black story like Bigger's could change something. By Jones's time, no hope is invested in the system. Black women are creating their own. In *Native Son*, Bessie's body is used to charge him for the murder of a white woman. This misuse of Bessie's body to perpetuate anti-Black violence is a problem for that reason, but also because Bigger is obscuring his own violation of her in this manipulative defense of her. The use of her body to incarcerate and kill a Black man is the only time she is made intelligible as a victim of a crime. This Afro-pessimistic reading of *Native Son* suggests that the system can always be manipulated to serve white supremacy. In *Corregidora*, the women are manipulating the body and language to create another justice system, which is also self-harmful and traumatizing.

Corregidora is a *Bildungsroman* that traces the early and mid-life of a young, Black woman named Ursa Corregidora, a blues singer in 1947 Kentucky who attempts to live with the remnants of a familial past steeped in Brazilian enslavement. Ursa's great grandmother, Great Gram, and grandmother, Gram, pass on the story of their enslavement through repeated sessions of oral storytelling. During these sessions, Ursa learns of their white Portuguese master/forefather, known only as "old man Corregidora," who subjected Gram and Great Gram to decades of sexual violence, including incest and coerced prostitution. By contrast, the case *State v. Little* results from a single incident. On an August night in 1974, a young, Black prisoner in Beaufort County jail, Joan (pronounced Jo-Anne) Little, was the victim of a sexual assault by her white guard, Clarence Alligood, whom she killed in self-defense. These plot summaries of both the novel and the legal case fail to capture the new reading that the historic trial offers to the contemporary critical landscape around Jones's *Corregidora*. As I mentioned when discussing the cases of Joan Little and Nafissatou Diallo, manipulation is at the foundation of Black women's relationship to the law when attempting to get justice for their sexual violations. Black women and their allies must find ways to manipulate the context of justice systems so as to change the outcomes in their favor.

"That's why they burned all the papers"

Because *Corregidora* spans generations of women, from enslavement in nineteenth-century Brazil to Jim Crow era Kentucky, the ideas around justice are much more abstract than those that appear in *State v. Little*. For

Little, there is a clear goal of systemic manipulation which is her liberation from imprisonment and possibly even the death penalty for the charge of first-degree murder. In *Corregidora*, Gayl Jones implicitly illustrates another element of Afro-pessimistic justice that represents a version of justice that is more expansive than the US legal system. This definition is mobile, one that is made to function for all Black women across international borders, historical time periods, and geopolitical circumstances. There are a number of scenes in the novel that illuminate the relationship between the Corregidora women and the criminal justice system. The first of these scenes is one that repeats in different ways throughout the novel: the scene in which Ursa recalls Great Gram telling her "the same story over and over again" when she was five years old, the story of her enslavement by old man Corregidora, who forced by her to prostitute herself and her daughter (known only as Gram) at young ages, and the suppression of this story by the Corregidora masters (11). Though the content of Great Gram's story is important, it is necessary to focus on her language, which is the source of her mode of systemic manipulation. The horrors that Great Gram describes are so surreal that young Ursa questions their veracity, prompting her Great Gram, the former slave, to outline the justice system that she has created:

> "You telling the truth, Great Gram?" She slapped me. ". . . don't you ever ask if I'm lying. Because they didn't want to leave no *evidence* of what they done—so it couldn't be held against them. And I'm leaving *evidence*. And you go to leave *evidence* too . . . we got to have *evidence* to hold up. That's why they burned all the papers, so there wouldn't be no *evidence* to hold up against them." I was five years old then. (14; emphasis added)

Great Gram's repeated use of the word "evidence" here is an important indication of not only her awareness of the criminal justice system, but also her investment in using it as a model for her own form of Afro-pessimistic justice, which is steeped in a Black millennialist view of time.[1] Black millennialism is a long-standing form of engaging with the notion of justice because it imagines that justice will be served even if it is not done in one's own lifetime. The Corregidora women form their own version of Afro-pessimistic justice (centered in a Black millennialist temporality) as a means of accessing justice that is both temporally and definitionally outside of the bounds of the US legal system. This outsider status is obviously a product of enslaved Black women's exclusion from the legal system. Out of necessity or not, Great Gram creates what I am referring to as an Afro-pessimistic justice system within which she redefines the meaning of "evidence" in hopes that this redefinition will one day be capable of repairing the crimes done against her by her masters/forefathers in an unlikely utopian future. She interprets her justice system as having an impact on serving future justice in a world in which men who enslave, rape their offspring, and coerce them into prostitution are punished to the fullest extent of the law. Though Great Gram cannot control the punishment of those who have violated her, she can redefine certain mechanisms of the law, such as what "evidence" means, to facilitate this future punishment.

Evidence holds a dual meaning for Great Gram. Evidence refers to both the offspring of the women and the "story" of brutalization that they pass down through those offspring.[2] These two pieces of evidence are inextricable from one another because, without offspring, the stories have no way of reaching the moment of hypothetical justice. Great Gram views it as the duties of the women to "make generations" that will act as proof, by their mere existence, of the rape and incest by their enslaver/forefather, old man Corregidora. Each woman must pass the story of sexual violence from mother to daughter, great grandmother to great granddaughter, and so on. The details of this system are vague, but telling; Great Gram says, "And when it come time to hold up the evidence, we got to have evidence to hold up" (14). Great Gram is aware that even in 1927, the year that she tells the story to Ursa, the time has not yet arrived at which holding up the only resources at their disposal—their capacity to reproduce and the oral storytelling of their memories—will be successful.[3] But when will it "come time"? And even if the time arrives, to whom would the evidence be "held up" and to what end? Great Gram's use of the word "evidence" implies that a standard judge and jury would be involved, but what would a successful outcome of such a trial look like?

Contemporary scholars of the novel often pay more attention to the pain that Corregidora women inflict on one another than on the pain they hope to inflict on those who have harmed them. And this is valid. The Corregidora women recycle their traumas through the system that is meant to be a source of healing. The mandate to reproduce as well as the endless retelling of the tales of their brutalization contribute to the same cycle of trauma that they endured. Nowhere is this cycle of pain more evident (or more complex) than in Ursa's mother, Irene. To fulfill the family mandate to reproduce, Irene, a virgin, seeks out non-consensual sex with a male acquaintance who later becomes an abusive husband. This ambiguous sexual act then produces a child, the protagonist Ursa, endangering her future ability to be intimate with others. Scholars Siréne Harb and Jennifer Cognard-Black use such excerpts to declare *Corregidora* as a novel about psychological trauma. Trauma is certainly one part of the novel. But *Corregidora* is also a novel about justice. Rather than dismiss Ursa's foremothers as broken spirits inflicting pain on one another, it is worthwhile to understand the logic of their methods for achieving the forms of liberation that they deemed accessible.

The time frame of their reproductive justice system illuminates the thought processes of the Corregidora women. The US justice system traditionally seeks to use evidence from a recent crime to produce a punishment for said crime in the "now."[4] Alternatively, Great Gram's justice system functions as a modified version of what Timothy E. Fulop calls "cultural millennialism," an offshoot of Black millennialism from the nadir, 1877–1901. The Reconstruction Era was the nadir of justice for Black Americans, yet another moment in Black history during which the promise of change was followed by the retrenchment of denial of justice.[5] Cultural millennialism still places God above all, but also puts "profound trust in American cultural principles and institutions" (96). Great Gram maintains most of the standard American language of trial ("evidence" "verdict" "guilt vs. innocence") to establish the notion that there will be a time on Earth when the evidence of her masters' brutality against her will be "held up" so that they may be appropriately judged for their crimes. The Afro-pessimistic underpinnings of the reproductive justice system are tailored to the needs of Black enslaved women, a group with a total lack of access to traditional forms of justice in their contemporary moment. However, this system is inherently hopeful, imagining a time in the future when this total deprivation of rights will no longer be the law of the land. The process relies heavily on a chain of inheritance which demonstrates that the Corregidora women believe that, if nothing else, at least their justice system having been modeled after the traditional US justice system, one so established and seemingly permanent, could therefore ensure the survival and efficacy of this justice system constructed for Black women.

Jones uses more explicitly millennialist language when Ursa's mother, Irene, invokes her own version of her inherited justice system: "But you got to make generations, you go on making them . . . And when the ground and the sky open up to ask them that question that's going to be ask. They think it ain't going to be ask, but it's going to be ask. They have the evidence and give the verdict too. They think they hid everything. But they have the evidence and the verdict too" (41). Here, Irene highlights a feature of their justice system that seems counterintuitive. There is an inevitable failure built into the millennialist system of justice that the Corregidora women have established. Not only is this approach to justice impossible, but also the women will never live to see justice served. And they cannot know to whom the evidence will be shown. The vague pronoun "they" that Irene uses ("They have the evidence and the verdict too. They think they hid everything") makes it difficult to discern those who could "have" the evidence, from those who "hid everything." This confusion between the saviors and the accused in this hypothetical justice scenario evinces the impossibility of this system actually functioning to bring the women justice. However, the doomed nature of this system does not mean that the women should not be lauded for their attempts. Jones is intent on the reader seeing Ursa and her foremothers as attempting to access liberation for themselves.

Great Gram is aware that evidence, in all of its forms, is at the foundation of the US criminal justice system. The Corregidora women wish to maintain a closed circuit around the evidence until "time come" to achieve hypothetical/millennialist justice. Great Gram views the "burning of the papers" as both an erasure of the crimes committed against her and her progeny as well as an implied admission of guilt on behalf of the enslavers. The bodies of Great Gram's children and those of her children's children therefore act as enforcers of guilt in place of the burned papers. But bodies can be a faulty substitute for paper evidence, evidence like documents of slave purchases or other evidence of enslavement that could be more easily publicized. Karla F. C. Holloway acknowledges this attitude toward evidence as a burden on slaves: "[Slaves are] caught in a brutal reality that would make [their] progeny also [their] documentary evidence of the rapes" (67). However, what Holloway characterizes as a brutal reality is just as much a precious, albeit doomed, opportunity. Using their progeny may not act as a solid testament to the burners' guilt. But the offspring are intentionally private forms of evidence until "time come." Only Great Gram, her "generations," and their masters can see the children of slaves as evidence of enslavement.[6] The privacy of this system allows the Corregidora women to feel some sense of control over a system that was built to exclude them. Great Gram's intense demand upon the specific term "evidence" points to a desire to publicize this guilt within the imagined boundaries of a millennialist justice system. Though this is a system that does not function to compensate the women for their various abuses, it gives them a sustained hope that one day it will.

Great Gram and Gram are born into slavery in Brazil where they serve Portuguese masters before migrating to Kentucky years after US slavery has legally ended. Although the migration from Brazil to America is not narrated overtly in the novel, the relocation implies a desire to both physically and mentally flee the space in which their sexual violation occurred, as well as seek out an entirely new land with an entirely new set of laws and an entirely new set of potential judges for whom to publicly exhibit the evidence of that violation. One would think that the women would use a set of logics around trial, verdict, and evidence that was specific to Brazil rather than those of their new home the United States.[7] But, in fact, the Corregidora women do not seem to be tracking the influence that national borders may have on their appeals for justice. The women never make references to location the way that they make references to time. This geographical adaptation of justice systems—an Afro-pessimistic strategy—further proves the extreme audacity of their project to not merely manipulate the law to gain restitution for enslavement and sexual violence, but to do so internationally and retroactively, outside of both the country and the time in which they were enslaved.[8]

The Corregidora women believe that they must attempt to manipulate the context in order to manipulate the outcome. The context that Great Gram attempts to manipulate is the definition of "evidence" at her disposal: her own body, the bodies of her offspring, and the stories that they tell one another.[9] The ways in which Great Gram centers her own body sit in somewhat stark contrast to the ways in which Bessie's body is used without her consent to exact "justice" (the killing of a Black man) in her name. The Corregidora women emphasize evidence within their control, operate on a Black millennialist time frame, and dismiss geography—these machinations of their system prove that the women must manipulate the justice system that excludes them in order to manipulate the outcome from one of injustice to one of a vague, Afro-pessimistic justice that exists on a millennialist time line—in hopes of obtaining a vague justice that is hoped for but will almost certainly never arrive. The Corregidora women, both by choice and the lack of choice forced on them by misogynoirist discrimination, become manipulators of the legal system. The efforts of this matriarchy to punish their rapists, enslavers, brutalizers demonstrate that *Corregidora* is not only about trauma but also about justice. And to view it as a novel about justice has direct implications on how one views the protagonist, Ursa Corregidora, the inheritor of this flawed reparations project.

Ursa's Future and the Barren Hope of Departing from the Past

When it becomes clear that *Corregidora* is a book about justice, assertions by scholars about Ursa come into question. Many scholars claim that Ursa is a victim of her family and its traumatic past. However, understanding the strategies of the Corregidora women as forms of justice-creation show that Ursa is not only a victim of her family's cycle of trauma, she is also the inheritor of a doomed-to-fail justice system. As enticing as it is to endow Ursa with agency over her relationship to her past, Jones does not allow for such clear-cut lines to be drawn. Neither the doom nor the potential hope that many scholars project onto Ursa is within her control. The entire novel centers on an act of domestic violence that Ursa's ex-husband, Mutt, commits against her. In a fit of jealousy, Mutt pushes a pregnant Ursa down the stairs of the club where she works.[10] As a result of her fall, Ursa suffers a miscarriage that also leads doctors to remove her uterus, rendering her infertile.

The rest of the novel follows Ursa as she wrestles with the loss of re-producibility, the very thing that fuels the familial justice system. However vague and improbable that project may be, it is still Ursa's inheritance. Cognard-Black claims that the telling and retelling of Ursa's horrific familial past retraumatize Ursa and that Ursa's silence, both reproductive (infertility) and vocal (there are several moments throughout the novel when Ursa chooses to remain silent) aim to counter the language-heavy, record-based, white male heteropatriarchal oppression (49). I agree with Cognard-Black that the Corregidora foremothers replicate the trauma by retelling the story of their enslavement so exhaustively. However, I do not agree that all attempts to physically record the past are executed under the auspices of white supremacy. Beyond the scope of this novel, there are many examples that refute the alignment between "recorded history" and white supremacy, such as the level of secrecy/anonymity within institutions like the Ku Klux Klan and reliance on the slave narrative as a record of great Black historical and evidentiary significance. But rather than reject Cognard-Black's advo-cacy of silence as an alternative rhetorical strategy, I want to insist that the Corregidora women act against injustice when they see that it is not neces-sarily the form in which the system operates—language, records, physical evidence—that is always the obstacle to justice so much as it is how white supremacy manipulates those forms to unequal, unlawful, and unjust ends.

Ursa's infertility is a kind of silencing but also an opportunity for her own voice to take center stage and for her to change the very definition of "public," another thing upon which the Corregidora women's justice system hinges. The Corregidora women point to a fundamental imbalance of justice by manipulating the very definition of "evidence." In the "private" world of the Corregidoras, of Black women, stories and offspring are as useful as paper or blood is to their oppressors. The family of women admits that stories and offspring are not very good forms of evidence, but they are the most readily available tools of systemic manipulation. Ursa is simultaneously of and apart from the "Corregidora women" because of how she shifts the definition of justice from one that is private and exists along a millennialist time line to one that is public and presentist/"real." The following analysis considers how Ursa reframes audience and the kind of justice that is possible for her from one that is doomed and mired in failure to another that is also doomed and mired in failure, but in a different way.

When Ursa is made infertile by domestic abuse that leads to a miscarriage and hysterectomy, the white heteropatriarchy, the burners of the papers, get what they wanted all along: a literal drowning out of the already fragile and faint message of the Black offspring-as-evidence. Ursa's infertility helps to undermine the viability of redefining evidence as a strategy for gaining justice. Not only does Ursa's barrenness make reproduction-as-justice impossible (because no more mixed-race Black children will be born under the Corregidora family name), but her lack of a womb also exiles the story of their violations from any public forum, forced to always maintain within the enclosed circle of the four generations of women. The procreative evidence will live and die with Ursa. This death of a kind of definition of evidence spells disaster of sorts for the justice project to which her family has been committed. The body (voice, existence, ability to reproduce, etc.) alone can no longer act as either subject or object of forensic analysis.[11] Many *Corregidora* scholars view Ursa's inability to reproduce as a positive end to a degrading cycle, but the end of reproduction does not mean that the story of brutalization will not be retold. Instead of ceasing the retelling of the story of her family's brutalization, because she no longer has offspring to whom to pass it on, Ursa changes the definition of "public" from the private public of Corregidora women to the public of her blues singing. This dichotomy between a private public and a public public is an adaptation of Deborah

McDowell's delineation between Black women's writing that is meant for a Black (female) audience (a private public) and writing that is meant for a majority white audience (a public public).

There is no representation of anyone who is described as white in the novel except for old man Corregidora, but Ursa sings her songs in a club therefore she is relinquishing control around the makeup of the audience to whom she hopes to pass her family history, as one excerpting of lyrics indicates: "*While mama be sleeping, the ole man he crawl into bed/ While mama be sleeping that old man he crawl into bed/ When mama have wake up, he shaking his nasty ole head*" (67). These lyrics do not speak directly to the brutal violence that her ancestors endured, but it is difficult not to see that Ursa uses the song as a replacement for the story of old man Corregidora raping his own daughter, Gram, while Great Gram was fully aware and can do nothing to stop it. Donia Elizabeth Allen reads the blues as a musical form that is evident in a "blues linguistics" that the entire novel takes on, but it is also a public forum through which Ursa can circumvent the Afro-pessimistic justice system of her foremothers. Ursa uses her singing to spread the mandate to physically reproduce, a forum through which she can create songs as evidence in a new kind of justice system. This is one way in which Jones never really allows us to see the cycle of violence end. Jones continues to represent evidence-based systems at crucial points in the novel, plaguing and helping Ursa to embrace hopelessness. However, the reader learns very late in the novel of a private memory that Ursa possesses, one which allows her to access yet another definition of justice that is presentist/real justice—and still Afro-pessimistic—that her foremothers never could.

Throughout *Corregidora,* nearly all of Ursa's memories are of conversations that she had with her Gram, Great Gram, or mother about their enslaved past, about their abuser and master old man Corregidora, or about their inherited mandate to reproduce. Jones makes the reader feel the same way that Ursa feels: deluged with the voices, opinions, and horrific memories of Ursa's family members. Whether in bed with a lover or talking to one of her girlfriends, the disembodied voices of her foremothers never stray too far from Ursa's mind.[12] It is therefore an enormous break from the previous tone of the novel when Ursa reveals a private memory more than two-thirds of the way through. The revelation of any private memory unique to Ursa would be significant on its own, but it is especially valuable to the role of justice in the novel that this memory pertains so immediately and exactly to the issues of race, sexual violence, and the law.

I couldn't have been more than ten the year the Melrose woman committed suicide. . . . I just sat down at the kitchen table and listened. "Yeah,
they found her over in Hawkins' alley," Mama was saying . . .

"Had to been some man," Gram said. "I ain't never known a woman
to take her life less it was some man." . . . *It wasn't until later that I knew
what they were talking about.* I was down at Mr. Deak's store, and him
and these men were talking. They weren't like Mama and Gram. They
didn't care if I was there or not . . . the girl was . . . one of Mr. Melrose's
girls. She was in her twenties . . . Melrose is up there now . . . he gon try to
find out what man's responsible . . . "How her daddy gonna find out, and
the whole police couldn't?"

"A daddy got ways the police ain't. Anyway, she wasn't nothing but a
nigger woman to the police. You know they ain't gon take they time to
find nothing about a nigger woman. "Here, put it in the nigger file.' That
mean they get to it if they can. And most times they can't. Naw, they
don't say put it in the nigger file, they say put it in the nigger *woman* file,
which mean they ain't gon never get to it . . .

It wasn't until I was about fifteen that I learned from reading back
papers in the school library that . . . now Mr. Melrose was in jail, and
the police had claimed they still didn't know whether the man he had
shot or knifed had had anything to do with his daughter. They still didn't
know why she'd killed herself. John Willie, of the police department, had
said, "There's some things them people just won't let be our business no
matter how hard we try. We still asking around though." . . . I don't think
anything ever worked me up so much as that woman, and I hadn't really
known her." (133–45)

From her encounter with the case of the "Melrose woman," Ursa learns a
valuable lesson about alternative approaches to justice that her foremothers
are either incapable of or refuse to expose her to. Other scholars of *Corregidora* might read the suicide of "the Melrose woman" in Ursa's town as yet
another instance of trauma and therefore a continuation rather than a disruption of the rhetorics of pain against Black women in the novel. In other
words, previous scholarship regards Ursa as learning nothing new in this
scene: the Melrose woman is another example of Black women as perpetual
victims of violence who cannot rely on the traditional channels for justice.
To be sure, for Ursa to learn of a young woman's demise (supposedly at the
hands of "some man") at such a young age is an emotionally challenging

experience. However, directing attention away from Ursa's emotional response to this "crime" (of which there is little textual evidence) and toward the way it informs her thinking about justice for Black women in the 1930s reveals the details of Ursa's departure from the reproductive justice system of her foremothers.

It is first important to establish the ambiguity around what exactly happened to the Melrose woman. This scene is one of many instances in the novel where Jones confuses societal expectations about women as victims of male violence. The first of these is in the novel's opening. The novel opens with Ursa in the hospital after being pushed down a flight of stairs by her possessive husband, Mutt. But was she pushed or did she fall? Even Ursa cannot give a clear answer. The Melrose woman's death is similarly confounding. Was the Melrose woman murdered or did she commit suicide? There is never a definitive answer. The distinction is important when viewing this scene as one that reveals to Ursa alternative approaches to justice. The presence of a crime is uncertain as every character discussing the case blurs the line between murder and suicide for Black women. As Gram says, "Had to been some man . . . I ain't never known a woman take her life less it was some man" (133). Gram's statement suggests that even if the Melrose woman committed suicide, it could still be considered a crime because it "Had to been some man." Mr. Deak echoes Gram's sentiments, asserting the issue of justice by assuming that anytime a Black woman is found dead, a crime of some kind must have been committed.[13]

Ursa is accustomed to justice that occurs on the specific terms of her foremothers. Redefinitions of the concept of evidence and a millennialist/ hypothetical justice time line are the central features of the Corregidora women's justice system. The story of the Melrose woman, however, offers concepts that are traditional to the US legal system, but new to Ursa as they are conceptions of evidence and a contemporary/real justice time line on which justice can (or can fail to) occur in the present. The presence of a dead body and police files, whether hidden or not, are markers that a justice system, however corrupt it may be, exists outside of the one that Ursa has inherited. Significantly, Ursa is introduced to a new kind of justice time line because, unlike the crimes committed against her foremothers, the Melrose woman's death as well as the fallout of the case occurs while Ursa is still alive. The foremothers speak of an impossible justice on a millennialist time line that they will never live to see, but Ursa, somewhat obsessively, tracks the case of the Melrose woman throughout her life. Though many of the circumstances are left open-ended, the system of justice is functioning in real time for Ursa, and therefore loses the hypothetical quality that Great Gram manifested or was forced to manifest in her own justice system.

Part of Ursa's tracking the case of the Melrose woman throughout her life involves a shift away from the alternative forms of evidence of the Corregidora women toward more traditional forms of evidence. Ursa acts as historian and critical race theorist of the case, seeking out an archive through which she might investigate the conclusion of a case whose implications for the relationships between the law, race, sex, and gender are so uncertain. The archive she seeks is one that she finds five years after the crime is committed and consists of "back papers in the school library" (144). When Ursa accesses a newspaper archive, she arms herself with a record of the crime. This tactic of using an archive runs directly contrary to her foremothers' system of using their bodies and oral histories to redefine the very meaning of evidence and use that as the foundation of a private approach to justice. And this is not the only way that Ursa uses "paper" records as evidence. The "nigger woman" file mentioned by Mr. Deak is another allusion to the use of paper records to keep track of crimes that places the victimization of a Black woman into recorded history as opposed to outside of it. This inclusion of Black women's pain in the record is not entirely unproblematic. As Mr. Deak says, "Anyway, she wasn't nothing but a nigger woman to the police . . . Somebody go down there and file a complaint, they write it down, all right, while you standing there, but as soon as you leave, they say, 'Here, put it in the nigger file . . . Naw . . . they say put it in the nigger *woman* file, which mean they ain't gon never get to it" (134).

Whether or not the Melrose woman receives justice for her death through the official channels is not of import in this instance; what matters is how Ursa's exposure to the case gives her access to the specific, traditional mechanisms of the US justice system. According to Mr. Deaks, in 1930s Kentucky the time has still not come when Black women can expect their abusers to receive just punishments. Mr. Deaks and the Corregidora women do not seem to possess the entire story. According to the police of Bracktown, Kentucky, the lack of justice is not the work of Jim Crow era white supremacy: "There's some things them people just won't let be our business no matter how hard we try. We still asking around though" (144). Over the span of 5 years, Ursa learns from Black onlookers who have become accustomed to the failure of a system to protect Black lives. She learns that there are other ways to not only define, but also uncover evidence as well as other time lines upon which justice can occur: both forms more tangible, albeit not necessarily more successful, than the forms that her foremothers construct. Much of this may seem obvious. Perhaps it seems obvious that, living in the United States, Ursa would inevitably be made aware of a more official justice system, one that consistently fails Black people yet maintains a formal approach to justice that differs from that of her family. But Ursa's departure from the Corregidora women is earth-shattering. Jones structures the narrative so that the reader is constantly bombarded with the sense that Ursa is trapped by her family's mentality. Ursa repeatedly insists that she has no other memories, no other connection to her individual past than those of her foremothers, nothing but an audio transcript of the brutality they suffered as slaves playing on an endless loop in her mind.

This scene in Mr. Deak's store, the memory of the Melrose woman, is an enormous break in the text. It is a moment unlike any other in the novel thus far, one in which Ursa is in command of her own memory and, rather than being the recipient of a story, is the teller of her own. Or rather, she tells her own story-within-a-story, the story of her experience of another woman's story. The death of the Melrose woman opens a new space of thought for Ursa in terms of how she defines justice, evidence, and the potential for Black women's pain to be recorded and then used for the transformation of another Black woman who does not just receive that record but is "worked up" by it so much that she changes her entire perspective about herself and the role that she plays in the story of her family.

Conclusion

Jones maps a psychological shift from hypothetical to real justice in her novel. The Corregidora women use their bodies, their stories, and the bodies of their children to formulate an Afro-pessimistic justice system that is intended to achieve justice at some vague point in the future. Whether she recognizes the fatalism of this justice system or is forced to alter her perspective because of her infertility is not of any major consequence because Ursa Corregidora still begins to break free from her ancestors by changing the definition of three key terms: "public," "story," and "evidence." Ursa begins to develop the tools needed to build a justice system that is "real" in the sense that it has the trappings of a system that could actually bring about some kind of change far more real and plausible than the system of Ursa's foremothers. When I say "real" justice, what I mean is that Ursa presents her justice work, albeit indirectly, to the public audience at her blues performances, whereas the Corregidora women maintain it among themselves; her infertility forces her to imagine a justice system that is not reproduced by her own body and therefore must begin and end with her, and, through the case of the Melrose woman's death, she explores the world of justice (or injustice) as it exists in a real case that has a beginning, middle, and end in her lifetime consisting of documented realities, witness testimonies, and the incarceration of the man who murdered the murderer.

Even if Jones does not allow us to see the capacity of the tools that Ursa develops to fully heal herself or to bring her to a point where she can "move on" from her traumatic familial past, there is triumph in the very fact of these changes in her perspective because they liberate her from a cycle of trauma from which she seemed previously incapable of escaping.

Though I want to align myself with previous scholars of Jones's novel to continue to seek the moments in which healing from trauma is possible, it is not possible to ignore the ways in which Jones limits healing. The novel ends with a sexual encounter between Ursa and her ex-husband, Mutt, that leaves the entire possibility of healing from the pain of sexual violence (and a familial history of violence) uncertain. In a bluesy refrain, Mutt tells Ursa that he does not want a woman who will hurt him and Ursa responds, "Then you don't want me." They go back and forth this way three times until "He shook me till I fell against him crying. 'I don't want a kind of man that'll hurt me neither,' I said. He held me tight" (185). Many read this scene as the moment of healing, the moment that Ursa is finally able to express herself emotionally. I would argue, however, that though it is certainly the beginning of some kind of transformation for Ursa, Jones intentionally leaves the reader in the dark about what form that transformation will take. Will it be one of healing? Will it be one of even more abuse between herself and Mutt? By ending the novel so indefinitely, Jones propels Ursa into a space that is not-yet-healed, but not quite as traumatized as it once was either. Similarly, all of the work that Ursa is able to accomplish to redefine the justice system that she inherited—from hypothetical to real, from story to song, from private to public—could contribute to a multiplicity of possibilities for her, ones that perpetuate the familial cycles of trauma in new forms or ones that could terminate those cycles for good.

Both Ursa and her foremothers incur a variety of traumas on their paths to create an Afro-pessimistic justice system that is also a reenactment of traditional US justice systems that rely on punishment as a means of resolving pain. The foremothers retraumatize themselves every time they tell the story of their abuse to one another. Ursa relives this familial trauma through song and is also exposed to brutal truths about Black women and justice at an early age through the Melrose woman. At the end of *Corregidora,* Jones offers something akin to a moment of closure, but with no definitive promise that the cycle of violence that Ursa's justice system hopes to end will actually do so. Jones therefore implies that there is no path to justice that is without trauma and so the only path forward that is presented is an Afro-pessimistic justice system, a system that Black women create in an effort to heal, but which continuously fails them, hurts them, and destroys the people they love in the process. Perhaps what Jones implies ultimately is that trauma is always an unhappy byproduct of Black women's attempts to find justice, especially in the quest to find justice for sexual violence. In the following chapter, we will see how, unlike the Corregidora women, Black immigrant women create new systems for healing that are completely outside of the traditional criminal justice system, but somehow continue to replicate the ways in which that system abuses and excludes them from accessing justice.

Chapter 6

IFEMELU'S SONG

To pivot from the Black American authors Richard Wright and Gayl Jones to the novel *Americanah* by the Nigerian author Chimamanda Ngozi Adichie may seem like an abrupt move, but it is necessary for this story of Black women, sexual violence, and justice.[1] As Diallo's story demonstrates, Black immigrant women interface with the criminal justice system in a particular way that calls for our specific attention. It is neither possible in one book nor in the interest of this project to draw a complete picture of the Black immigrant woman's story. Adichie herself has famously publicly discussed in her TED Talk, "the danger of a single story" looms especially large over those most marginalized in the literary canon. To tell the whole story of women like and unlike Nafissatou Diallo (chapter 3) is not in the purview of this chapter because it would mean to cover all of the ways in which Black women from all around the globe find themselves in the United States.

There are stories of undocumented women, stories of women who marry to gain citizenship, stories of Black women who lost their lives in transit, stories of Black women from Panama, from Haiti, Black women from the United Kingdom and Greece and South Korea, stories of Black women who migrated when rights for immigrants seemed briefly expanded. Black women like my grandmother, Sylvia Hislop, who left her home, her husband, and her children in Trinidad & Tobago at age 47 and entered the United States in 1968, a few years after the Hart-Cellar Act of 1965 profoundly altered immigration law and removed decades of discrimination against non-Western groups. Thus I would be remiss to act as if the story of Diallo, the story of an African refugee who was sexually assaulted and sought justice for that assault, told a full story of Black immigrant women looking to the law in the twenty-first century. In that vein, I turn to Chimamanda Ngozi Adichie's 2013 breakout novel *Americanah* to offer the story of Ifemelu as offering another part of the puzzle. For the purposes of talking about Black immigrant women and sexual violence, the class differences between Diallo and Ifemelu suggest how we can understand the complexities of Afro-pessimistic justice when the identities of its purveyors change.

In many ways, this final chapter is both a return to and a twist on the beginning of part 2. In chapter 4, which opened part 2, I remarked upon a paradox in *Native Son*: the way that Richard Wright evacuates Bessie's voice from the novel makes it difficult for us to understand her place in Afro-pessimistic justice, but his insistence on the ability of the legal system to believe in its own power to speak for her attempts to fill the void her death causes. In the twenty-first century that *Americanah* represents, Black immigrant women are the stewards of their own stories, and the law is almost entirely eliminated from the equation and replaced by other, new systems created through new technologies. More specifically, this chapter argues that Ifemelu, the protagonist of *Americanah*, explores how digital writing spaces act as one of the portals to Afro-pessimistic justice for Black immigrant women who experience sexual violence. Through Ifemelu's story of her life online, Adichie's novel elucidates the law's failure to capture the character's violation itself, a failure so acute that her assault cannot be legally categorized as such, as I will explain. My reading of *Americanah* as a trauma-centered work is a departure from dominant scholarly readings of the novel, which tend to focus on the political significance of Black hair or the novel's participation in the "Afropolitan literature" genre, a genre on which scholars like Taiye Selasi, Achille Mbembe, Simon Gikandi have commented. Ifemelu's experience is, implicitly, the result of systemic failings, but she sees the internet—specifically blogging—as a chance to not only express her feelings about the failings of systems, but also to totally control that mode of expression.

Afro-pessimistic Justice in Americanah

Ifemelu, the Nigerian protagonist of *Americanah*, is a college student in Philadelphia on an F-1 visa. Upon arriving in the United States around 1993, Ifemelu is almost immediately struck with the realities of severe financial deprivation. One of the stipulations of her student visa is that she cannot work. She can earn money through the work-study job provided on campus, but this barely covers her rent let alone other living expenses.[2] And the student visa forbids recipients from working off campus. Somewhat fortunately, Ifemelu has an informal knowledge network through her aunt and a friend, Ginika, who migrated to the United States years before

Ifemelu. These women offer their guidance and tools of survival: Aunty Uju gives Ifemelu the Social Security card of a friend so that she can apply for jobs which require such a document. Ginika helps Ifemelu edit her resume so that it looks like she has far more work experience than she does. Like Diallo, with such actions, Ifemelu participates in the culture of lying that the immigration system conditions through its limited definitions and standards. However, unlike Diallo, Ifemelu is presumably of a different class of immigrant because of the ways in which she is resourced through her aunt and the international student support system that her university provides.

Despite her access to all of this knowledge and support, Ifemelu cannot get a job. And she does not have wealthy parents back in Nigeria to send her money to fill in the gaps. Amidst all of this financial strife, Ifemelu is also thrust into a Black identity that she does not yet have all of the tools necessary to navigate or even articulate. Both her lack of funds to support herself and a mounting identity crisis form the backdrop of a deep depression for our protagonist. The narrator describes the pain and anxiety of this period in Ifemelu's life so vividly that it is almost physically painful to experience alongside her, such as when she must borrow books from a fellow student because she cannot afford to buy them. "It stung her, to have to beg . . . the students walking past the large grey sculpture in the middle; they all seemed to have their lives in the shape that they wanted, they could have jobs if they wanted to have jobs, and above them, small flags flapped severely from lampposts" (136). Nearly everything in this period is described this way, as "grey," "severe," and shapeless with spots of light being Ifemelu's phone conversations with her boyfriend Obinze, who encourages her, and her younger cousin, Dike, whose innocence inspires her. But her joblessness still hovers over these moments of levity.

After what seem like months of searching endlessly for waitress, home service care provider, and babysitter jobs, Ifemelu happens upon a want ad in a local newspaper. The ad reads, "Female personal assistant for busy sports coach. . . communication and interpersonal skills required" (146). The first time Ifemelu visits the sports coach to inquire about the job, he tells her that he needs someone to help him "relax." She thinks to herself, "He was not a kind man. She did not know exactly what he meant, but whatever it was, she regretted that she had come" and leaves only to continue to suffer for want of income (146). She even briefly considers an "ESCORTS" ad in the newspaper but remembers Ginika's warning about such ads: "Forget that escort thing. They say it isn't prostitution, but it is and the worst thing is that you get maybe a quarter of what you earn because the agency takes the rest. I know this girl who did it in freshman year" (153).[3] Ifemelu does not call.

In this moment, Ifemelu's knowledge network saves her from one kind of exploitation, but after her roommates complain about her paying the rent late again, Ifemelu returns to the office of the tennis coach a second time. She is still uncertain about what the sports coach wants from her; but as we hear her internal monologue during their encounter, it is clear that, for her, her mere presence acts as a form of consent for what happens next.

> "Come over here," he said. "I need to be warm."
>
> She should leave now. The power balance was tilted in his favor, had been tilted in his favor since she walked into his house. She should leave. She stood up.
>
> "I can't have sex," she said. Her voice felt squeaky, unsure of itself . . .
>
> "Oh no, I don't expect you to," he said . . . She moved slowly toward the door, wondering if it was locked, if he had locked it, and then she wondered if he had a gun.
>
> "Just come here and lie down," he said. "Keep me warm. I'll touch you a little bit, nothing you'll be uncomfortable with. I just need some human contact to relax."
>
> There was, in his expression and tone, a complete assuredness; she felt defeated . . . He knew she would stay because she had come. She was already there, already tainted. She took off her shoes and climbed into his bed. She *did not want* to be here, *did not want* his active finger between her legs, *did not want* his sigh-moans in her ear, and yet she felt her body rousing to a sickening wetness. Afterwards, she lay still, coiled and deadened. *He had not forced her.* She had come here on her own. She had lain on his bed, and when he placed her hand between his legs, she had curled and moved her fingers. Now, even after she had washed her hands, holding the crisp, slender hundred dollar bill he had given her, her fingers still felt sticky; they no longer belonged to her. (156; emphasis added).

Ifemelu seems to make up her mind that this is a consensual encounter when she thinks, "He had not forced her. She had come here on her own."

But many other moments in the scene belie this binary view of consent, such as when she thinks, "The power balance was tilted in his favor" or "She moved slowly toward the door . . . wondered if he had a gun." These phrases demonstrate that Ifemelu is frightened and is in a position of powerlessness, making it impossible to discern consent in a legal sense. Though some states have recently chosen to define consent by differentiating "freely given consent" from "affirmative consent," Pennsylvania law does not. Like most states, Pennsylvania instead defines the absence of consent, what is called "forcible compulsion," as "compulsion by use of physical, intellectual, moral, emotional or psychological force, either express or implied. The term includes but is not limited to compulsion resulting in another person's death, whether the death occurred before, during or after sexual intercourse" (Pennyslvania Consolidated Statutes § 3101).[4] According to this definition, the tennis coach does not legally commit sexual assault because he does not forcibly compel Ifemelu to perform a sexual act. But the reader knows that even if the tennis coach is not legally to blame, he benefits from the complex circumstances that *are* forcibly compelling Ifemelu to exchange money for sexual touch. Though Ifemelu legally consents to be with the tennis coach, her language clarifies that she does not desire to be with the tennis coach.

Adichie seems to be conscious of the fine line that the scene walks between consent and desire. Perhaps the sentence that best encapsulates the ambiguous line between consent and desire is the repetitive phrasing toward the end of the passage: "She did not want to be here, did not want his active finger between her legs, did not want his sigh-moans in her ear, and yet she felt her body rousing to a sickening wetness." In a single sentence we get a sense of the paradox that Ifemelu faces: at the same time that she consented, she did not desire; at the same time that she mentally rejected this man's touch, her physical response might be interpreted as desire, something her internal monologue reveals it is not. This contradiction of affect and action causes Ifemelu to feel deep self-loathing, depression, and isolation in the immediate aftermath of this trauma. All of these confusing and contradictory details set Ifemelu's experience in steep contrast with Diallo's, which was, in Diallo's account, a more straightforward case of sexual assault: in a legal sense, the sports coach's actions did not meet the legal definition of sexual assault, whereas Strauss-Kahn's, in Diallo's account, did.

But even if it is true that Ifemelu is not sexually assaulted in a way that would be intelligible to the law, this does not mean that she does not experience severe trauma. Her trauma is so severe, in fact, that she goes into a deep depression, immediately cuts off communication with those closest to her who are in Nigeria: her boyfriend, Obinze, and, for a shorter time, her parents. The severity of this silencing cannot be overstated. It is not only a silencing of others, but also a silencing of her own story of her trauma for herself: "She would never be able to form the sentences to tell her story" (160). I would argue, however, that Ifemelu finds a way to tell this story without telling it. In this way, these various forms of silence are what prompt Ifemelu to explore blogging as a form of expression through which to heal and possibly reap a form of justice—if not directly for the sexual trauma she has experienced, then indirectly for the burden of racial trauma she takes on upon migrating to America and becoming Black.

Adichie hints at the capacity of the blog to give language to things that neither Ifemelu nor the law can. We get a glimpse of this language and of the future blog that Ifemelu will write when she is near tears with her friend, Ginika, who drives her home from finally getting a babysitting job:

> Ginika said, "I think you're suffering from depression."
>
> Ifemelu shook her head and turned to the window. Depression was what happened to Americans, with their self-absolving need to turn everything into an illness. She was not suffering from depression; she was merely a little tired and a little slow. "I don't have depression," she said. Years later, she would blog about this: "On the Subject of Non-American Blacks Suffering from Illnesses Whose Names They Refuse to Know." A Congolese woman wrote a long comment in response: She had moved to Virginia from Kinshasa and, months into her first semester of college, begun to feel dizzy in the morning, her heart pounding as though in flight from her, her stomach fraught with nausea, her fingers tingling. She went to see a doctor. And even though she checked "yes" to all the symptoms on the card the doctor gave her, she refused to accept the diagnosis of panic attacks because panic attacks happened only to Americans. Nobody in Kinshasa had panic attacks. It was not even that it was called by another name, it was simply not called at all. Did things begin to exist only when they were named? (160)

This past future tense ("Year later, she would . . .") disrupts the normal, simple past narrative flow a number of times throughout the novel, particularly in the chapters that narrate Ifemelu's pre-blog life. Usually, the past future tense gives a glimpse into the blog either by talking about the title of a post or an experience that Ifemelu has that prompts a blog post, some of which is then excerpted for the reader. Adichie's nonlinear storytelling is a nod to the ways in which Afro-pessimism looks at time because it frames the past as never past. This temporal disruption is especially remarkable because even as the narrator turns the focus to mental illness, the comment on naming here could easily apply to the sexual trauma that occurred only pages before: "It was not even that it was called by another name, it was simply not called at all. Did things begin to exist only when they were named?" One could easily replace the vague pronouns "that" and "things" with the term "sexual trauma" to see that the blog post is implicitly about Ifemelu's experience with the tennis coach: "It was not even that the sexual trauma was called by another name, it was simply not called at all." Does sexual assault only exist when it is called "sexual assault"? This attention to naming recalls the legibility or intelligibility of Black women as victims of sexual violence, as victims of sexual crimes, explored in the previous chapters.

The line of narration that nearly ends the chapter excerpted above (chapter 15), "She would never be able to form the sentences to tell her story," is therefore at odds with the blog post. This is not only literally untrue because Ifemelu tells Obinze about her sexual trauma when they are reunited in Lagos more than a decade later, but it is also figuratively untrue because the blog that Ifemelu writes about depression is an implicit reference to the depression that resulted from her experience with the tennis coach. Therefore, though Ifemelu's silence results from the assault, this moment of disruption acts as a clear indication that the blog is, in one way or another, connected to the assault.

The blog functions as a mode of expression through which Ifemelu can verbally lambast the systems that made her nonforcible assault possible. Once she begins blogging, many years have passed since her encounter with the sports coach. She now has a regular job in Baltimore at a public relations office and a white and wealthy boyfriend, Curt, through whom she gets the job which, fortunately, includes a work visa and a path to a green card.[5] Having such an intimate relationship with a white and privileged man and existing in such a white, corporate space, Ifemelu confronts microaggressions that induct her into a common Black American experience of a white or non-Black person asking uncomfortable questions about her hair, skin color, or accent. These microaggressions are so named because they do not fit under the category of macroaggressions, such as acts of explicitly violent racism. Because there is seemingly no legal recourse, the microaggressed must deal with their discomfort and pain through interpersonal confrontation and emotional labor that can be psychologically and physically draining to perform on a constant basis.[6]

Ifemelu is sometimes capable of responding to microaggressions in real time, but given the difficulty of doing, she seeks alternative spaces through which she can express her emotions. She begins to explore the natural hair community online, first as an observer and later as a participant, commenting on the stories of other Black women, learning tips on hair care, and generally building a sense of community. This online community is not only explicitly Black and dominated by women, but it is also steeped in African American ritualistic traditions, as Ifemelu implies after leaving a comment on happilykinkynappy.com.

> She wrote: *Jamilah's words made me remember that there is nothing more beautiful than what God gave me.* Others wrote responses, posting thumbs-up signs, telling her how much they liked the photo she had put up. She had never talked about God so much. Posting on the website was like giving testimony in church; the echoing roar of approval revived her.
>
> On an unremarkable day in early spring . . . she looked in the mirror, sank her fingers into her hair, dense and spongy and glorious, and could not imagine it any other way. That simply, she fell in love with her hair. (215)

The natural hair community becomes a source of positive affirmation for Ifemelu. And this esteem-building functions as an antidote to the poison of self-hatred, shame, and silence she incurs and self-inflicts as a result of her sexual trauma. It particularly reforms the relationship with her body that Ifemelu at least partially gained after her noncoerced sexual assault, as denoted in the way she physically dissociates: "her fingers still felt sticky; they no longer belonged to her" (156).[7] Many scholars who have written on the novel, such as Beauty Bragg and Cristina Cruz-Gutiérrez, emphasize the role that hair plays in the novel; hair is a political and sociocultural lens through which Ifemelu observes and is observed by the world.[8]

In both her experiences of the natural hair blog and creating her own blog, Ifemelu is taking back some form of narrative control about herself. An important difference (and one which, perhaps, propels Ifemelu to create her own blog) is that Ifemelu feels the need to perform in what could be described as recognizably Black ways on the natural hair blog—for example, she refers to her strong Christian identity which is in truth nonexistent—whereas her own blog permits her to embody some of the more messy intersections of her identity as she constantly refers to herself as a "non-American Black" woman. The natural hair community has its own cultural blind spots. If Ifemelu has an experience that is particular to her identity as a non-American Black woman, the natural hair community does not seem to provide an outlet for it.

For Ifemelu to indirectly confront the sexual trauma she experienced, she must turn toward her particularity, toward her identity as an immigrant. Through this turning inward, Ifemelu also uses the blog to turn outward, toward the immigration system that put her in a position in which her vulnerability can be neither legally nor emotionally processed. In other words, when seizing the opportunity to have a somewhat public platform through her blog, it is no surprise that Ifemelu chooses to concentrate her energy on her perspective as a "non-American Black" woman because of the ways in which her un-Americanness and non-citizen status are at the root of the trauma that compelled her to seek new forms of healing online in the first place. It therefore makes sense that Ifemelu starts her own blog. The Black blog is a special space that, as Catherine Knight Steele asserts, "creates alternate publics that use covert methods to interrogate issues politically critical to the resistance of oppression" (113). Unlike the online hair community, Ifemelu's blog exists outside of the confines of the law; she can use it to create alternatives to master narratives about immigrant women of color, alternatives that she writes, produces, and owns.

Other scholars such as Safiya Umoja Noble and Alondra Nelson write at length about the powers, both liberative and structurally problematic, of the internet for Black and brown people. Steele's writing about "black blogs" is largely positive, but Noble's recent book, *Algorithms of Oppression: How Search Engines Reinforce Racism*, points to the ways in which search engines specifically, and the internet more broadly, maintain the same racially and sexually oppressive structures that they purport to neutralize. However, Nelson also discusses the internet as a positive tool for social justice organizing as evinced by the #BlackLivesMatter Twitter hashtag and other social movements that grew traction on the internet.

Even prior to publishing *Americanah*, Adichie seemed primed to enter this discourse about the liberative and/or oppressive powers of the internet for people of color and other marginalized identities given her own "viral" explosion on the internet. Adichie rose to prominence not only as a novelist, but also as a public figure when her TEDxEuston talk, "We Should All Be Feminists," went viral on YouTube in 2012 (it now has 4.7 million views); and when, only a year later, Beyoncé included a sound bite from this talk in one of her most popular songs, "Flawless," on her fifth album, *Beyonce*.[9] Adichie therefore reads the internet more subjectively than the academics with whom she is in conversation as she uses fiction to test the limits of its powers through Ifemelu and her blog, *Raceteenth or Various Observations About American Blacks (Those Formerly Known as Negroes) by a Non-American Black*.

The liberating aspects of Ifemelu's blog resemble those of the natural hair community. The blog is collaborative from beginning to end, including the voices of other women. And Ifemelu is almost never alone in her blog posts. She uses the platform to offer humorous yet politically profound retellings of interactions she has had with others, as is clear from the titles of some of these blog posts: "Not All Dreadlocked White Guys Are Down," "Badly-Dressed White Middle Managers from Ohio Are Not Always What You Think," (4–5) and an ongoing series of "Understanding America for the Non-American Black." This last title is especially helpful as it shows how Ifemelu often uses the blog to perform a sarcastic mode of cultural authority, instructing while entertaining her non-American readers on how to best navigate the experience of becoming Black in America.

Everything about the blog gives Ifemelu space to not only potentially unconsciously reverse the pain surrounding her sexual trauma, but also to offer others the emotional tools that she believes may have diverted her from ever being in that room with the tennis coach in the first place. Whereas the trauma caused Ifemelu to feel completely isolated and alone, the blog creates community. Whereas the trauma made her feel powerless, Ifemelu has total creative control over the blog. Whereas trauma turned Ifemelu's immigrant status into something exploitable, Ifemelu uses the blog to point out the aspects of existing as a non-American Black that are empowering, funny, and culturally profound.

Most important, Ifemelu can use long-form blogging to offer more complex, contradictory counternarratives to the simplistic master narratives that exist about immigrant women of color. An outcome, I might add, that accords with Adichie's own discussion of "The Dangers of a Single Story," in another one of her famous TED talks. In one such blog post, titled "To My Fellow Non-American Blacks: In America, You Are Black, Baby," Ifemelu sarcastically unpacks the unspoken "rules" and codes that a non-American Black person who has just arrived can use to navigate this brave, new racialized world called the United States:

Dear Non-American Black, when you make the choice to come to America, you become black. Stop arguing . . . America doesn't care . . . We all have our moments of initiation into the Society of Former Negroes. Mine was in a class in undergrad when I was asked to give the black perspective, only I had no idea what that was. So I just made something up . . . So you're black, baby. And here's the deal with becoming black . . . In describing black women you admire, always use the word "STRONG" because that is what black women are supposed to be in America . . . When a crime is reported, pray that it was not committed by a black person, and if it turns out to have been committed by a black person, stay well away from the crime area for weeks, or you might be stopped for fitting the profile . . . If you go to eat in a restaurant, please tip generously . . . You see, black people have a gene that makes them not tip, so please overpower that gene . . . Most of all, do not be angry. Black people are not supposed to be angry about racism. Otherwise, you get no sympathy. (222–23)

This post is among the best at capturing how drenched in hilarious sarcasm and irony *Raceteenth* is.

But there are also several indirect links to Ifemelu's assault beneath the top layer of humor. The very first line of this blog post is full of implicit references to Ifemelu's experience with the tennis coach. Unlike other blog posts, this one is directly addressed to the reader, who she presumes to be a non-American Black person. The epistolary form is reiterated in this opening line as well as in the more academic format of the title. At the same time as the addressee is faceless and nameless, reduced to their race and immigrant status, there is also something tender and caring in the form of address ("Dear"). To address her blog reader with such tenderness speaks to the lack of tenderness that Ifemelu received from her Aunty Uju after Ifemelu told her about the assault without telling her. Immediately after the sexual encounter, Ifemelu calls Aunty Uju: "I went to work for a man in the suburbs today. He paid me a hundred dollars." "Ehn? That's very good. But you have to keep looking for something permanent" (157). In that moment, Aunty Uju reacts to her niece in the most practical of ways. This is understandable, given that Aunty Uju does not get the full story of what happened and she has her own financial and personal struggles. But who knows what healing Ifemelu may have been able to access had she been received with more tenderness, less judgment, more warmth, less severe practicality? Who knows, in other words, what would have become of Ifemelu had she had a blog like *Raceteenth* with which to anonymously express herself as a commenter or even motivate her to go to therapy, a cultural abnormality that the earlier blog post on mental illness works to normalize. Ifemelu, consciously or not, performs the tenderness that she never received for her reader, cajoling them with humor and a certain disingenuousness into the horrifying yet profoundly absurd experience of becoming Black in America.

The opening line, however, also obfuscates the coercive elements of the immigration system. When she says, "when you make the choice to come to America, you become black," she is speaking to Ifemelu's own contradictory relationship to her privileged status as a student at an American university, which is at odds with her long-suffering impoverishment. In some ways Ifemelu chose to migrate, but in other ways she did not: her options were a constantly shut-down university in Nsukka, Nigeria, or a functioning one, thousands of miles away. Ifemelu either broadly applies choice to the migration narratives of her reader or is using "choice" here to ironically undermine the choicelessness of becoming Black for the non-American Black who arrives in the United States. This choiceless choice is something we have also observed in Diallo's navigation of the criminal justice system because, as is true for many refugees, we do not have a real sense of what separates her desire to migrate from her necessity. Despite their different migrant statuses—one is a student, and the other is a refugee—and the class differences that are typically entailed, both Diallo and Ifemelu exemplify the ways in which both the immigration system and the criminal justice system turn Black women into objects rather than subjects of their own destinies. Additionally, class differences among Black immigrant women (and Black women more generally) influence how each defines Afro-pessimistic justice and uses strategies that suit her specific needs.

Ifemelu's introduction of her readers to the horrors of being Black in America is also telling of how the blog is a means through which she can work out her own healing, how she can mend the wounds wrought by a system that cannot make visible what the tennis coach did to her. As she writes, "When a crime is reported, pray that it was not committed by a black person . . . you might be stopped for fitting the profile" (223). Here, Ifemelu uses humor to ironize the brutal reality of "stop and frisk" police surveillance, under which Black Americans (particularly young Black American men) live, and nearly empties it of its systemic valence, of violence, of the fear of death, and of imprisonment. Instead of representing the brutality,

Ifemelu renders it a nuisance to be under such constant surveillance, something against which prayer is the only thing keeping the criminal from being Black. By vanishing the system around which racism is implemented while laughing at it, Ifemelu both deflates and misrepresents the situation. This aligns with Steele's reading of the "black blog," whose creator gets to imagine a new and adjacent reality to the one they are actually living. In Ifemelu's imagined reality, she does not pretend that racism disappears when we laugh at it, but rather leaves room for the impact of systemic racism to be weakened if it is transformed into something silly, something minimal, something manageable. Ifemelu thus uses humor to transpose two sets of anguishes—the anguish of her racialized and gendered trauma and the anguish of becoming Black—from one context to another: from the context of private, internal suffering to the context of public, external expression. The fact that Ifemelu is able to perform the role of racial and cultural ironist so publicly while also maintaining anonymity plays with the limits and possibilities that traditional definitions of "public" impose upon Black women writers.

Noble argues that search engines, and the internet more broadly, perpetuate racist and sexist myths, especially about Black and Latinx women and girls, who are the least represented in the technology industry. In this way, Noble indirectly reads anonymity as one of the dangers of the internet, something that allows largely white and male companies to perpetuate a masculinist and white-centric lens without anyone knowing. For example, though Google responded to criticism about the top hits for searching for "Black girls" or "latina girls" being porn sites, the tech conglomerate dismissed it as a problem with how their algorithm interacts with "users" (avoiding any kind of specific identification markers) rather than a problem with the race and gender makeup of their employees and CEOs. Noble sees this persistence of stereotyping as a result of the way that corporations like Google sell themselves as politically neutral or even in service of doing good in the world. (Google's motto is "Don't be evil.") These companies can sell themselves as neutral because their owners and employees remain relatively anonymous.[10] Though Noble situates the argument around anonymity within the arena of technology juggernauts, a similar battle has been raging around anonymity and the internet since its inception: Some argue that access to online anonymity is the only way to truly protect free speech, while others are adamant that online anonymity actually ends up protecting hate speech.

Ifemelu's experience writing her anonymous blog, *Raceteenth*, leads her to enter the fray to speak from both sides of the issue of anonymity and, in turn, speaks to both the limits and possibilities of blogging as a space for immigrant women of color to heal their trauma. Anonymity is both personally and logistically crucial to how Ifemelu operates her blog. Her readers know she is a non-American Black woman, but they do not know her country of origin. She mentions the import of her anonymous status when relating the story of her conversation with an Ethiopian cab driver in Baltimore: "When, years later, she wrote the blog post 'On the Divisions within the Membership of Non-American Blacks in America,' she wrote about the taxi driver, but she wrote of it as the experience of someone else, careful not to let on whether she was African or Caribbean, because her readers did not know which she was" (208). Here, Ifemelu implies that there is a voice missing from the debate around anonymity online. There are not only intergroup reasons why anonymity becomes controversial (i.e., white men decry a loss of anonymity as a loss of freedom while people of color claim that less anonymity might mean less horrific hate speech online), but also intragroup reasons for anonymity to act as a protective shield. Ifemelu is aware that if her readers know that she is Nigerian, all of her perspectives on race, culture, and politics will be read as skewed, inflected with special interest, with the bias of national origin.

Ifemelu garners a certain pleasure from being anonymous online that she and other immigrant women of color can never have in the analog world, as is illustrated in the story of her first meeting the friends of white and wealthy Curt: "[Curt's] friends were like him. . . To them, she was interesting, unusual in the way she bluntly spoke her mind. They expected certain things of her, and forgave certain things from her, because she was foreign. . . [she realized] that Curt and his friends would, on some level, never be fully knowable to her" (209). Here, Ifemelu feels the twoness of hypervisibility. On the one hand, Curt's friends put Ifemelu into a special category of "foreign"; on the other hand, her "blunt" way of speaking is forgiven more easily because of this category. In other words, though this twoness can be pleasurable, the things that they will expect and the things that they will forgive are out of Ifemelu's control. Online, Ifemelu has total control over everything: she can delete comments, block users, respond or not respond, delete posts, edit posts even after publishing, and limit the amount of personal information that she makes public.

It is worth noting that Ifemelu may have access to or desire a kind of total control that Nafissatou Diallo does not because of their class differences, thus pointing once more to the varieties of approaches to Afro-pessimistic justice. Nevertheless, the kind of control Ifemelu wields is not merely something she can exercise as a means of revenge against what the tennis coach took from her, but also against the way that systems of oppression, and agents of those systems, classify her as "immigrant woman of color" without her consent and without her being able to control the characteristics and assumptions that follow from that classification. Not allowing her readers to know what kind of non-American Black she is is one way Ifemelu asserts control not only over the narratives about immigrant women of color, but also over the very concept of a narrative existing about any group.

The longer that Ifemelu has her blog and as the blog becomes a serious means of income, however, her anonymity becomes less fixed as a liberating possibility and emerges as a limiting aspect of blogging while Black, immigrant, and a woman. *Raceteenth* effectively becomes an emotional burden that bears some resemblance to the emotional burden that the nonforcible sexual assault represents to Ifemelu. The blog is with Ifemelu through a number of personal and political life changes: when she breaks up with Curt and begins dating Blaine, a young Black professor (whom she serendipitously meets, for the second time, at a Blogging While Brown convention); when she quits her corporate job; when she decides to return to Nigeria; and when the United States elects its first Black president. Not only is the blog a witness to several important life events, but it is also responsible for many of them. After gaining a certain amount of notoriety, Ifemelu begins to monetize the blog, selling enough ad space and receiving enough donations from readers that she can live off of the money that she makes as a full-time blogger.

But this new financial success has consequences, as Ifemelu explains, when she receives an email after giving a speech called "How to Talk About Race with Colleagues of Other Races" to an all-white audience of employees at a small company in Ohio: "That evening she received an e-mail: YOUR TALK WAS BALONEY. YOU ARE A RACIST. YOU SHOULD BE GRATEFUL WE LET YOU INTO THIS COUNTRY. That e-mail . . . was a revelation. The point of diversity workshops . . . was not to inspire any real change but to leave people feeling good about themselves" (307). Ifemelu receives comments that she is racist before monetizing her blog, but now that the blog makes money and is more accessible to a larger, whiter audience, it is also even more vulnerable to these kinds of attacks. The emailer's final line about Ifemelu being grateful that "we" gave her entry to America is especially relevant. The popularity of her blog leads to Ifemelu appearing in public, her photo being posted on other blogs that profile her. Now that she is embodied for her audience, there are more opportunities for her complex ideas to either be misunderstood or undesired, as she says: "They did not want the content of her ideas; they merely wanted the gesture of her presence" (307). Ifemelu's body is in fact all that the audience really wants, precisely because her body speaks to a simplistic multiculturalist narrative that they can digest, a narrative about good white folks trying to understand the perspectives of those who are different from them.

Ifemelu is demanding much more from her audience, but when she begins to be an embodied public intellectual, she learns how to code-switch, how to distinguish between her public person and her private public persona:

> As she gave more talks at companies and schools, she began to say what they wanted to hear, none of which she would ever write on her blog, because she knew that the people who read her blog were not the same people who attended her diversity workshops. During her talks, she said: "America has made great progress for which she should be very proud." In her blog she wrote: *Racism should never have happened and so you don't get a cookie for reducing it.* Still more invitations came. She hired a student intern, a Haitian American, her hair worn in elegant twists, who was nimble on the Internet, looking up whatever information Ifemelu needed, and deleting inappropriate comments almost as soon as they were posted. (307)

The consequence of the blog's popularity here is a division of Ifemelu's self. Ifemelu divides herself in two to satisfy the needs of her distinct audiences and arenas. On the one hand, this seems like an act of surrender because she acquiesces to the demands of a more conservative audience. In a way, Ifemelu behaves here like a politician.[11] On the other hand, she treats a complicated situation with the kind of care and specificity of which most of the systems at play in this novel and in *New York v. Strauss-Kahn* are incapable. If the legal system, for example, could always stay constantly attuned to how specific circumstances make certain populations vulnerable to certain kinds of violence, perhaps the assaults committed both against Diallo and

Ifemelu would be legible as crimes. Whether one sees Ifemelu's strategy here as subversive or accommodationist, it remains true that upon relinquishing some of her anonymity, Ifemelu also relinquishes some of the control that she has over the blog and its impact on others.

The blog gives Ifemelu a sense of control that allows this technological space to function as a mode of therapeutic expression. The tennis coach makes Ifemelu feel like she has no control over her body and the blog gives her total control, or at least the illusion of total control, over a narrative and community of immigrant women of color. This control allows Ifemelu to complicate overly simplistic notions of immigrant women of color as either romantically oppressed, as represented by the white liberal perspective of Kimberly, the woman whose children she cares for as her first job in America, or from the conservative perspective of some of her blog readers, as criminals hell-bent on taking over the country.

Ifemelu hints at this increasing lack of control as the blog's popularity increases: "The blog had unveiled itself and shed its milk teeth; by turns it surprised her, pleased her, left her behind" (305). Here, she describes the blog as a child who grows not just apart but beyond her. Because the novel opens on Ifemelu just as she is shutting down the blog, the reader gets a sense of how the blog disappoints Ifemelu long before we are even aware of her long journey to creating it.

As Ifemelu describes her decision to shut the blog down, it is only upon rereading that the reader sees that the blog has grown from being an innocent adolescent into an all-consuming nightmare.

> All those readers, growing month by month . . . they had always frightened and exhilarated her . . . Readers like SapphicDerrida, who reeled off statistics and used words like "reify" in their comments, made Ifemelu nervous, eager to be fresh and to impress, so that she began, over time, to feel like a vulture hacking into the carcasses of people's stories for something she could use. Sometimes making fragile links to race. Sometimes not believing herself. The more she wrote, the less sure she became. Each post scraped off yet one more scale of self until she felt naked and false. (5)

The blog evolves once again from something over which Ifemelu has lost control, what was once a somewhat harmless child, into something that has consumed her, turning her into a frightening animal that objectifies its interactions with other human beings.[12] At the same time that Ifemelu is consumed by the blog, it strips her, "[scraping] off yet one more scale of self until she felt naked and false." The description of herself as "naked and false" is the most horrifying yet because it is reminiscent of her scene with the tennis coach, not only because of the nudity but because of the dissociation from her body she experienced after performing a sexual act with him. It therefore makes sense that once the blog begins to reenact the time in her life when she was least in control, she decides to shut the blog down.

Despite being shut down, however, the blog lives on as an archive. We find out that although Ifemelu has ceased posting on the blog, this does not mean that the blog ceases to exist, as is clear when we see that her ex-love, Obinze, reads the blog for clues about Ifemelu's life (374). *Raceteenth*, therefore, continues to live beyond and without Ifemelu, but she seems to be at peace knowing that its sustained life is no longer her responsibility. Despite the many limits that the blog comes to place on Ifemelu, its strength as a space of healing cannot be underestimated: it gives Ifemelu a way to express her rage against systems of racial oppression, a community through which she can share in the experiences and perspectives of immigrants of color and immigrant women of color, and, most important, a space over which she, initially, has total control.[13]

Conclusion

In her groundbreaking 1996 essay "Textual Healing: Claiming Black Women's Bodies, the Erotic and Resistance in Contemporary Novels of Slavery," Farrah Jasmine Griffin argues that Black women authors of that era, like Sherly Anne Williams and Michelle Cliff, were adamant about using literature to represent the alternative ways that Black women find healing in their experiences with one another. Griffin is explicitly enthralled by the ways that these authors highlight physical touch between Black women, whether platonic, familial, romantic, or otherwise, as a means of finding closure after violent or violating experiences or to survive the double marginal experience of existing as a Black woman in the world. Griffin is staunchly in the "recovery" camp if we accept the overly simplistic but helpful recovery/acknowledgment split between Black studies practitioners and scholars that I have mentioned earlier in this book. Griffin's purpose in the essay is to collect the ways in which Black women literally lean on one another to recover from pain and to explore how Black women-identified authors represent this communal support as an alternative to other, perhaps more white-male-dominant means of compensating trauma, such as through the fight for political rights or through the struggle for social justice. In many ways, Griffith extends the Black feminist political work of the Combahee River Collective and other groups who were intent upon finding ways to heal that had not yet been imagined by the mostly white feminist and the mostly male Black rights movements from which the Black feminist movement emerged.

I propose that Afro-pessimistic justice acts as yet another way for Black women to "recover" from sexual trauma, but, because these methods are mired in a failure that is baked into what it means to inhabit a Black body, the strategies exist in a cycle of failure, triumph, and failure again. Specifically, because the Black women of this book, whether by their own design or not, are unable to escape the systems within which they are operating—the criminal justice system, the immigration system—and are attempting to exact justice for crimes committed against bodies that have historically been exiled from being intelligible as victims of sexually violent crimes, this cycle between failure and triumph is endless and doomed to never be sutured enough to the point where it could ever heal. A novel like *Americanah* is an outlier in the collection of other novels presented here because it lacks reference to a criminal justice system—no language of trial, no courtroom, no eye toward the law—yet it still functions as a contributor to the strategies that exist under Afro-pessimistic justice.

CONCLUSION

Where Have We Been, and Where Are We Going? An Ambivalent Future between Afro-pessimism and Abolition

When I began the research and writing that set the foundation of *Bodies in the Middle*, it was 2014, three years before the #MeToo and #TimesUp movements had erupted online, more than 5 years before the Black uprisings of 2020 and a global pandemic that claimed the lives of millions of people. We are at a pivotal historical moment at which many bodies are in various kinds of crises with seemingly little to no avenues for solutions. Afro-pessimism offers a way out of the notion that it is the responsibility of marginalized people, namely Black people, to find solutions to the horrific problems of inequality and devastating global and systematic oppression. Instead of seeking recovery, Afro-pessimism encourages us to acknowledge the mess that we are actually in, a mess that has never actually escaped from the confines of enslavement and never will. If the goal is no longer escaping or undoing inequality, what must the new goal become? *Bodies in the Middle* proposes that when we follow the stories that raped Black women and their defenders tell us about their violations, we are invited to explore the spaces that exist between recovery and acknowledgment, spaces that other Black studies scholars like Christina Sharpe, Saidiya Hartman, Fred Moten, Hortense Spillers, and June Jordan have been digging into for decades.

Throughout the chapters in this book, I have outlined the ways in which Black female victims of sexual violence (and their defenders) have created their own justice systems, whether they were manifesting such a creation out of an already-existing system or imagining one that did not exist at all. Out of these stories of Black women and systems emerge what I call Afro-pessimistic justice, a collection of strategies through which Black female victims—real and fictional—of sexual assault, rape, and other kinds of sexual violence attempt to receive healing or compensation for the crimes committed against them. These strategies range from generating liberal activist movements to placing pressure on governing bodies, manipulating the machinations of a trial system to the benefit of a poor and Black incarcerated woman, and manifesting public sympathy for one's victimization through the advent of televised news. The Black women's stories told here structured their strategies around and in defiance of existing justice systems, but the resulting system, an Afro-pessimistic justice system, centered the physical body, reproduction, and voice; another system functioned primarily around the death of the rape victim; or healing and justice from the virtual world. The intricate details of each system are important and satisfy the needs of each victim's circumstances, but it is most important that they all share a common thread of failure. All of the systems fail.

None of the systems that Black women manifest for themselves "work" to bring about the full healing and fair justice that they want, deserve, and need. When we talk about the failure of justice in the context of a rape case, we are most often talking about the failure to bring the person or people responsible "to justice," the failure to "make the rapist(s) pay" for the crime that they committed by going to jail as the law states. The very fact that Black women have been denied access to not only any kind of compensation for the sexual crimes committed against them, but also to any kind of recognition as victims for so long brings an inherent sense that what Black women are owed is precisely the incarceration of those who have committed wrongs against them.

But what if Afro-pessimistic justice, in its seeming desire for failure, is functioning precisely as intended? What if we were to see the way forward for Afro-pessimistic justice was not for Black women to find new methods for nonfailing kinds of justice and not for the criminal justice system to be reformed so as to serve the needs of Black women? Later in this conclusion I suggest how these Afro-pessimistic questions which interrogate systemic injustice may lead us to a meditation on the prison abolition movement, but first I will situate Afro-pessimism and discuss the argument as a whole.

Recovery Work and Acknowledgment Work

As I mentioned in the introduction to this volume, there are very broadly speaking two approaches to African American literary and historical study: recovery work and acknowledgment work. On the one hand, recovery work aligns with resistance work and other kinds of justice work in that it aims to uncover the (sometimes historical) truth of Black beauty, hope, future, and Black excellence to counter the dominant racist narratives of Black people as ugly, hopeless, without future, inferior. Acknowledgment work is where scholars and other public writers have opted to push for an awareness and a consciousness-raising of just how complex and deeply troubling the systems of oppression around us are and just how anti-Black the anti-Black violence is. I would argue that Afro-pessimism is acknowledgment work because it is not very interested in showcasing how we have progressed from our past; it acknowledges how little progress (or perhaps no progress) has been made. If we stay within the acknowledgment frame, we may ask what happens to a struggle for Black lives with no end goal other than, perhaps, acknowledging that the struggle for Black lives will never cease, particularly in a country in which anti-Blackness and the pursuit of global capital are so tied?

Bodies in the Middle argues that twentieth and twenty-first century legal cases and novels which centered raped Black women prove that Black women are not merely the objects of a neglectful, racist, and sexist "criminal justice" system. The cases of Recy Taylor, Joan Little, and Nafissatou Diallo, the novels *Native Son*, *Corregidora*, and *Americanah* show how Black women or their defenders/allies, in history and literature, find ways, both productive and destructive, to act as subjects by manipulating the legal system, creating their own legal systems, or replacing justice with other modes of expression. But what remains constant throughout is that in between all of these attempts are the nonattempts, the failures, and the deaths. There is no justice for Black women who have experienced sexual violence. Contrary to previous scholarship on this topic, Black women are not trapped in a binary of being either subject or object, and the authors who write about them resist this reductive binary as well.

Reading Danielle McGuire's book, *At the Dark End of the Street*, was the first time I encountered the stories of Recy Taylor and Joan Little. As a young queer Black woman in my first few years of graduate study, these stories were life changing. Not only did Recy Taylor fail to get justice for the blatant sexual crime committed against her, this violation was not even seen as a crime, as made evident by the utter and total failure of the grand jury in Abbeville, Alabama, to indict her rapists not just once, but twice. Though the specifics of this case—geography, racial identities of the rapists, and so on—are key to its "failure," Taylor introduces the concept of intelligibility to this project and reinforces the ugly truth that Black women are often left out of the status of "victim of rape" to which white women typically have easier access.

Perhaps partially obscuring the failure of Taylor's case is the case of clear triumph in the Betty Jean Owens case of 1959, in which a young Black woman was raped by four white men in Tallahassee, Florida, and those men received life sentences. I did not tell Owens's story in-depth because, given the number of cases that I was reading about in which no justice or some kind of modified justice was handed out to a raped Black woman, the Owens case seemed like an exception to the pattern I was noticing rather than exceptional in how it was starting its own pattern. In other words, Joan Little's story is more representative of a number of Black women's experiences (the mixture of triumph and loss). The important takeaway is that for the length of the twentieth century and beyond, Black women have not had total and complete access to justice for sexual violence. The wins have often been exceptions and the losses expected parts of a long-standing American tradition. Another corner of the picture of Afro-pessimistic justice is peeled back when the case of Recy Taylor is placed in conversation with *Native Son*.

Richard Wright's *Native Son* was published in 1940; Recy Taylor received the devastating news that her case would not go to trial once in 1944, and again in 1945, after more than a year of hundreds if not thousands of people fighting in defense of her equal right to justice. Obviously, Wright could not have known about Taylor's specific case when he wrote the novel, but his creation of Bessie showcases a desire to portray Black women and the sexual violation that they experience or are threatened with daily. Wright demonstrates that he was well aware of the ways in which Black women were vulnerable to violence, not only from white men and women, but also from Black men. For Wright to conclude that Black women would have to die for the injustices against them to be named as such is potentially the most extreme strategy of Afro-pessimistic justice. The strategy asserts that Black women will never access anything close to justice for the crimes committed against them from a white supremacist justice system unless they are dead and their corpses can be made valuable to prosecute a crime committed against a white woman. Clearly Wright is being extreme for effect and to confront politically passive white and Black audiences with the unbelievable violences being waged against Black women. However, Wright's insistence on death as Bessie's destiny also demonstrates the same insight that Recy Taylor's case reveals: systems of power do not see Black women as victims of violence, specifically sexual violence.

What Taylor's case unveils is that Wright seems disinterested in the possibilities that exist outside the law—namely within interracial social justice coalition work—for Black women to be made legible as victims of sexual violence. The Committee for the Equal Justice of Mrs. Recy Taylor is able to temporarily make Recy Taylor intelligible as a Black woman *and* the victim of a sexual crime, but the propaganda in support of Taylor's case also demonstrates the ways in which such movements are plagued by the universalism of human rights rhetoric, forcing them to divorce Taylor from her Blackness in order to prove herself worthy of justice. Taylor's status as a mother, a churchgoer, and a wife are ways of deracinating her, inviting her into middle class echelons in which she could access a version of femininity in need of defense. The intersections between Taylor and Bessie reveal that although Taylor does not need to physically die to be made intelligible as a victim of sexual violence, liberal supporters of her cause kill off parts of her identity that they regard as detrimental to her being publicly accepted as a victim of sexual violence. In other words, within this liberal framework, Black women are incapable of accessing the kind of normative forms of justice we associate with a triumphant case without incurring physical or psychological harm. Despite the massive wave of support for Taylor, she received so many death threats from white people in her town that she was forced to move to Florida; she never returned to Alabama. Both Bessie and Taylor serve as familiar examples of the ways in which systems and collective organizations act upon Black women not necessarily centering the holistic healing of their hearts, bodies, and minds. Wright's novel and Taylor's case reveal the corner of Afro-pessimistic justice in which death and the denial of Blackness are integral to the new kinds of systems Black women and their allies are building.

Running both with and counter to the notion that we make progress over time, the connections between Taylor's case and that of Joan Little invite some new levels of intelligibility and legibility to be discovered. Little and Ursa of Gayl Jones's *Corregidora* present the possibilities for Black women attempting to create justice for themselves. Each opens up what Afro-pessimistic justice is and what it means to practice it. And this conversation between Little and Ursa is happening in a number of registers, but, perhaps most primarily, in the register of time. Time is key to Afro-pessimism. To position oneself in an Afro-pessimistic stance is to position oneself in a particular way with and against the past. Frank B. Wilderson III and others have investigated the ways in which Black people have never and will never be free from their slave status, under the current white supremacist and global capitalist systems; they are saying in effect that the past has never left us. Afro-pessimism charges us to consider, from the perspective of Black life, that "the past is not dead, it is not even past," as William Faulkner famously said. Both Little and Jones also charge us to consider that the past is never past. Or, better said, the novel *Corregidora* questions the possibility for Black women to escape their past and appears, ultimately, to decide that they cannot: therein lies the Afro-pessimism. In some ways Little's case offers a more promising and hopeful vision for relating to the past, as much of Little's defense was built around a relatively new and academic take on the past from a Black perspective. Her attorney, Jerry Paul, talked extensively in his closing statement about the ways in which the United States used and abused Black women during enslavement and how our inability to grant them equal consideration under the law is a continuation of that centuries-old abuse. Following the logic of both Paul and McGuire in her book, if Little triumphs, the stereotypes around Black women as "rapeable" without consequence can be vanquished. However, even as they used their position toward history in the hopes of undermining systems of oppression, Joan Little's defense also acknowledged the ways in which the past is never past especially where Black people and justice are concerned.

Little and Jones differ when it comes to the question around the escapability of that past. Afro-pessimism, again, prompts us to consider that there is no escape from the enslaver-enslaved dynamic for white and Black people. I would argue that, at the very least, Jones is ambiguous on the question of whether escape from enslavement and therefore some kind of liberation is possible. And contrarily, the defense team of Joan Little and Joan Little herself consider the win in her case a step forward, a sign of progress along a straightforward historical continuum. This divide between Little and *Corregidora*'s Ursa offers a dynamic way to think about the relationship between Black women who have been raped and "justice." Black women who have experienced sexual violence and are seeking justice are never operating within a binary between abjection and triumph (and who, perhaps, are never even in agreement about what binary they are never in). One of the throughlines of this project is the way in which the women are forced or choose to use their bodies in the search for or creation of justice for themselves. As I conclude this study, I offer a continued meditation on the divergences between the cases and the novels I have examined. These divergences both center and decenter the body from their versions of Afro-pessimistic justice.

Bessie's body is used as evidence both for and against her own interests; Recy Taylor's body is divided up into the pieces of her identity that various audiences deem intelligible or legible as victim; Ursa's body, in its barrenness, becomes incapable of being useful as the site upon which the Afropessimistic justice system of the Corregidora women can be exacted; and Joan Little's body is made intelligible as raped but also as inescapably criminal. All of the cases I've been summarizing thus far here examine Black women's physical bodies' capacity as containers for alternative justice systems. That is to say, all of the cases until Ifemelu in Chimamanda Ngozi Adichie's *Americanah*. This novel marks Adichie's attempt to move beyond the body through the blogosphere where that Ifemelu creates a blog in an attempt to heal herself after a sexual assault. This move "beyond the body" is vital for understanding the significance of a major divergence along class lines that exists between Ifemelu and Nafissatou Diallo, the Guinean victim of Dominique Strauss-Kahn's assault. As discussed in the final chapter of part 1, Diallo centers her body and its image-making powers as well as her voice and its sonic powers to explore their capacities for enacting an Afro-pessimistic justice system that counters dominant misogynoirist narratives of Black immigrant women as whores, as money-hungry prostitutes, and therefore as non-victims of sexual violence. Adichie tells a story very similar to Diallo's about a Black immigrant woman who is the victim of an assault and who searches for a way to use technology to, indirectly, heal that trauma. Why, then, does Adichie choose to do the opposite of Diallo and decenter the body through the digital portals of the blog?

Part of the answer is located in the class differences between Diallo and Ifemelu that emerge almost entirely from their differing migrant statuses. As a refugee and an asylum-seeker, Diallo was forced to endure a much more rigorous process to get to the United States, but, upon arrival, actually had access to a number of resources and services that allowed her to get employment, housing, a pathway to a green card, and access to other social services that other migrant statuses do not have access to. The flip side of the refugee's access, however, is that they are, typically, thrust into a position of financial precarity precisely because they are forced into low wage employment and not often given much opportunity for upward mobility. In many ways, especially legally, Ifemelu's status as an immigrant living in the United States on a student visa is directly opposite of Diallo's refugee status. Ifemelu's visa permits her to stay in the country for a temporary amount of time, just long enough for her to complete her studies; it provides little to no track to permanent residency. Additionally, under her student visa, Ifemelu has no access to employment outside of work study. Adichie establishes this lack of access to employment through the painstaking examination of Ifemelu's period of poverty, during which, before finding work, she had difficulty sustaining her most basic needs, such as food and shelter. Despite its difficult limitations, Ifemelu's student visa is not one that marks its recipients as destined to live in poverty and, if anything, receiving undergraduate degree at an Ivy League university permits Ifemelu to enter many echelons of middle-class society. Diallo may now have access to some kind of class mobility because of the money she received from her civil suit against Strauss-Kahn which enabled her to open a restaurant, but even as a small business owner, Diallo and Ifemelu differ in their class statuses because of their difference in education.

A lot has to happen in the plot of *Americanah* for Ifemelu to end up with a high-paying job that grants her a green card. Despite the ways in which Adichie manipulates plot mechanics to make her immigrant protagonist seem quite lucky, Ifemelu's path as a somewhat privileged class of immigrant does not differ so much from reality as to make the story completely unbelievable. International students are often regarded as being on a track toward the middle or upper middle class; such is the social capital attached to certain kinds of education and degrees. The stories of Diallo and Ifemelu inscribe the impact of migration status—whether one is legally considered either a refugee or a student—on class position, restricting or broadening access to employment.

I am specifically asserting that both Diallo and Ifemelu seek out the kinds of Afro-pessimistic justice that they do—one embodied, one disembodied—because of their different class statuses. As a refugee, Diallo is thrust into a socioeconomically lower position and, therefore, perhaps, must rely on her body as the means through which to prove her innocence (when accused of being a prostitute), which in turn should work to prove her status as a victim of sexual violence. Diallo, in other words, must use her body to access a class position which Ifemelu may desire to reject, obscure, or imagine through her anonymity. However, at the same time as Ifemelu's Afro-pessimistic justice appears to require disembodiment and anonymity, the very practice of blogging coincides with a number of middle- to upper-class trappings: she must own a computer, the blog discusses the inner workings of social life in such academic prose that it could be inaccessible to some; even the spaces in which Ifemelu often travels (taking taxis, going to dinner parties) in her blog recall a kind of class status. This class binary gets much more complicated when we consider that Ifemelu is in fact the one of the two who actually does receive money for sex, so perhaps her desire to detach from the body stems from trauma rooted in the monetary evaluation of her body. And we must also remember that Diallo attempted to remain anonymous, only entering the public eye once she felt forced to clear her name after newspapers spread lies about her being a sex worker.

What all of this suggests is that the relationship between a Black woman and her body in the wake of sexual trauma is varied. Whether her body is a source of healing or a source of retraumatization, whether her body itself bears signals of access or a lack of access to resources, whether her body is present or not, the body is central to Afro-pessimistic justice systems that Black women create for themselves precisely because of the body's fallible nature. Bodies shift, change, grow, evolve, and are therefore worrying sites for justice systems, which require some amount of stability. Additionally, even in the process of using or rejecting the body, every woman seems to harm herself, her defenders, and her loved ones in the attempt to be a site for a new kind of justice system to emerge. Ultimately any kind of justice system that requires Black women to harm themselves to receive compensation for the violations of their bodies, minds, and psyches is an Afro-pessimistic justice system precisely because it cannot function. The mobius strip of harm that Afro-pessimism presents us with brings us to a concluding question and meditation: what is the afterlife of a world without traditional forms of justice in which the assailant is punished and the wronged is presumably healed through this punishment? The prison abolition movement offers us a way forward and through such lines of questioning.[1]

Abolition and Afro-pessimistic Justice

First a bit of background: the movement to abolish prisons is far older than one may think. Philosophers, artists, scholars, and others have been trying to imagine alternative approaches to "crime" and "punishment" for thousands of years. However, the modern movement to abolish prisons in the United States began in the 1970s precisely because, prior to this moment, the carceral system was far smaller and less advanced than the prison industrial complex we know now. As Angela Y. Davis elucidates in her foundational text *Are Prisons Obsolete?* the notion of the modern prison is relatively new. A modern prison is one in which hundreds if not thousands of people are incarcerated for long periods of time. Prison sites are located great distances from the "civilian" population, and there is not merely one of these in each locale but often several correctional facilities or detention centers for every small locale—though this obviously can depend on the state. Many politicians and average citizens who support incarceration as a "solution" to crime likely imagine that the construction of prisons coincided with a rise in crime. Following this line of thought, the proliferation of prisons is a response to an increase in crime that must be "contained" [within the prison]. But this is not true.

We have experienced unbelievably low crime rates across states and nationally while incarceration rates have never really decreased; in fact, new prisons and carceral facilities are being built constantly.[2] It is almost definitely true that incarceration does not limit or reduce crime. In fact, as both Hartman and Khalil Gibran Muhammad clearly argue, how we define "crime" is entirely socially constructed and often made up so as to prioritize and center the desires of upper middle class white people in power.[3] The demographics of people most often imprisoned and those who have the most difficult time escaping the poverty-to-prison pipeline reflect these desires to keep "undesirable" elements of society out of sight and to maintain the oppression of poor people, Black and Brown people, queer and trans people, disabled people, and many other marginalized people.

The first point of alignment between Afro-pessimistic justice and the prison abolition movement is this: the notion that to reform the system, we need to talk to the people most impacted and knowledgeable about incarceration—currently or formerly incarcerated people. In other words, what happens when incarcerated or formerly incarcerated people, who have been most negatively impacted by or neglected by the systems meant to mete out justice, are now in charge of them? What happens when the victims of an oppressive system become the arbiters of how that system functions? This is one point of alignment between Afro-pessimistic justice and prison abolition. Afro-pessimistic justice consists of raped Black women asking: what happens when we, the people who have historically been most neglected by justice systems, become the arbiters of it, in full control of its mechanics? The respective works of great prison abolitionists such as Davis's *Are Prisons Obsolete?*, Mariame Kaba's *We Do This 'Til We Free Us*, and Andrea Ritchie's *Invisible No More: Police Violence Against Black Women and Women of Color* ask and attempt to answer precisely these questions by bringing our attention to just how much harm the prison system causes Black, brown, and poor families who are broken apart, whole communities are stigmatized and discriminated against, and the over-policing of communities dictates who goes to jail for what crimes and for how long, often resulting in the excessive incarceration of Black, brown, or poor people.

The prison abolition movement goes on to ask additional questions. What happens when those who have historically been completely left out of deciding what happens to them and to their abusers get put in charge? What happens when both victims and "offenders" (in the language of transformative and restorative justice) are treated as victims in need of care, attention, healing? In other words, how do justice systems get reimagined when they begin to center the care for the most marginalized and vulnerable to being harmed, violated, and cyclically oppressed by a system? How can these "justice systems" be reimagined to include rather than exclude victims of them as well as their abusers? What does a world in which there are no police and no prisons require? Afro-pessimistic justice calls for (and calls out) the failure of systems that have never "functioned" properly for Black women precisely because, so often when they do function, they not only hurt Black women but also the people who love Black women and who Black women love. But this is the most sensitive part of any intersection between not only Afro-pessimistic justice and abolition, but also justice for rape victims and abolition.

In a project that centered on the topic of Black women and rape, it's only fair to ask: where does abolition fit when we are talking about crimes like sexual violence? In fact, many of those who are suspicious of or outright against prison abolition and the abolition of police fixate on the crimes of rape and murder as the ones that make prison abolition most impossible. What do we do with the rapists and the murderers? And this is a fair question. Abolitionists often approach any and all crime as rooted in something much deeper than the crime itself and are more interested in discussing whether or not imprisonment solves rape and murder or keeps it from happening. We know that imprisonment does not solve rape and murder. If the prison industrial complex could solve our most abhorrent crimes, it would have done so long ago. Indeed, given the rate of incarceration, it should have kept those crimes from ever happening again. One of the counterarguments to this then re-focuses the argument: Do victims of violent crimes deserve some level of peace which the incarceration of their abuser could provide? Would a victim be able to heal through their victimization better knowing that the person who harmed them could not do so to another person?

The answer to this line of questioning is unbelievably complicated, especially when we center Black female victims of sexual violence. On the one hand, Black women who are victims of rape or sexual assault may be generally against the carceral system because of the ways they may have seen it ravage their own families and communities. This anti-reporting approach is one which abolition obviously encourages, but it also tends to isolate instances of harm that occur between two or more people who are in the same community. While it is true that most rapists are people who the victim knows or is intimate with, this does not cover the broad spectrum of violence that can occur. And even within communities, abolition seems to forestall a space for the rage that a victim may feel or a collective need for the violator to be excluded from the community. Abolition and other kinds of restorative and transformative forms of justice point again to not involving the police or the prison system at all and see whether a community of care can provide resources for both a victim and an abuser. Is it possible to prioritize the needs of a victim of rape while also acknowledging that her abuser is likely also a victim?

On the other hand, there are plenty of instances in which we have seen Black women not only desire, but also demand the incarceration of their abusers and violators. We have seen this in the cases of Recy Taylor, the case of Nafissatou Diallo, and the case of Bessie Mears. If abolition and Afropessimistic justice are attempts to center the needs and desires of Black female victims of sexual violence, what happens when the victims want incarceration? Abolitionists would say that individual needs of victims may change when abolition is a real and mature option. Currently we do not live in a world in which Black women can look at abolition as a reality, and so it seems unfair to demand that they imagine forms of healing that do not yet exist on a more massive level.[4] Afro-pessimistic justice and abolition therefore arrive at an impasse around the issue of attending to the needs of individual victims and whether such a thing is feasible when it comes to conversations about the destruction of whole systems or whether all individual needs must be resisted to prioritize radical and revolutionary action against oppression.

Thinking beyond the tension between Afro-pessimistic justice and abolition momentarily, the former is still a viable and worthwhile lens through which to consider how and what Black women are thinking about justice. I want to live in a world in which Black women who are harmed feel that there is at least a creative and liberative space available to them, to dream of a future where not only are they visible as victims, but where their pain is prioritized and acted upon in a way that is healing for them. This project has focused on stories of Black women and their defenders who have been creating justice for themselves in ways that are sometimes healing, but also sometimes destructive, in ways that sometimes maintain their individual wholeness and also in ways that break them apart again and again. This project therefore has no closure other than abolition which prompts us to dream not of a fantasy world in which no one ever harmed another person ever again, but rather to imagine and build the world we wish to see in which systems of harm are disempowered and disenfranchised rather than the individuals most vulnerable to oppression. The only way forward is to continue dreaming with Recy, with Joan, with Nafissatou, with Bessie, with Ursa, with Ifemelu. I say their names. I say their dreams. Out loud.

NOTES

Introduction

1. See Moya Bailey's 2013 article, "New Terms of Resistance: A Response to Zenzele Isoke." Bailey originated the term in a 2010 article "They Aren't Talking About Me." Since the advent of Bailey's term, there have been several other scholars, writers, artists, and activists who have continued to contribute to the rape-race conversation that puts Black women at the center. I want to take a moment to laud the recent documentary works covering the now-convicted rapists Bill Cosby and R. Kelly, *We Need to Talk About Cosby* by W. Kamau Bell and *Surviving R. Kelly* by dream hampton respectively. I will not be talking about the cases surrounding these high-profile rapists largely because they put the rapists at the center of the conversation rather than the victims. But I do want to acknowledge the significance of the filmmakers who have changed the public conversation around Black women and rape for the better.

2. To be clear, I am not suggesting that the conversation around Black women and sexual violence has always been mired in abjection. Scholars like Joan Morgan, Deborah McDowell, Tera Hunter, Claudrena Harold, Saidiya Hartman, and Hortense Spillers have sought to depict Black women throughout history in a way that is honest, rich, and complex. However, even within this complexity, Black studies scholars agree that even in exceptional moments when Black women overcame their circumstances, the time of enslavement was one of legal and social abjection for Black women, especially because of their vulnerability to rape and other forms of sexual violence. Additionally, most would agree that the legacy of enslavement is still felt as Black women continue to be more vulnerable to violence of all kinds, particularly state violence. See also Joan Morgan, *When Chickenheads Come Home to Roost: A Hip-hop Feminist Breaks It Down;* Deborah McDowell, *"The Changing Same": Black Women's Literature, Criticism, and Theory;* Tera Hunter, *To 'Joy My Freedom: Southern Black Women's Lives and Labors After the Civil War;* Saidiya Hartman, *Wayward Lives, Beautiful Experiments: Intimate Histories of Riotous Black Girls, Troublesome Women, and Queer Radicals.*

3. See Higginbotham, *Righteous Discontent: The Women's Movement in the*

Black Baptist Church 1880–1920; Hazel V. Carby, *Reconstructing Womanhood: The Emergence of the Afro-American Woman Novelist*; Michele Mitchell, *Righteous Propagation: African Americans and the Politics of Racial Destiny After Reconstruction*; Combahee River Collective, "A Black Feminist Statement."

4. Too many scholars to name have commented on the marked difference between the definition of justice in the civil rights era and what is commonly referred to as the "post-Soul era." For decades, they have asked: What becomes of a mainstream justice movement when the rights that were presumably at the center have been, at least on paper, "granted"? The discourse on the differences between a rights-based justice movement, an abolition of oppression justice movement, and a reformist justice movement can be seen in Nelson George's *Buppies, B-boys, Baps and Bohos*. See also Keeanga-Yamahtta Taylor, *From Black Liberation to Black Lives Matter*; Mariame Kaba, *We Do This 'Til We Free Us*.

5. See Lisa Lowe, *Immigrant Acts: On Asian American Cultural Politics*; Mae Ngai, *Impossible Subjects: Illegal Aliens and the Making of Modern America*; Nils Christie, "The Ideal Victim."

Chapter 1: Justice in the Abstract

1. #TimesUp is a hashtag as well as a movement which began in January 2018 as a response to the growing number of accusations of sexual violence being made against powerful men in Hollywood. #TimesUp consists of a group of Hollywood actresses, activists, and legal consultants who are outspokenly dedicated to ending sexual harassment in their own industry, to providing anti-violence groups with grants, and to supplying women with funds to cover their legal costs for those seeking justice for sexual crimes committed against them. #MeToo began in 2006 with Tarana Burke, a Black woman and longtime anti-violence activist, but gained a resurgence of popularity when the famous white actress, Alyssa Milano, tweeted the hashtag in October 2017. The story of #MeToo is itself a microcosm of the story of Black women that my project tells.

2. Winfrey uses the word "persecuted" in her speech, but it is likely that she meant to say "prosecuted."

3. Perhaps the best example of this usage of "abstraction," as I am using it, is in Marlon B. Ross's "Race, Rape, Castration: Feminist Theories of Sexual Violence and Masculine Strategies of Black Protest," "Rather than assuming an equal, reciprocal, or analogous relation between rape and castration, however, I want to consider the equivocal imbalances and disruptions operating in this cultural logic, which equates graphic racial violence against Black men with an abstraction of men's sexual violence against women" (306). See also Orlando Patterson's *Slavery and Social Death*; Stefano Harney and Fred Moten, *The Undercommons*; Gayatri Chakravorty Spivak, "Can the Subaltern Speak".

4. The discourse of sexual violence and race requires a more flexible definition of the "state." When I use the term "state," I am referring to individuals and institutions who represent local, state and/or federal power. The 'state' can refer to a range of people: elected officials, governing bodies, juries, lawyers, and/or activists, though I will parse those various groups when necessary. The idea behind this usage of the term is that activists can play as much of the role as agents of the state as those who are elected and/or hired to such governmental positions. The various activist groups represented in this project see themselves as exemplary agents of the state, advocating for the preservation of the Union, at the same time that they are railing against the state to motivate change.

5. There are troubling things about calling the people who raped Taylor "boys," so I have refrained from doing so. To grant this gang of white male rapists a kind of boyhood innocence which their whiteness assumes would be to detract from the heinousness of the crime that they committed. But, as an abolitionist, I want to acknowledge that this gang of white male rapists was made up of teenagers, and this is also significant. To be clear, I am not interested in the destruction of these young lives as payback for the ways in which they destroyed Taylor's life.

6. I am using the language of legible/intelligible because it is the language that I find best fits the context of Taylor's case. Both her white liberal defenders and the Deep Southern grand jury are literally and metaphorically misreading her body according to anti-Black and/or liberal universalist values deeply embedded in the systems operating around her. But I recognize that there are other theoretical framings for these concepts. In the realm of biopolitics, scholars such as Michel Foucault, Hannah Arendt, and Giorgio Agamben theorize that political power is ultimately about who is permitted to live and who is not. On the other hand, in his article "Necropolitics", Achille Mbembe asserts that "the ultimate expression of sovereignty resides, to a large degree, in the power and capacity to dictate who may live and who must die . . . But under what practical conditions is the right to kill, to allow to live, or to expose to death exercised?" (11–12) Mbembe rightly states that the primary theorists of biopolitics centered the Holocaust in their thinking. In his own work, Mbembe asks what happens when the "practical conditions" are not a late-modern genocide carried out in Western and Eastern Europe, but rather the pre-colonial/colonial/post-colonial eras. Both scholars of the biopolitical and necropolitical, however, inspired by Marx and Hegel, think in terms of subjecthood and agency. Who gets to be a subject? Who gets to be an agent? These positions are largely determined by whether or not one is in control of or at the mercy of biopolitical or necropolitical powers. The concepts of "subject" and "agent" align somewhat with my terms of "legible" or "intelligible," but I insist that the terms I'm using are more specific to the context of the relationship between Black women who are interested in a certain kind of recognition from the public and/or the state. Alexander

Weheliye and Sylvia Wynter also theorize around notions of power, race, and being, but use the "human" as their focal point. Finally, Afro-pessimists like Jared Sexton and Frank B. Wilderson may opt for the language of master/slave to describe Black/white power dynamics across history and in our current moment.

7. The binary I'm setting up between "recovery" work and "acknowledgment" work is by no means fixed, but there are some valuable examples of each. Examples of recovery work are Tera Hunter's *To 'Joy My Freedom;* Farrah Jasmine Griffin's article, "Textual Healing: Claiming Black Women's Bodies, the Erotic and Resistance in Contemporary Novels of Slavery," and William L. Andrews's foundational book on slave narratives, *To Tell a Free Story: The First Century of Afro-American Autobiography 1760–1865.* Examples of acknowledgement work include Fred Moten's *In the Break,* Saidiya Hartman's *Scenes of Subjection,* and Khalil Gibran Muhammad's *The Condemnation of Blackness: Race, Crime, and the Making of Modern Urban America.*

8. The entire country was not shifting its attitudes in any unified sense. But Taylor reported her rape at a time when the entire country—some areas at a quicker pace than others—was slowly beginning to see the destructive nature of both *de jure* and *de facto* racism; this was playing out with especial vigor on the national media stage as a fight between the "integrated" North and the "uncivilized" South in 1944, the year of Racy Taylor's rape.

9. I do not want to valorize Governor Chauncey Sparks. He was a pro-segregationist governor and did little to improve the lives of his Black constituents during his time in office. However, the circumstances were complicated. He probably could have done more than he did to help Taylor, but the people of Abbeville are primarily to blame for the failure of the case to be seen as a criminal case.

10. The importance of the work done by the Governor and the Office of the Attorney General of Alabama at this time cannot be overstated. The "Report" and "Supplemental Report" produced by their investigations are the only reason we have Recy Taylor's account of the events that took place the night of her rape. Whether these reports were attempts to appease a complaining public or not, they are of enormous historical and archival significance.

11. I want to be cognizant of the way that my project exists outside of a prison abolitionist framework. On Tuesday, March 27, 2018, Angela Davis gave a speech in Charlottesville as a part of the University of Virginia's Excellence Through Diversity Speaker Series, Angela Davis remarked on the #MeToo movement. She expressed support for survivors, but simultaneously expressed wariness of any proposed solutions to rape that focus on imprisonment. My analysis of Taylor's case and *Native Son* (chapter 4) does not take an abolitionist stance; I define justice for raped Black women as including some form of punishment of the rapists. But I am eager to use future opportunities to engage with modern and contemporary abolitionist scholarship regarding crimes of sexual violence.

12. In *To 'Joy My Freedom: Southern Black Women's Lives and Labors After the Civil War,* Tera W. Hunter touches on the overly sexualized, savage pastness projected upon the Black female body.

13. To qualify the Committee's strategies as conservative may seem unfair and anachronistic. I do so fully aware of this problem. The Committee was quite radical for its time. However, there are always precedents for radical thought that were well-known during the same historical period upon which we have projected a kind of shrug-inducing backwardness.

14. Buckmaster's framing of Taylor as racialized *and* defendable do not exist in a vacuum. It is important to pay special respect to the work of Ida B. Wells for publicizing this kind of defense of Black women in her 1892 pamphlet, *Southern Horrors: Lynch Law in All Its Phases.*

Chapter 2: Manipulating Bodies

1. In the 2017 book *How We Get Free: Black Feminism and the Combahee River Collective,* Keeanga-Yamahtta Taylor interviews Barbara Smith. Smith, a pioneer of Black feminism, distinguishes the "women's movement" from what the National Black Feminist Organization (and its later offshoot, the Combahee River Collective) so I am purposefully using the women's movement here to reference a largely upper middle class white women's movement.

2. I want to make a distinction between Black women as manipulators and Black women as agents. In her foundational 1997 work, *Scenes of Subjection,* Saidiya Hartman argues against limiting notions of enslaved women as passive objects. Hartman makes a convincing case for the agency of both enslaved and newly freed women. Only now are African American literary scholars eager to deflate what has become a fetishization of agency as the magical cure to abjection/objecthood. In this project, to see Black women as manipulators is a way of assuming their agency without pretending that it cures them of being denied rights.

3. I am detaching "voice" from "body" in a way that I hope is reminiscent how this disconnect arose for Recy Taylor and Bessie Mears in *Native Son* in the previous chapters. More often than not, the Black woman's body is discussed without her being able to voice dissent whether that is because she is physically incapable or silenced in other ways. See Darlene Clark Hine's 1989 article "Rape and the Inner Lives of Black Women in the Middle West: Preliminary Thoughts on the Culture of Dissemblance" for more on the dissemblance of silence.

4. One of the most salient details from the story of this covert removal of Little from her hiding place is that Margie Wright insisted that Little wear one of her wigs as she walked from the hiding place to Paul's car. The wig was used to disguise her from the gaze of Beaufort County police who were constantly surveilling and directed to "shoot on sight" if they discovered Little. McGuire tells the story of the wig

in her book, but listening to Margie Wright tell the story in her own words infused a level of humor that I had not anticipated. Wright was a Black sex worker in North Carolina. I was able to hear her tell this story when I listened to James Reston's recorded interview with her in the Southern Historical Collection at UNC Chapel Hill, thanks to funding from the Power, Violence, Inequality Collective of the University of Virginia.

5. For more in-depth detail on the racial politics of North Carolina and in the nation more broadly in the 1970s, see Danielle McGuire's *At the Dark End of the Street* and Christina Greene's excellent article, "'She Ain't No Rosa Parks': The Joan Little Rape-Murder Case and Jim Crow Justice in the Post–Civil Rights South." Genna Rae McNeil also offers incredibly helpful context and insight into Little's case in her article.

6. Emily L. Thuma does an excellent job showcasing the ways in which organizations with many different allegiances—mostly white women's movements, prisoner rights movements, Black power movements, and so on—came together to prove Little's innocence (and thus her rapist's guilt) in her book *All Our Trials: Prisons, Policing, and the Feminist Fight to End Violence*.

7. By "racial-sexual precedent" I mean to say that, prior to *State v. Little*, race as well as other facets of identity had not been successfully used to argue the existence of jury bias and relocation of a trial. Notable and relevant examples include the all-white jury in Mississippi that acquitted Emmett Till's murderers in 1955 as well as the multiple juries, even one including a single Black man, that repeatedly found the Scottsboro Boys guilty of rape in multiple counties in Alabama to no avail. *State v. Little* was the first time that a lawyer successfully argued for trial relocation based not only upon the race of the defendant, but also their gender.

8. McKinnon's reasoning aligned with the prosecutors, Griffin and Wilkinson, who also wanted the case moved because of high publicity. However, Griffin and Wilkinson wanted the case moved to Pitt County, one of the six options available. The defense wanted the case moved to Orange County, "the liberal seat of North Carolina" according to Mullin. Mullin wanted to investigate Pitt County because she suspected that she could prove that it had similar attitudinal problems as Beaufort in terms of race. But Mullin knew that in order to ensure that this research was compelling evidence of bias to Judge McKinnon, she would have to also prove that the majority of residents held specific prejudices against Little because of how it was being used to turn them into a national enemy of racial justice. Mullin did both in another attitudinal survey of Pitt County (*The Innocence of Joan Little* by James Reston, 192–93).

9. A little more than a decade after Little is acquitted, *Batson v. Kentucky* (1986) ruled that prosecutors may not use race alone to dismiss jurors under peremptory challenge. Prior to this, each side in a trial had a certain amount of jurors that they

could dismiss without having to state a reason why. It was found through *Batson* that many of those jurors were being dismissed to curate the racial makeup of juries.

10. Rosa Parks's staged attempt to sit at the front of a bus in Montgomery, Alabama, in 1955 is probably the most famous version of an activist organization using the public failure of a system to demand social change. However, as McGuire argues, the case of Recy Taylor (1944–45) predates it and ties an anti-rape and anti-racist rhetoric to the foundations of civil rights movements. Recy Taylor was gang raped in Abbeville, Alabama, and an all-white and male jury failed to indict her rapists twice. Rosa Parks and other members of the NAACP used this systemic failure to begin The Committee for the Equal Justice of Mrs. Recy Taylor.

11. *State v. Little* was no average rape trial, and it cannot be representative of all rape cases for Black women. Not only was it a case that landed in the right place at the right time with the right amount of resources, but also it is technically not a rape case. Joan Little is on trial for the murder of her rapist. Though this invariably means that Little's character and her capacity to be visible as a victim of rape are on trial, it is ultimately a unique case in this regard. The jury has to choose between jailing a woman who is lying about being raped and who killed for malicious reasons and freeing a woman who has been the victim of a crime on the grounds of self-defense.

12. This is a slight oversimplification of the highly complex nature of consent, but I am being hyperbolic because this is often the kind of oversimplification that rape laws make: one can only demonstrate that one resisted sex through a verbal rejection or proof that they were physically forced (defensive bruising, etc.). Though the definition of consent varies somewhat across states, most state prosecutors must maintain this narrow view of consent because they may be the only determining factors that they have at their disposal (RAINN).

13. Even Taslitz's distinction between "women's language" and Black women's demeanor reproduces a misconception that Black feminists Akasha (Gloria) T. Hull, Patricia Bell-Scott, and Barbara Smith, have attempted to combat with their edited anthology, *All the Women Are White, All the Blacks Are Men, But Some of Us Are Brave*. For more on the mistreatment of rape victims in criminal courts see the article by Jonathan M. Golding et al., "Impeaching Rape Victims in Criminal Courts".

14. "Misogynoir" is a term created by writer and activist, Moya Bailey which she defines as "[a word] I made up to describe the particular brand of hatred directed at black women in American visual & popular culture" ("They Aren't Talking about Me," 3).

15. There are so many other interesting ways that Little's voice is manipulated. In fact, there are too many to recount here. But one other aspect that is worth mentioning is how Griffin tries to use Little's diary and correspondence with friends or family members, her own written voice, to ventriloquize the stereotype of a Black woman he hopes to invoke for the jury. At one point in his questioning, he asks

Little to read a passage from a letter in which she says that "the jailers are being very nice to me." He tries to use her note about the kindness of the jailers to deflate the defense's argument that Little suffered poor conditions in the jail and that she in fact invited Alligood's sexual advances.

16. For more on the explicit use of United States history to defend Joan Little, see Jerry Paul, "Argument to the Jury."

Chapter 3: "I love this country, but sometimes I'm not sure where I am"

1. Some of the material from this chapter first appeared as Maya Hislop, "'I Love This Country, but Sometimes I Not Sure Where I Am': Black Immigrant Women, Sexual Violence, and Afropessimistic Justice in New York V. Strauss-Kahn and Chimamanda Ngozi Adichie's *Americanah*," *Law and Literature* 34, no. 3, 2022, pp. 337–62. Some of the material from this chapter will also appear in the anthology *Modern Migrations, Black Interrogations*, Temple University Press, forthcoming January 2024.

2. On February 9, 2017, Irvin Gonzalez, a trans woman, was met by ICE agents at a courthouse after her case for a protective order against her extremely abusive boyfriend (P.R. Lockhart, "Immigrants Fear a Choice Between Domestic Violence and Deportation"). On February 10, 2015, a white man, Craig Hicks, murdered Deah Barakat, Razan Abu-Salha, and Deah's wife, Yusor Abu-Salha (Reema Kharis, "Shaken by Shooting, North Carolina Muslims Emerge 'Proud' One Year Later"). The term "anchor child" was first used in reference to the children of the second wave of Vietnamese refugees from 1987. The term "anchor baby" gained new relevance in 2006 as the immigration debate grew hostile, particularly targeting Mexican immigrants. Especially relevant to this project is the way in which the rights of immigrants as well as slaves born in the United States were conferred through the Fourteenth Amendment, which grants citizenship to anyone born on US soil, or *jus soli*. See Kelly Frances, "A Profile of a Lost Generation"; Marc Lacey, "Birthright Citizenship Looms as Next Immigration Battle."

3. Congress passed the Patriot Act a little over a month after the September 11, 2001, attacks as a means of beefing up national security. Of the many things that the act did, one of the most alarming was expanding the power of the FBI to search telephone, email, and financial records without a court order (Orin S. Kerr, "Digital Evidence and the New Criminal Procedure").

4. One of the reasons that Strauss-Kahn's lawyers were able to argue for his house arrest (despite state arguments that he was a potential flight risk) was Strauss-Kahn's lack of prior criminal convictions. However, this seemingly unblemished history elides the fact that Strauss-Kahn had been accused of sexual assault before, in 2008, by an employee of the International Monetary Fund. The fund carried out an investigation but did not fire Strauss-Kahn, claiming to have found no evidence for

what they deemed a "sexual affair," despite the employee's claims that Strauss-Kahn abused his power to coerce a relationship. One of the contentions of this section is that it is very difficult to find evidence that proves that someone has abused power to force another person to perform sexual favors.

5. Dotson and Gilbert define "complex social identities" as those which are socially readable, defining them against those identities that individuals apply to themselves internally. This term is certainly indebted to Kimberlé Crenshaw, whose work in two early articles "Mapping the Margins" and "Demarginalizing the Intersection of Race and Sex" outline the term "intersectionality" as a framework for approaching systems of power (i.e. racism and sexism) and how they intersect to disenfranchise individuals whose identities are impacted by more than one form of systemic oppression. Crenshaw clarifies that people who live under two or more intersecting systems of oppression are not legible to legal systems, particularly in terms of discrimination law, because such systems are incapable of legislating more than one form of discrimination in a single case. It is unfair to put Crenshaw alone as the only person doing this work at the time; another invaluable contributor to intersectionality was Patricia J. Williams' *Alchemy of Race and Rights*. Additionally, the work around intersectionality has advanced considerably in the last ten years. Recently, Black feminist scholars like Jennifer C. Nash, Brittney C. Cooper, and Crenshaw herself have lamented the misappropriation of the term "intersectionality." Many feminists, especially online, use the term "intersectional" when they really mean "diverse" or "considering multiple perspectives." Therefore, a more accurate term for this than "intersectional" would be inclusive of "complex social identities."

6. In her interview with ABC News, Diallo tells another story of gendered violence: "When I was seven years, they cut me in my private area . . . My daughter was only seven or eight years old . . . I don't want her to get cut and I don't want her to get raped. If that happen there, you don't tell nobody. I know I have a better life here. That's why I make mistake on my asylum. I make mistake because I want to be here" (00:58:01). Diallo recounts her experience of female genital mutilation (FGM) in Guinea at the same time that she tells the story of her rape in the restaurant. Diallo acknowledges the necessity of lying to have one's asylum application approved but is still guarded about the content of the lie. This portion of her interview gives us some insight into the kinds of narratives that asylum seekers presume may be most compelling to United States officials. FGM and a gang-rape committed by civilian men were allegedly not the stories that Diallo used on her asylum application precisely because they do not satisfy the requirements of "political" violence as the portion of the form in figure 6 outlines. For more on the context around the asylum application process, see Audrey Macklin's "Truth and Consequences. . . ."

7. Aside from the many American news outlets covering the case that I mention here, there were hundreds of others spanning far and wide across the globe. To note,

the case has had a resurgence in publicity due to the recent release of a docuseries about the case, *Room 2806: The Accusation,* produced by Netflix.

8. Martha Evans and Ian Glenn offer a definition of Afropessimism along these same lines in their 2010 article, "'TIA–This Is Africa,'" 14–15.

9. For more on the ways in which immigrants make themselves visible in the public sphere, see Judith Butler's 2009 lecture "Performativity, Precarity, and Sexual Politics" in which Butler revisits the theory of performativity made famous in their groundbreaking 1990 book *Gender Trouble.*

10. It is important to recognize that Guinea gained independence from France in 1958 and is a trading partner of the United States. In the years leading up to Diallo's case, the small West African country had experienced several decades of military coups of authoritarian leaders. This history of internal violence culminated in the country's first democratic elections in 2010, but conflict still plagues the country. In 2011, the United States spoke out against what they considered human rights violations, namely the harming of women and children by security forces. This context demonstrates that Diallo's narrative as a victim of a politically motivated act of sexual violence fits a script that the United States already has for Guinean women and therefore makes her legible as someone needing political asylum.

11. I refer here to a brilliant critical analysis of Black LGBTQ families, which uses The Moynihan Report as a basis for its arguments. See Juan Battle and Colin Ashley, "Intersectionality, Heteronormativity, and Black Lesbian, Gay, Bisexual, and Transgender (LGBT) Families."

12. The jury is an important facet of Diallo's civil suit against Strauss-Kahn, as Noreen Malone points out in her article for *New York Magazine,* "Why DSK's Accuser Might Have Decided to File Her Civil Suit in the Bronx" because it allowed Diallo to be judged by "other immigrants, more minorities, and less wealthy than it might be in Manhattan" (Malone, 1). It is also key to mention that Diallo filed two civil suits at once, one against Strauss-Kahn for compensation for damages done to her body and reputation and another against the *New York Post* for libel and damages (Rushe et al.).

13. It is appalling that, for so long, the assumption that sex workers cannot be raped has been maintained by systems and agents of systems. This is an avenue of thought that I explore in this book.

14. In an article entitled "From 'Frog' to 'Fraud!': How the *New York Post* Told the DSK Story," Joe Coscarelli reported on the *Post*'s many headlines on the case.

15. The leak of this letter and other statements that discredited Diallo in the eyes of the press form a core part of Thompson's civil case filing, in which he claims that the DA failed to protect Diallo from the release of her personal information.

16. For more on this, see Grace Chang's *Disposable Domestics: Immigrant Women Workers in the Global Economy.*

17. Soon after the publication of these stories of sex work, Diallo sued the *Post* for libel, claiming that the reporters reported that Diallo was performing sexual acts for money knowing that it was not true. This case never went to trial.

18. Rape shield laws not only protect victims' identities if they choose to report their sexual violations, but it is also meant to protect them from having their sexual history used against them during the trial. Diallo reveals a loophole in US Rape Shield law when she tells Robin Roberts that a female French journalist called her cellphone the night that she was assaulted, asking her questions. It is quite remarkable that this overseas journalist already knew the story and how to contact Diallo even before the police had fully processed her report. It is possible that international journalists are not beholden to these federal rules around anonymity. There may also have been extenuating circumstances in this case given the high-profile status of Strauss-Kahn in his native France. For more on rape shield laws, see Cassia Spohn and Julia Horney, *Rape Law Reform: A Grassroots Revolution.*

19. It is unlikely that Diallo decided to come forward totally independently. Her lawyer, Ken Thompson, the first African American district attorney of Kings County, New York, probably strategized this public reveal with Diallo. Sadly, Thompson passed away from cancer in 2016 at the age of 50. Many speculated that, had he not passed away, he could have been a strong contender for Vance's job as the NYDA. It is almost certain that Thompson played a large role in helping Diallo to tell her story on ABC News and in shaping her as an "ideal victim" that could be legible to such a large audience. A helpful source for more on the ways in which Black women are pushed out of "ideal victim" status is an article by Kali Holloway, "When You're a Black Woman, You're Never Good Enough to Be a Victim".

20. In September 2011, Strauss-Kahn sat down for several interviews with French media outlets to discuss what happened in New York. His first was with Claire Chazal, a close friend of his wife's, and it was visibly uncomfortable for both of them. Strauss-Kahn continues to experience legal trouble and reports of sex scandals to this day.

21. In some respects, this focus on Strauss-Kahn is fair because he was gearing up to run for President of France and so his moral indiscretions were of great interest to his fellow citizens. However, the media's intense focus on those who commit sexual assault creates a culture in which the voices of the victims are marginalized in favor of the spectacular fall of a person in power.

22. It may seem unforgiving to call Diallo's use of the media a "strategy" if, following a pro-victim stance, her status as a truthteller is to be maintained. However, as has been demonstrated in the previous chapter, the Black woman who has experienced sexual violence must manipulate a system for that system to even minimally function in her defense.

23. There is a long and important history around assimilation as both an

unfortunate side effect of white supremacy's stranglehold on racial progress as well as reality of survival modes Black, Brown, and indigenous folks have been using for decades. When I reference Lowe and Ngai and the "good immigrant" narrative, I am also referencing a deep well of scholarship on assimilation which ranges from cultural to racial. For more on the Black history of assimilation and/or justice, see Michele Mitchell, *Righteous Propagation,* and James Weldon Johnson, *Autobiography of an Ex-Colored Man.*

24. It is necessary to note that all kinds of women may use rape shield laws to remain anonymous during a rape trial for all kinds of reasons. Rape shield laws were created for many reasons, one of which was to make the identity of the rape victim (especially not her sexual history) a non-issue in the public's consumption of the trial; although this is well-intentioned, it can mask the ways in which the victim's identity (race, class, citizenship status, etc.) can be central to her victimization. Rape shield laws also can lead one to imagine that maintaining anonymity could potentially improve one's chances to a just opinion in court because public opinion cannot weaponize the victim's identity or past against her in the same way, but the high-profile 2016 Brock Turner case distorts this assumption. In 2016, Brock Allen Turner, a white Stanford swimmer, was convicted of three counts of sexual assault for assaulting Chanel Miller, a Chinese American woman who maintained her anonymity throughout the trial. The judge in the case controversially sentenced Turner to only six months in jail (of which he only served three) even though he was caught in the act of assault in public and basically admitted to it. Many accused the judge of "affluenza," treating Turner with kid gloves because of his whiteness and financial privilege. The judge was recalled two years later. This case is an example of anonymity failing to necessarily bring about the "justice" that a rape victim may have wanted. For more on this case, see Chanel Miller's memoir, *Know My Name.* For an interesting update on how women in Turner's geographical location are using the digital spaces of Tik Tok and Reddit to alienate Turner as a replacement for jail/imprisonment, see Jay Barmann, "Convicted Stanford Assaulter Goes Viral Again Via 'Whisper Network' in Ohio."

25. Evelyn Brooks Higginbotham, whose work *Righteous Discontent,* is mentioned in an earlier chapter, is the historian who made the phrase "respectability politics" commonplace. Higginbotham defines this term as a kind of assimilation tactic that Black people have used for decades to garner sympathy and support for their human rights from a middle-class, white public. Judith Butler's lecture "Performativity, Precarity, and Sexual Politics" builds on her theory of gender performativity (which outlined the ways in which all genders are a performance that has to be consistently maintained, often to the detriment of all involved) to include additional kinds of identity performance, homing in on immigrant identity by close reading the public assertions of rights of undocumented activists.

26. There is a sizable portion of Chimamanda Ngozi Adichie's *Americanah*—which this study explores in its final chapter—that touches on accents. Early on during her time in America, Ifemelu loses her Igbo-dialect–inflected accent and takes on an American one. She then retrains herself to lose the American accent. This is especially interesting because of how Ifemelu puts the learning/unlearning of accents in terms of authenticity. She is motivated to lose her American accent after a phone call with a telemarketer who compliments her undetectable accent: "Only after she hung up did she begin to feel the stain of a burgeoning shame spreading all over her, for thanking him, for crafting his words 'You sound American' into a garland that she hung around her own neck . . . Her fleeting victory had left in its wake a vast, echoing space, because she had taken on, for too long, a pitch of voice and a way of being that was not hers. And so she finished eating her eggs and resolved to stop faking the American accent" (177).

27. Here I am recalling the work of Andrew Taslitz (*Rape and the Culture of the Courtroom*), referenced in the previous chapter, in which he touches on the double-edged sword that the courtroom presents for Black women who cannot easily access the kind of soft femininity that white women have access to through their voices and demeanor. I extend Taslitz's interpretation of how race, gender, and voice operate in the courtroom to how race, gender, citizenship status, and voice operate in the televised news interview.

28. Diallo invokes God several times throughout her interview with Robin Roberts, citing a divine power as the ultimate bearer of justice and truth, "I think why people have to believe what I say God as my witness I'm telling the truth" (01:05:49).

Chapter 4: Bessie's Song

1. I understand that many scholars in Black studies like Alexander Weheliye and others are interested in de-centering the work of white philosophers Arendt, Agamben, Foucault, and others to center Black feminist political and philosophical thought from scholars like Sylvia Wynter and Hortense Spillers. My emphasis on JanMohamed is an attempt to do this kind of re-centering, but I understand that it is not yet as progressive as it could be.

2. Scholars of critical rape studies, like Sabine Sielke and Regine Michelle Jean-Charles, place rape and sexual assault at the center of a critical race discourse not merely because such woman-centric/race-centric stories are historically underrepresented, but because American history demands it. As stated in the introduction of this dissertation, the history of lynching proves that rape, race, and death are some of the most entangled and fundamental building blocks of national identity formation in the United States.

3. Richard Wright began to work on another novel while he finished *Native Son* in 1939. The never-published novel, *Little Sister* would have been an updated

retelling of the "tragic mulatto" centered on the Black female protagonist, Maude, who passes as white to get a better job. We can see that Wright desired to center the Black female experience in another novel, but, lacking an actual copy of the unfinished book, we must seek ways to center the Black female in *Native Son*. For more on Wright's unpublished works, see Michel Fabre's *The Unfinished Quest of Richard Wright*. Guttman offers a parallel, albeit different, reading of the novel as one about the success of political organizing. She analyzes the elimination of women from the novel as necessary to Wright's larger communistic project of interracial labor organizing among men (171).

4. I am applying "Afro-pessimism" to *Native Son* somewhat anachronistically as this was not yet a term that Richard Wright or his contemporaries were using to discuss their work. Instead, they were using terms like "social realism" or "naturalism" which touch on aspects of Afro-pessimism but are devoid of the specifically racial theorization. For more on Richard Wright and social realism, see J. J. Butts's *Dark Mirror: African Americans and the Federal Writers' Project*. It is also important to state here that Afro-pessimism differs from my own term, "Afro-pessimistic justice," which I will touch on later in the chapter.

5. On the topic of other novels in which Black women are represented as mere ciphers or stereotypes, it is important to acknowledge that *Native Son* is not the only novel of the African American literary canon in the 1940s that touches on the subjects of Black women, sexual violence, and justice. Ann Petry's foundational novel *The Street* (1946) is an extremely important work that, in many ways, reverses Richard Wright's myopic framing of the Black man and recenters the action on Lutie Johnson, a Black woman struggling to escape the dangers of slum living with her eight-year-old son Bub. Petry's *The Street* is a crucial paratext to my exploration of *Native Son,* but to try to insert it into this study would do a disservice to Petry (who is too often compared and contrasted with Wright); nor would it fit with the ultimate goal of this project, which is to understand how literature represents the raped Black women interacting with the legal system and, specifically, the criminal justice system. There are glimpses into that relationship in Petry when we see another Black woman defend her against rape by Supe and then again when we see her defend herself against rape by killing her attempted rapist, Boots Smith. But systems through which "justice" could be achieved (and probably foreclosed) are never realized, which is, of course, one of the novel's central Afro-pessimistic messages: the neglect of the state will ultimately kill Black people in a slow and petty way if space is not made for them as full participants and recipients of fair treatment in the American imaginary.

6. The prosecutor, Buckley, wants to foment mob violence as well as advance his own political career by pinning two additional rape/murders on Bigger Thomas (283).

7. Max renders Bigger and Bessie as animals with the phrase "with his own kind," thus endorsing racist stereotypes about Black people as savage beasts. This proves that Max is only going as far as is necessary to try to keep the Chicago jury from executing Bigger.

Chapter 5: Ursa's Song

1. Nineteenth-century abolitionist Isaac Sheen explains that millennialism is a more literal interpretation of a section of the Book of Revelation, "The Millennial state will be the renewed state, which will precede the eternal state" (1). John D. Fitzpatrick adds detail to this notion and portrays the millennial state as one that will arise when Jesus returns causing a golden age of "new hope and promise . . . [of] a better day . . . would come and bring the world new hope" (3). This sense of hope and renewal lends itself extremely well to the African American Christian tradition as Timothy E. Fulop lays out in his article, "'The Future Golden Day of the Race': Millennialism and Black Americans in the Nadir, 1877–1901." Fulop argues that Black millennialism of the postbellum period took a variety of shapes that distinguished this ideology of nadir era Christians from the quietist millennialism of enslaved peoples. Within the various approaches to millennialism was a disagreement about whether America was the location in which this golden age would arise: "A large segment of black millennial thought did locate the millennium in America, which was congruent with the dominant ideology of America as a redeemer nation" (81). In light of the faith in America that Fulop describes, it is not difficult to understand how Black approaches to justice through the legal system are millennialist. The combination between law and theology is evident in how Jerry Paul and other civil rights movement leaders and organizations like the National Association for the Advancement of Colored People (NAACP) used the law. In the cases of Joan Little, Recy Taylor, Rosa Parks, and countless others, lawyers and organizers knew that justice for that individual plaintiff was probably impossible, so the focus was instead on a much larger, broader sense of justice that would come "some day" as the lyrics of the protest song "We Shall Overcome" voice. Paul reveals this attitude toward the legal system in much more cynical tones than one would think given the hopefulness of millennialism. These civil rights movement strategies were millennialism because they held onto a faith in the US legal system as a problematic albeit useful tool that could be used to the advantage of oppressed groups.

2. Jones is very consciously twisting many nineteenth-century tropes, such as that of the "tragic mulatta" and of what is termed "a slave-breeder's mentality" in *Corregidora* inside out here (20). The "tragic mulatta" could be the result of a consensual relationship between an enslaved woman and her master or a nonconsensual relationship, but her downfall was almost always inevitable either way. The Corregidora women are declaring their light skin (and possibly other phenotypical

features that they share with their white antecedents) as another layer of their evidence against their abusers. Similarly, reproduction is being turned on its head. The Corregidora women turn reproduction from being a means of torturing enslaved women to breed more slaves to being a means of evidence-production to feed their reproductive justice system.

3. Time is infrequently marked in the novel. Jones's novel opens in 1947 and ends in 1969, but the chronology of the action in between is difficult to historically pinpoint. A few other time markers are used, but overall Jones is largely disinterested in marking time in the novel. This is significant because it speaks to an overall desire to make the past, be it enslavement or the Jim Crow era, not only relevant, but also not past, to use Faulkner's phrase. Though the novel is set in multiple, overlapping temporalities, this lack of temporal markers makes it difficult to read as necessarily historically specific. Though it helps to feel the urgency of Ursa's life choices as a very recent descendant of enslaved women, it is not difficult to see how Jones saw herself and other Black women of the 1970s as beset with those same choices and questions: how do we engage with or disengage from the history of enslavement in our country, in our own families, and in our ourselves?

4. There is the rare "cold case" occurrence in which new evidence emerges about cases from the past and previous rulings are changed or revoked. But, for the most part, justice is on a timeline that exists in the present or the very immediate future.

5. The hopeless failure narrative around Reconstruction is not quite fair because of the massive steps forward that were taken in the way of Black education and land reallocation (in some cases), as W.E.B. Du Bois flawlessly argues in his timeless classic, *Black Reconstruction in America 1860–1880*.

6. The progeny of masters and slaves do not necessarily act as evidence of sexual violence because not only was it difficult for enslaved women to argue that they had the right to resist sex with their masters, but also some of the children born to enslaved women were born out of consensual relationships. The bodies of the children do not themselves act as proof of nonconsensual sex between enslaved women and masters.

7. As an aside, I do not want to suggest that the Corregidora women innately know the ins and outs of the US criminal justice system. Nor do I want to suggest that the women know that the criminal justice system is unfair because they are Black and enslaved. They learn that they have no access to justice when they hear the story of a woman on a neighboring plantation who, when she killed and castrated her white rapist in self-defense, was forced to watch the brutal lynching and castration of her husband and then lynched herself (67). This is a fictionalization of a real case, *The State of Missouri v. Celia, A Slave* (1855), recounted recently in a 2017 *Washington Post* article by DeNeen L. Brown. The University of Michigan also

contributed beautifully to our understanding of Celia through The Celia Project. The tale of this woman in the context of *Corregidora* teaches Gram and Great Gram that American justice is vengeful: a white man is castrated and murdered, a Black man must be castrated and murdered. White supremacy demands that something fill the lack. In a similar vein, the Corregidora women are performing a revenge-based justice: because their white masters burn the papers, they must fill that lack with story and offspring. *State v. Little* tells the story of racialized rape-revenge, but somewhat in reverse when, in his closing statement, Jerry Paul declares that Joan Little's triumph would be a small albeit necessary balm on centuries of sexual violence perpetrated against enslaved Black women. Despite this seeming obsession with revenge inside and outside of the legal system, the 1970s were home to debates between criminal justice reformers interested in rehabilitative justice and those who maintained the importance of retributive law. I will cover this notion of retributive justice briefly in the coda.

8. In *Bridging the Americas: The Literature of Paule Marshall, Toni Morrison, and Gayl Jones* Stelamaris Coser argues that despite the shift in geography, Jones is working within the broader context of the "Americas" when she blurs the lines between American and Brazilian institutions of slavery. I think Coser's point is well taken, but the fact remains that the legal jurisdictions would have been different.

9. Karla F.C. Holloway refers to this use of the body and its progeny as "pitiful" and, although it is unfortunate, it is one of the important results of slavery to attend to. Enslaved people created their own ways of "moving without moving" says Trueblood, a character in Ralph Ellison's *Invisible Man* says, a concept that Houston A. Baker expounds upon in his essay, "To Move without Moving: An Analysis of Creativity and Commerce in Ralph Ellison's Trueblood Episode" (837). It is also relevant that the character of Trueblood develops what Baker calls a symbolic euphemism when describing the incestuous sex he has with his daughter, around which the parameters of consent are questionable.

10. There is significant debate about whether Mutt pushes Ursa down the stairs or if her fall is an accidental result of their physical struggle. I would argue that Mutt's intent is not as important as the fact that his sexual jealousy turns Ursa into a target of violence.

11. This language around forensics comes from Eyal Weizman's *Forensis*.

12. Jones separates the voices of Ursa's foremothers (and other voices) from the rest of the narrative by italicizing the conversations that occurred in the past. My own archival research of Jones's papers reveals that the italicization was likely the result of an editorial note that Jones received after she had already written two drafts of the manuscript.

13. This is an interesting reversal of the dominant narrative around Black women and sexual violence that I have been tracing. The dominant narrative portrays Black

women as incapable of having their sexual violations seen as crimes. Mr. Deak and the Corregidora women seem to overcorrect by asserting a new narrative, that any kind of violence that befalls a Black woman is a crime.

Chapter 6: Ifemelu's Song

1. This chapter expands on an article previously published in *Law and Literature*. See Maya Hislop, "'I Love This Country, but Sometimes I Not Sure Where I Am': Black Immigrant Women, Sexual Violence, and Afro-pessimistic Justice in New York V. Strauss-Kahn and Chimamanda Ngozi Adichie's Americanah." Some of the material from this chapter will also appear in a forthcoming anthology from Temple University Press, *Modern Migrations, Black Interrogations*.

2. Immediately after the Hart-Cellar Act of 1965, which removed the language of numerical quotas from immigration policy, there was one wave of Black immigrants from both Africa and the Caribbean who arrived in America not only looking for work, but also invested in Pan-African modes of racial solidarity. A second wave of Black immigrants from Africa were less interested in political racial solidarity, but not necessarily disinterested. Ifemelu falls into what Shane McCoy calls the "new" wave of the African diaspora, given that she migrates to the United States around 1993. At this time, institutions of higher education were opening their doors to Black international students to increase diversity. Ifemelu is therefore the beneficiary of decades of struggle for diversity at the level of higher education while also acting as a model minority against which Black Americans are judged. All of this is important to understanding her financial deprivation because, on the one hand, she is privileged (she is in the United States; she is getting a good college education), but, on the other hand, the F-1 visa puts her into a less privileged place because of the limits on employment. The limits on employment are intended to allow international students to focus on their studies while also removing a population of smart, educated immigrants from competing with (white) citizens in the American job market. There are other kinds of visas that purposefully "brain drain" other countries such as India, Pakistan, and Nigeria of their most talented to reap the benefits of their labor in specific areas, such as engineering, medicine, and other STEM fields. From the perspective of undergraduate institutions, the F-1 visa works to benefit the diversity aims of American universities. It is clear that the student visa limits employment options for international students while claiming them as part of the diverse university community precisely because it is part of the visa process. For recipients of the F-1 visa to receive their visa, they must sign a statement that promises that they will return to their country of origin upon completion of their studies. In other words, once universities have benefitted from Black and brown bodies as increasing their numbers of minority students, the country hopes to be rid of them. Though applicants break this promise all of the time, it is a strong indication of just

how badly the US immigration system does not want international students to have full-time employment while they are in school.

3. The flippant tone with which Ginika addresses the idea of sex work is somewhat striking because Ginika is more concerned with how little money one makes than the potential emotional trauma one could incur from doing that sort of work out of financial desperation. However, such indifference toward relationships between men, women, and money is a common tone for several characters throughout the novel. When Aunty Uju is still in Nigeria, her role as The General's mistress involves financial dependence. When Ifemelu returns to Lagos more than a decade later, her friend Ranyinudo is in a similar position as a mistress of a wealthy man, but she also searches for alternative suitors. Both Obinze and Ifemelu have direct and indirect experience with the exchange of money for sex/romantic attachment. Ifemelu's assault demonstrates this exchange; while living as an undocumented person in London, Obinze has an experience trying to pay some shady men to find a woman who is a British citizen he can marry so that he may get a visa to stay in London. Obinze's marriage plot is unfortunately discovered by immigration agents, and he is deported. On the one hand, the multiplicity of this triangle between money and sex/love normalizes an exchange that is typically seen as problematic. On the other hand, perhaps Adichie features so many of these entanglements as a way of glorifying a troubled part of the plot: the affair between Ifemelu and Obinze at the end of the novel. The reader is clearly meant to feel conflicted about the affair between our primary characters, but perhaps the extent of this conflict is lessened when the "pure love" relationship between Ifemelu and Obinze is compared to the affairs "contaminated" by money.

4. Many legal scholars, such as Hannah Brenner and Michael Bucchandler-Raphael, argue that a consent-based definition of sexual violence is inadequate precisely because it imagines that there are no power differentials between people who can or cannot "give freely" of their consent. Brenner and Bucchandler-Raphael respectively argue for a power-based definition of sexual violence that acknowledges power as a mighty force in any situation in which one or many people use force to violate the body of another. See Hannah Brenner, "Beyond Seduction: Lessons Learned about Rape, Politics, and Power from Dominique Strauss-Kahn and Moshe Katsav" and Michael Bucchandler-Raphael, "The Failure of Consent: Re-Conceptualizing Rape as Sexual Abuse of Power."

5. Adichie narrates Ifemelu's access to citizenship with little fanfare, therefore corroborating the arguments of Shane McCoy and others that Adichie is very purposefully writing against older migrant narratives in which the path to citizenship is arduous and at the center of the protagonist's life. This is not to say that Ifemelu is not pleased with her good fortune, but she is a more complex migrant figure because she has misgivings about this privilege as she compares herself to her college

friends from the African Students Association: "It was good news, and yet a sober-ness wrapped itself around her. Wambui was working three jobs under the table to raise the five thousand dollars she would need to pay an African American man for a green-card marriage, Mwombeki was desperately trying to find a company that would hire him on his temporary visa, and here she was, a pink balloon, weightless, floating to the top, propelled by things outside of herself. She felt, in the midst of her gratitude, a small resentment: that Curt could, with a few calls, rearrange the world, have things slide into the spaces that he wanted them to" (204). Without psycho-analyzing Ifemelu too directly, it would seem that the assault continues to leave its imprint upon her as she has a difficult time accepting that she is deserving of victory especially after suffering financial indignity and a sexually traumatizing experience. But Ifemelu's recognition of injustice here is appropriate. She is right. It *is* unfair that Ifemelu's single connection to wealth makes the immigration system bow at her feet whereas others must wrangle it into a shape that will permit them to stay in the country. This is one of many ways that Ifemelu begins to sharpen her culturally critical and observant eye in service of acknowledging racial and national systems of oppression.

6. There have been several studies on microaggressions and how they (and other stressors) cumulatively contribute to an imbalance in Black–white experience of anxiety as well as mortality. One such study examined what is called the "allostatic load," or "the accumulation of physiological perturbations as a result of repeated or chronic stressors in everyday life" (2). This "load" could result from the virulence of constant gun violence in one's neighborhood, stop-and-frisk police surveillance, microaggressions, etc. The study concludes that the allostatic load partially explains higher mortality rates amongst Blacks when variables such as socioeconomic factors and health behaviors remain constant. See Duru et al. "Allostatic Load Burden and Racial Disparities In Mortality." See also Claudia Rankine, *Just Us.*

7. I say "partially" because Ifemelu's migration also changes her relationship with her body, as we see when she begins gaining weight.

8. The role of hair appears throughout the novel in numerous ways. *America-nah* opens on Ifemelu as she makes her way from Princeton, New Jersey, where she works on fellowship to an African hair salon in Trenton, New Jersey, to get her hair braided before her return to Lagos, Nigeria (which is subsequently delayed because of a suicide attempt by her younger cousin, Dike). Hair also arises as a topic when the narrator recounts Ifemelu's teenage years in Lagos and the ways that her best friend's looks are praised because she has naturally long and wavy hair whereas Ifemelu gets her hair relaxed. When Ifemelu decides to go natural, she is met with questions from her white coworkers about whether she is making a political state-ment. At the same time, her Black boyfriend Blaine questions the political signifi-cance of her blog, seeing it as talking only about frivolous things like hair and the idiosyncratic and mundane unusualness of living as a Black person in American.

9. In several interviews, Adichie remarks that her enormous popularity and rise to fame in America was part of the impetus for writing *Americanah*. Adichie also shares a good deal in common with her protagonist, which makes it difficult for readers to separate them from one another, as Nora Berning suggests (3).

10. The faces of the CEOs of companies like Microsoft, Apple, and Facebook are relatively well-known (Bill Gates, Tim Cook, and Mark Zuckerberg, respectively). But what about the rest of their employees? What about other people with a great deal of power at these seemingly omniscient companies? These people are not so publicly visible and therefore obscure the extent to which these companies can achieve the kind of public good that they purport to do or desire to do. And what about other omnipresent companies like Google, Wikipedia, Reddit, and so forth? Is it in the best interest of their CEOs to maintain a level of anonymity so as to maintain the charade of "do-gooderism"?

11. Ifemelu's politicianlike behavior is appropriate given the particular role that President Barack Obama plays in the novel. It is clear that Obama raises the specter of the Black politician as someone who must have a range of cultural fluencies, which was on especially public display during Obama's presidential campaign. Ifemelu has conversations with Blaine and his friends about Obama while he is campaigning for the Democratic nomination. This leads her to write a blog post about Obama that is seemingly apolitical, but is in fact very political: "Why Dark-Skinned Black Women—Both American and Non-American—Love Barack Obama" (264) and "Is Obama Anything but Black?" (418) and "This is Why Obama Will Do It Better" (439).

12. This transformation of the blog from an innocuous to a monstrous creature could also be read as Adichie's own critique of the internet and the way that internet fame has spun her own public image almost entirely out of her hands.

13. A peripheral interpretation of Ifemelu's control arises when the novel is paired with Noble's *Algorithms of Oppression*. Noble claims the racial bias that is inherent in the structure of the internet because of who its owners are. In some respects, Ifemelu "owns" her blog and has control over it because she decides its output. However, because Ifemelu runs her blog through a corporation called Wordpress, she enjoys the illusion of control while a larger company is in fact in control. This issue of control does not arise in the novel in any explicit way, which is why I do not address it, but it is an important avenue of thought for other scholars of Adichie's work to explore in the future.

Conclusion

1. Several terms refer to different alternatives to the traditional criminal justice system as it exists in the United States. Abolition, transformative justice, and restorative justice are just a few of the most common terms that people in decarceral movements use. All of these terms may differ in their meaning depending on

how they are weaponized and for which political discourses. But they all serve as alternatives to what their practitioners have determined to be an overly punitive and violently coercive "justice" system. In this conclusion, I discuss "abolition" only because it presents the most radical vision for a world without incarceration, but I want to acknowledge that some may see abolition as just one form of transformative or restorative justice, whereas others may say those are reformist terms that stand in opposition to abolition. As John Braithwaite writes in his article, "Restorative Justice: Assessing Optimistic and Pessimistic Accounts," "Restorative justice is a process where all the stakeholders affected by an injustice have an opportunity to discuss how they have been affected by the injustice and to decide what should be done to repair the harm" (28). Braithwaite articulates this further to explain that restorative justice calls for the victim and offender to work together with mediators and counselors to determine what justice for both may look like. Transformative justice takes a slightly different tack. "While coming from the same background as restorative justice, transformative justice (TJ) takes a bit of a bolder approach. Instead of simply seeking to restore the actors, TJ sets out to transform them for the better. As expressed by Wozniak (Transformative Justice: Critical and Peacemaking Themes Influenced by Richard Quinney), TJ seeks to change the larger social structure as well as the personal structure of those involved. Realizing the unjustness of our current criminal justice system, transformative justice wants to be productive by providing victims with answers for why they were victimized, recognizing the wrong that has occurred, providing restitution, and restoring/establishing peace and security. Highly influenced by Richard Quinney and his writings regarding critical criminology and peacemaking criminology, TJ is aware of the injustices of the world as well as the need to spread peace" (Admin, "Restorative Justice and Transformative Justice: Definitions and Debates"). Given this, abolition is a kind of transformative justice whereas restorative justice refers to a host of other, less drastic strategies for bringing healing to a victim–offender relationship.

2. For more on the proliferation of prisons in the United States, see findings from a study conducted by the Vera Institute for Justice, Chris Mai, et al., "Broken Ground: Why America Keeps Building More Jails and What It Can Do Instead." Also see organizing materials and resource database of Stop Cop City (stopcopcity. org), a protest movement that began in late 2021 against the building of the largest police training facility in the United States, the Weelaunee Forest in Atlanta, Georgia (Mira Sydow, "Abolitionists and Environmentalists in Atlanta Band Together to "Stop Cop City").

3. As I've mentioned earlier, Saidiya Hartman asserts in her book *Scenes of Subjection* that enslavement is the root of the stereotype around Black people as criminals or having tendencies toward crime. As enslaved people, Black people were literally unable to petition on their own behalf as victims of crimes in a court of law

but were more than welcome to be petitioned against as criminals. Khalil Gibran Muhammad continues the logic of this historical argument in his book *Criminalizing Blackness* by looking at the Jim Crow era and the specific ways in which laws were created to target and incarcerate Black people. Michelle Alexander also covers similar ground in her book *The New Jim Crow*.

4. There are several organizations enacting the goals of abolition and transformative/restorative justice at the local level. These organizations largely create spaces for victims and their assailants to participate in mediated dialogues with the hope of receiving the much-needed healing that can abate or stop the violence.

BIBLIOGRAPHY

Adichie, Chimamanda Ngozi. *Americanah*. New York: Alfred A. Knopf, 2013.

Adichie, Chimamanda Ngozi. "Chimamanda Ngozi Adichie: The Danger of a Single Story." TED, July 2009. www.ted.com/talks/chimamanda_ngozi_adichie_the _danger_of_a_single_story/transcript.

Admin. "Restorative Justice and Transformative Justice: Definitions and Debates." Sociology Lens Insights, March 5, 2013. https://www.sociologylens.net/topics /crime-and-deviance/11521.

Agamben, Giorgio. *Homo Sacer: Sovereign Power and Bare Life*. Stanford U. Press, 1998.

Alexander, Michelle. *The New Jim Crow: Mass Incarceration in the Age of Colorblindness*. New York: New Press, 2010.

Allen, Donia Elizabeth. "The Role of the Blues in Gayl Jones's *Corregidora*." *Callaloo* 25, no. 1 (January 2002): 257–73.

Andrews, William L. *To Tell a Free Story: First Century of Afro-American Autobiography 1760–1865*. Urbana: University of Illinois Press, 1986.

Antony, Pemberton. "Dangerous Victimology: My Lessons Learned From Nils Christie." *Temida* 19, no. 2 (2016): 257–76.

Arendt, Hannah. *On Violence*. Harcourt, Brace, Jovanovich, 1970.

Atwater, Fred. "$600 To Rape Wife? Ala. Whites Make Offer to Recy Taylor Mate!" *The Chicago Defender*, January–October 1944. Image provided by the Alabama Department of Archives and History, Montgomery, AL.

Bailey, Moya. "They aren't talking about me." Crunk Feminist Collective, March 14, 2010. www.crunkfeministcollective.com/2010/03/14/they-arent-talking-about -me/.

Bailey, Moya. "New Terms of Resistance: A Response to Zenzele Isoke." *Souls: A Critical Journal of Black Politics, Culture and Society*15, no. 4 (2014): 341–43.

Baker, Houston A. "To Move Without Moving: An Analysis of Creativity and Commerce in Ralph Ellison's Trueblood Episode." *PMLA* 98, no. 5 (October 1983): 828–45.

Balseiro, Isabel, and Zachariah Rapola, eds. *The Passport That Does Not Pass Ports: African Literature of Travel in the Twenty-First Century*. Michigan State University Press, 2020. https://doi.org/10.14321/j.ctv14t482q.

Barmann, Jay. "Stanford Rapist Brock Turner Goes Viral Again on TikTok in Ohio." *SFist*, August 22, 2022. www.sfist.com/2022/08/22/stanford-rapist-brock-turner -goes-viral-again-on-tiktok-in-ohio/.

Batson v. Kentucky, 476 U.S. 79 (1986).

Battle, Juan, and Colin Ashley. "Intersectionality, Heteronormativity, and Black Lesbian, Gay, Bisexual, and Transgender (LGBT) Families." *Black Women, Gender, and Families* 2, no. 1 (2008): 1–24.

Bell, Kamau W., director. *We Need to Talk About Cosby*. Showtime, 2022.

Berning, Nora. "Narrative Ethics and Alterity in Adichie's Novel Americanah." *CLCWeb: Comparative Literature and Culture* 17, no. 5 (2015): 9. https://doi.org /10.7771/1481-4374.2733.

Bragg, Beauty. "Racial Identification, Diaspora Subjectivity, and Black Consciousness in Chimamanda Ngozi Adichie's Americanah and Helen Oyeyemi's Boy, Snow, Bird." *South Atlantic Review* 82, no. 4 (2017): 121–38.

Braithwaite, John. *Restorative Justice & Responsive Regulation*. Oxford University Press, 2002.

Brenner, Hannah. "Beyond Seduction: Lessons Learned about Rape, Politics, and Power from Dominique Strauss-Kahn and Moshe Katsav." *Michigan Journal of Gender & Law* 20, no. 2 (2014): 225–90.

Brooks, Gwendolyn. "A Bronzeville Mother Loiters in Mississippi. Meanwhile, a Mississippi Mother Burns Bacon". *The Bean Eaters*. 1960. Hassell Street Press, 2021.

Brown, DeNeen L. "Missouri v. Celia, a Slave: She killed the white master raping her, then claimed self-defense." *Washington Post*, October 19, 2017.

Buchhandler-Raphael, Michael. "The Failure of Consent: Re-Conceptualizing Rape as Sexual Abuse of Power." *Michigan Journal of Gender and Law* 18, no. 1 (2011): 147–228.

Buckmaster, Henrietta. "Western Union Telegram from Henrietta Buckmaster to Governor Chauncey Sparks," December 29, 1944. Alabama Governor (1942–1947: Sparks) administrative files. SG012505, folder 4. Alabama Department of Archives and History, Montgomery, AL.

Buckmaster, Henrietta. "Foreword." *Equal Justice Under Law*. 1945 January–October. Alabama Governor (1943–1947: Sparks) administrative files. SG012505, folder 4, page 2. Alabama Department of Archives and History/, Montgomery, AL.

Buirski, Nancy. *The Rape of Recy Taylor*. Widescreen ed. DVD. New York: The Orchard, 2018.

Butler, Judith. *Gender Trouble: Feminism and the Subversion of Identity*. New York: Routledge, 1990.

Butler, Judith. "Performativity, Precarity and Sexual Politics." *Antropólogos Ibero-americanos en Red* 4, no. 3 (2009): i–xiii.

Butts, J. J. *Dark Mirror: African Americans and the Federal Writers' Project*. Columbus: Ohio State University Press, 2021.

Carby, Hazel. *Reconstructing Womanhood: The Emergence of the Afro-American Woman Novelist*. New York: Oxford University Press, 1987.

Catt, Carrie Chapman. "Letter from Carrie Chapman Catt to Governor Chauncey Sparks." January 19, 1945. Alabama Governor (1943–1947: Sparks) administrative files. SG012505, folder 4. Alabama Department of Archives and History, Montgomery, AL.

CBS News. "40th anniversary of Joan Little's pivotal murder acquittal". Published YouTube August 14, 2015. https://www.youtube.com/watch?v=z-rUIpcjIhQ&t=140s.

The Celia Project. University of Michigan College of Literature, Science, and the Arts, 2014. sites.lsa.umich.edu/celiaproject/.

Chang, Grace. *Disposable Domestics: Immigrant Women Workers in the Global Economy*. Chicago: Haymarket Books, 2016. (Original work published 2000). Ebook.

Christie, Nils. "The Ideal Victim." In *From Crime Policy to Victim Policy*, edited by E. A. Fattah, 17–30. Basingstoke, UK: Macmillan, 1986.

Cognard-Black, Jennifer. "'I said nothing': The Rhetoric of Silence and Gayl Jones's *Corregidora*." *NWSA Journal* 13, no. 1 (April 2001): 40–60.

Combahee River Collective. "A Black Feminist Statement," April 1977. *Monthly Review* 70, no. 8 (2019): 29–36.

Cooper, Brittany. *Eloquent Rage: A Black Feminist Discovers Her Superpower*. St. Martin's Press, 2018.

Coscarelli, Joe. "From 'Frog' to 'Fraud!': How the *New York Post* Told the DSK Story." *New York Magazine*, August 23, 2011. www.nymag.com/intelligencer/2011/08/dsk_case_new_york_post.html.

Coser, Stelamaris. *Bridging the Americas: The Literature of Paule Marshall, Toni Morrison, and Gayl Jones*. Philadelphia: Temple University Press, 1995.

Crenshaw, Kimerblé. "Demarginalizing the Intersection of Race and Sex: A Black Feminist Critique of Antidiscrimination Doctrines, Feminist Theory and Antiracist Politics." *University of Chicago Legal Forum* 140 (1989): 139–67.

Crenshaw, Kimerblé. "Mapping the Margins: Intersectionality, Identity Politics, and Violence Against Women of Color." *Stanford Law Review* 43, no. 6 (July 1991): 1241–99.

Cruz-Gutiérrez, C. "Hairitage" Matters: Transitioning & the Third Wave Hair Movement in 'Hair', "Imitation" & Americanah. In *A Companion to Chimamanda Ngozi Adichie*, edited by E.N. Emenyonu, 245–61. Woodbridge, England: Currey, 2017.

Davis, Angela. *Are Prisons Obsolete?* New York: Seven Stories Press, 2010. Ebook.

Davis, Angela. Lecture. Excellence Through Diversity Distinguished Learning Series, March 27, 2018, University of Virginia, Charlottesville, VA. www.youtube
.com/watch?v=-CdK1MTHfMA&t=5120s.

Delgado, Richard, and Jean Stefancic. *Critical Race Theory: An Introduction*. 2nd ed.
New York: New York University Press, 2012.

Diallo, Nafissatou. Interview with Robin Roberts. *ABC News Good Morning America*. Air Date: July 25, 2011. https://www.youtube.com/watch?v=lxc8rmcNr9A.

Dotson, Kristie, and Marita Gilbert. "Curious Disappearances: Affectability Imbalances and Process-Based Invisibility." *Hypatia: A Journal of Feminist Philosophy*
29, no. 4 (2014): 872–88.

Douglass, Frederick. *Narrative of the Life of Frederick Douglass, an American Slave*.
1845. Penguin Classics, 2014.

Du Bois, W. E. B., *Black Reconstruction in America, 1860–1880*. New York: Touch-
stone, 1995.

Duru, O. Kenrik, Nina T. Harawa, Dulcie Kermah, and Keith C. Norris. "Allostatic
Load Burden and Racial Disparities in Mortality." *Journal of the National Medical
Association* 104, no. 1–2 (2012): 89–95.

Erdley, Sabrina. "A Rape on Campus." *Rolling Stone*, November 14, 2014.

Evans, Martha, and Ian Glenn. "'TIA–This Is Africa': Afropessimism in Twenty-
First Century Narrative Film." *Black Camera: An International Film Journal* 2, no.
1 (Winter 2010): 14–35.

Fabre, Michel. *The Unfinished Quest of Richard Wright,* second ed. Urbana: University of Illinois Press, 1993.

Feimster, Crystal N. *Southern Horrors: Women and the Politics of Rape and Lynching*.
Cambridge, MA: Harvard University Press, 2009.

Frances, Kelly. "A Profile of a Lost Generation," *Los Angeles Time Magazine*, December 13, 1987.

Fulop, Timothy E. "'The Future Golden Day of Race': Millennialism and Black Americans in the Nadir, 1877–1901." *Harvard Theological Review* 84, no. 1 (1991): 75–
99.

George, Nelson. *Buppies, B-Boys, Baps and Bohos: Notes on Post Soul Black Culture*.
New York: HarperPerennial, 1992.

Gikandi, Simon. "On Afropolitanism." *Negotiating Afropolitanism*, BRILL, 2011,
https://doi.org/10.1163/9789042032231_003.

Gobry, Pascal-Emmanuel. "The Strauss-Kahn Defense: It Was Consensual." *Business
Insider*, May 17, 2011. https://www.businessinsider.com/.

Golding, Jonathan M., Kellie R. Lynch, and Nesa E. Wasarhaley. "Impeaching Rape
Victims in Criminal Court." *Journal of Interpersonal Violence* 31, no. 19 (2016):
3129–49.

Gordy, Cynthia. "Recy Taylor: A Symbol of Jim Crow's Forgotten Horror." The Root,
February 9, 2011. www.theroot.com/.

Greene, Christina. "'She Ain't No Rosa Parks': The Joan Little Rape-Murder Case and Jim Crow Justice in the Post–Civil Rights South." *The Journal of African American History* 100, no. 3 (Summer 2015): 428–47.

Greene, Christina. *Free Joan Little: The Politics of Race, Sexual Violence & Imprisonment.* UNC Chapel Hill Press, 2022.

Griffin, Farrah Jasmine. "Textual Healing: Claiming Black Women's Bodies, the Erotic and Resistance in Contemporary Novels of Slavery." *Callaloo* 19 (1996): 519–36.

Gross, Kali N. *Colored Amazons: Crime, Violence, and Black Women in the City of Brotherly Love, 1880–1910.* Durham, NC: Duke University Press, 2006.

Guttman, Sondra. "What Bigger Killed For: Rereading Violence Against Women in Native Son." *Texas Studies in Literature and Language* 43, no. 2 (2001): 169–93.

Hamilton, Brad. "Dominique Strauss-Kahn 'Refused to Pay' Hooker Maid for Sex." *New York Post,* July 3, 2011. www.nypost.com/2011/07/03/.

hampton, dream, executive producer. *Surviving R. Kelly.* Lifetom, 2019.

Hansberry, Lorraine. *A Raisin in the Sun.* 1959. Hampton-Brown, 1998.

Harb, Siréne. "Memory, History and Self-reconstruction in Gayl Jones's *Corregidora.*" *Journal of Modern Literature* 31, no. 3 (March 2008): 116–36.

Harney, Stefano, and Fred Moten. *The Undercommons: Fugitive Planning and Black Study.* Wivenhoe, UK: Minor Compositions, 2013.

Hartman, Saidiya. *Scenes of Subjection: Terror, Slavery, and Self-Making in Nineteenth-Century America.* New York: Oxford University Press, 1997.

Hartman, Saidiya. *Wayward Lives, Beautiful Experiments: Intimate Histories of Riotous Black Girls, Troublesome Women, and Queer Radicals.* New York: W.W. Norton, 2019.

Higginbotham, Evelyn Brooks. *Righteous Discontent: The Women's Movement in the Black Baptist Church, 1880–1928.* New York: ACLS History E-Book Project, 2005. (Original work published 1993)

Hine, Darlene C. "Rape and the Inner Lives of Black Women in the Middle West: Preliminary Thoughts on the Culture of Dissemblance." *Signs* 14 (1989): 912–20.

Hislop, Maya. "'I Love This Country, but Sometimes I Not Sure Where I Am': Black Immigrant Women, Sexual Violence, and Afropessimistic Justice in *New York v. Strauss-Kahn* and Chimamanda Ngozi Adichie's *Americanah.*" *Law and Literature* 34, no. 3 (2022): 337–62.

History.com Editors. "Carrie Chapman Catt." *History,* August 28, 2023. www.history .com/topics/womens-history/carrie-chapman-catt.

Holloway, Kali. "When You're a Black Woman, You're Never Good Enough to Be a Victim." *Jezebel,* September 11, 2014. www.jezebel.com/.

Holloway, Karla F. C. *Legal Fictions: Constituting Race, Composing Literature.* Durham, NC: Duke University Press, 2013.

hooks, bell. *Ain't I a Woman.* New York: South End Press, 1999.

Hull, Akasha (Gloria T.), Patricia Bell Scott, and Barbara Smith, eds. *All the Women Are White, All the Blacks Are Men, But Some of Us Are Brave.* New York: Feminist Press, 2015. (Original work published 1982)

Hughes, Langston. "Harlem". *The Collected Works of Langston Hughes.* 1951. Vintage Classics, 1995.

Hunter, Tera W. *To 'Joy My Freedom: Southern Black Women's Lives and Labors After the Civil War.* Cambridge, MA: Harvard University Press, 1997.

Illuzzi-Orbon, Joan, and John McConnell. "Letter to the Defense." June 30, 2011. New York Times: Documents in the Strauss-Kahn Case. Digital archive. https://archive.nytimes.com/www.nytimes.com/interactive/2011/08/22/nyregion /dsk-documents-and-court-filings.html?ref=nyregion. (This document has since been removed from this archive.)

Image of the cover of the Committee for the Equal Justice for Mrs. Recy Taylor pamphlet "Equal Justice Under the Law." May 1945. Alabama Governor (1943–1947: Sparks) administrative files. SG012505, folder 4. Alabama Department of Archives and History, Montgomery, AL. Digital. https://digital.archives.alabama.gov /digital/collection/voices/id/13940/rec/2.

INCITE!. "INCITE!–Critical Resistance Statement." 2001. www.incite-national.org /page/.

Jacobs, Harriet. *Incidents in the Life of a Slave Girl.* 1861. Dover Publications, 2001.

James Reston Jr. Collection of Joan Little Trial Materials, 1975–1976. Collection Number 04006, box 1, folder 14–16. Southern Historical Collection, The Wilson Library, University of North Carolina at Chapel Hill.

JanMohamed, Abdul R. *The Death-Bound-Subject: Richard Wright's Archaeology of Death.* Durham, NC: Duke University Press, 2005.

Jean-Charles, Régine Michelle. *Conflict Bodies: The Politics of Rape Representation in the Francophone Imaginary.* Columbus: Ohio State University Press, 2014.

Johnson, James Weldon. *The Autobiography of an Ex-Colored Man.* New York: Penguin, 1990. (Original work published 1912)

Jones, Gayl. *Corregidora.* Boston: Beacon Press, 1986. (Original work published 1974)

Kaba, Mariame. *We Do This 'Til We Free Us: Abolitionist Organizing and Transforming Justice,* edited by Tamar K. Nopper. Chicago: Haymarket Books, 2021.

Katersky, Aaron. "Dominic Strauss-Kahn's Accuser Speaks Out." ABC News, July 25, 2011. https://abcnews.go.com/US/dominique-strauss-kahns-accuser-speaks /story?id=14150192.

Kerr, Orin S. "Digital Evidence and the New Criminal Procedure." *Columbia Law Review* 105, no. 279 (2009): 279–318.

Kharis, Reema. "Shaken By Shooting, North Carolina Muslims Emerge 'Proud' One Year Later." NPR, February 10, 2016. www.npr.org/sections/codeswitch/2016 /02/10/466287677/.

King, Martin Luther Jr. "Letter from Birmingham City Jail". American Friends Service Committee, 1963.

King, Wayne. "Joan Little's Lawyer Smirks at 'Justice.'" *Charlotte Observer*, October 21, 1975.

Lacey, Marc. "Birthright Citizenship Looms as Next Immigration Battle," *New York Times*, January 4, 2011. www.nytimes.com/2011/01/05/us/politics/05babies.html.

Lockhart, P. R. "Immigrants Fear a Choice Between Domestic Violence and Deportation." *Mother Jones*, March 20, 2017. www.motherjones.com/politics/2017/03/.

Lorde, Audre. "Afterimages". *The Collected Poems of Audre Lorde*. Norton, 1997.

Lowe, Lisa. *Immigrant Acts: On Asian American Cultural Politics.* Durham, NC: Duke University Press, 1996.

Macklin, Audrey. "Truth and Consequences: Credibility Determination in the Refugee Context." Conference paper. Ottawa: International Association of Refugee Law Judges, 1998, pp. 1–7, http://alturl.com/a4szt.

Mai, Chris et al. "Broken Ground: Why America Keeps Building More Jails". *Vera Institute of Justice.* November 2019. https://www.vera.org/downloads/publications/broken-ground-jail-construction.pdf.

Malone, Noreen. "Why DSK's Accuser Might Have Decided to File Her Civil Suit in the Bronx." *New York Magazine*, August 10, 2011. www.nymag.com/intelligencer/2011/08/why_dsks_accuser_might_have_de.html.

Mbembe, Achille. "Necropolitics." *Public Culture* 15, no. 1 (2003): 11–40. doi: https://doi-org.libproxy.clemson.edu/10.1215/08992363-15-1-11.

Mbembe, Achille, and Sarah Balakrishnan. "Pan-African Legacies, Afropolitan Futures." *Transition (Kampala, Uganda)*, no. 120, 2016, pp. 28–37, https://doi.org/10.2979/transition.120.1.04.

McDowell, Deborah E. *"The Changing Same": Black Women's Literature, Criticism and Theory.* Bloomington: Indiana University Press, 1995.

McGuire, Danielle L. *At the Dark End of the Street: Black Women, Rape, and Resistance—A New History of the Civil Rights Movement from Rosa Parks to the Rise of Black Power.* New York: Alfred A. Knopf, 2010.

McNeil, Genna Rae. "The Body, Sexuality, and Self-defense in State vs. Joan Little, 1974–1975." *The Journal of African American History* 93, no. 2 (April 2008): 235–61.

Miller, Chanel. *Know My Name: A Memoir.* New York: Penguin, 2014.

Mitchell, Michele. *Righteous Propagation: African Americans and the Politics of Racial Destiny After Reconstruction.* Chapel Hill: University of North Carolina Press, 2004.

Morgan, Joan. *When Chickenheads Come Home to Roost: A Hip-Hop Feminist Breaks It Down.* New York: Simon and Schuster, 2017. (Original work published 1999)

Morrison, Toni. *Beloved.* 1987. First Vintage International edition, 2004.

Moten, Fred. *In the Break: The Aesthetics of the Black Radical Tradition.* Minneapolis: University of Minnesota Press, 2003.

Muhammad, Khalil Gibran. *The Condemnation of Blackness: Race, Crime, and the Making of Modern Urban America*. Cambridge, MA: Harvard University Press, 2010.

National Organization for Women (NOW). "*NY Post* Stoops Lower Than Usual to Discredit the DSK Accuser." *NOW*, July 13, 2011. https://now.org/blog/.

Nelson, Alondra, et al., editors. *Technicolor: Race, Technology, and Everyday Life*. New York University Press, 2001.

Netflix. *Room 2806: The Accusation*, 2020.

New York State Senate. Penal Chapter 40, Part 3, Title H, Article 130, Section 130.05 (Sex offenses; lack of consent). www.nysenate.gov/legislation/laws/PEN/130.05.

Ngai, Mae M. *Impossible Subjects: Illegal Aliens and the Making of Modern America*. Princeton, NJ: Princeton University Press, 2004.

Noble, Safiya Umoja. *Algorithms of Oppression: How Search Engines Reinforce Racism*. New York: New York University Press, 2018.

Office of the Attorney General. "Report." December 14, 1944. Alabama Governor (1943–1947: Sparks) administrative files. SG012505, folder 4. Alabama Department of Archives and History, Montgomery, AL.

Office of the Attorney General. "Supplemental Report." December 27, 1944. Alabama Governor (1943–1947: Sparks) administrative files. SG012505, folder 4. Alabama Department of Archives and History, Montgomery, AL.

Patterson, Orlando. *Slavery and Social Death: A Comparative Study*. Cambridge, MA: Harvard University Press, 2018.

Paul, Jerry. Argument to the Jury. August 14, 1975. James Reston Jr. Collection of Joan Little Trial Materials. 4006, box 1, folder 9, pp. 16–22. Southern Historical Collections, Wilson Library, University of North Carolina at Chapel Hill, NC.

Pennsylvania Consolidated Statutes. Title 18, Chapter 31, § 3101. www.legis.state.pa.us/CFDOCS/LEGIS/LI/.

Petry, Ann. *The Street*. Boston: Beacon Press, 1985. (Original work published 1946)

Puar, Jasbir K. *Terrorist Assemblages: Homonationalism in Queer Times*. Durham, NC: Duke University Press, 2007.

Rankine, Claudia. *Just Us: An American Conversation*. Minneapolis: Gray Wolf Press, 2020.

Rape, Abuse & Incest National Network (RAINN). "Public Policy: How Does Your State Define Consent?" March 27, 2016. www.rainn.org/news/how-does-your-state-define-consent.

Reston, James, Jr. *The Innocence of Joan Little: A Southern Mystery*. New York: Times Books, 1977.

Ritchie, Andrea J. *Invisible No More: Police Violence Against Black Women and Women of Color*. Boston: Beacon Press, 2017.

Ross, Marlon B. "Race, Rape, Castration: Feminist Theories of Sexual Violence and Masculine Strategies of Black Protest." In *Masculinity Studies and Feminist Theory: New Directions,* edited by Judith Kegan Gardiner, 305–43. New York: Columbia University, 2002. Ebook.

Rushe, Dominic, Ed Pilkington, and Angelique Chrisafis. "Strauss-Kahn Case Maid Sues New York Post Over Prostitute Allegation." *The Guardian,* July 5, 2011. www.theguardian.com/world/2011/jul/05/.

Sexton, Jared. "Afro-pessimism: The Unclear Word." *Rhizomes: Cultural Studies in Emerging Knowledge*, no. 29 (2016). www.rhizomes.net/issue29/pdf/sexton.pdf.

Sheen, Isaac. *The Millenial State* Issues 1–2. True Latter Day Saints' Herald, (exact date of publication unknown but between 1850–1874).

Sielke, S. *Reading Rape: The Rhetoric of Sexual Violence in American Literature and Culture, 1790–1990.* Princeton, NJ: Princeton University Press, 2002.

Spillers, Hortense. "Mama's Baby, Papa's Maybe: An American Grammar Book". *Diacritics* 17, no. 2 (1987): 64–81.

Spivak, Gayatri Chakravorty. "Can the Subaltern Speak?" In *Marxism and the Interpretation of Culture,* edited by Cary Nelson and Lawrence Grossberg. Basingstoke, 271–313. New York: Macmillan, 1988.

Spohn, Cassia, and Julie Horney. *Rape Law Reform: A Grassroots Revolution and Its Impact.* New York: Springer Science + Business Media, 1992.

Steele, Catherine Knight. "Black Bloggers and Their Varied Publics: The Everyday Politics of Black Discourse Online." *Television and New Media* 19, no. 2 (2018): 112–27.

Stop Cop City, 2022. stopcopcity.org.

Supreme Court of the State of New York. "The People of the State of New York against Dominique Strauss-Kahn." *New York Times*, August 22, 2011. https://www.documentcloud.org/documents/238252.

Sydow, Mira. "Abolitionists and Environmentalists in Atlanta Band Together to "Stop Cop City". *Yes!* March 22, 2022. https://www.yesmagazine.org/environment/2022/03/22/.

Taslitz, Andrew E. *Rape and the Culture of the Courtroom.* New York: New York University Press, 1999.

Taylor, Keeanga-Yamahtta, ed. *How We Get Free: Black Feminism and the Combahee River Collective.* Chicago: Haymarket Books, 2017.

The People of the State of New York. "Recommendation for Dismissal of Strauss-Kahn Case" in *New York vs. Dominique Strauss-Kahn,* Indictment No. 02526/2011. https://archive.nytimes.com/www.nytimes.com/interactive/2011/08/22/nyregion/dsk-recommendation-to-dismiss-case.html?hp.

Thompson, Ken. "Complaint and Demand for Jury Trial". *Nafissatou Diallo vs.*

Dominique Strauss-Kahn. Filed 08 August 2011. Bronx, NY. https://archive
.nytimes.com/www.nytimes.com/interactive/2011/08/22/nyregion/dsk-documents
-and-court-filings.html?ref=nyregion.

Thuma, Emma L. *All Our Trials: Prisons, Policing, and the Feminist Fight to End Violence.* Urbana: University of Illinois Press, 2019.

U.S. Citizenship and Immigration Services. I-589, Application for Asylum
and for Withholding of Removal". doi: https://www.uscis.gov/sites/default/files
/document/forms/i-589.pdf.

U.S. House of Representatives, Resolution 194: Expressing Regret for the State of Al-
abama's Involvement in the Failure to Prosecute Crimes Committed Against Recy
Taylor, H.J. Res. 194, 112th Cong. (2011). www.arc-sos.state.al.us/ucp/B11122AA
.AP5.pdf.

Walker, Alice. *The Color Purple.* First Washington Square Press Printing, 1983.

Watorski, Al. "Postcard from Bronx Resident to Governor Chauncey Sparks."
August 15, 1945. Alabama Governor (1943–1947: Sparks) administrative files.
SG012505, folder 4. Alabama Department of Archives and History, Montgomery,
AL. Personal scan. [postcard image]

Weheliye, Alexander. *Habeas Viscus: Racializing Assemblages, Biopolitics, and Black
Feminist Theories of the Human.* Duke University Press, 2014.

Wells, Ida B. *Southern Horrors: Lynch Law in All Its Phases.* New York: New York Age
Print, 1982. (Original work published 1892) www.archive.org/details/southern
horrors14975gut.

Weizman, Eyal. *Forensis: The Architecture of Public Truth.* Berlin: Sternberg Press,
2014.

Wilderson, Frank B., III. *Afropessimism.* New York: Liveright, 2020.

Wilderson, Frank B., III. *Incognegro: A Memoir of Exile & Apartheid.* South End
Press, 2008.

Wilderson, Frank B., III, Hartman, Saidiya, Steve Martinot, Jared Sexton, and
Hortenese J. Spiller. *Afro-pessimism: An Introduction.* Minneapolis: Racked &
Dispatched, 2017.

Williams, Patricia J. *The Alchemy of Race and Rights: Diary of a Law Professor.* Cambridge, MA: Harvard University Press, 1991.

Winfrey, Oprah. 75th Annual Golden Globe Awards, January 7, 2018, Beverly Hilton
Hotel, Beverly Hills, CA. Cecil B. DeMille Award Acceptance Speech. NBC, 30
December 2019, www.nbcnews.com/pop-culture/tv/. Transcript.

Wozniak, John F. *Transformative Justice: Critical and Peacemaking Themes Influenced by Richard Quinney.* Lexington Books, 2008.

Wright, Richard. *Native Son,* Revised and abridged edition. New York: Harper Pe-
rennial Modern Classics, 2003. (Original work published 1940)

Wynter, Sylvia, and David Scott "The Re-enchantment of Humanism: An Interview with Sylvia Wynter." *Small Axe* 8 (September 2000): 119–207.

X, Malcolm, and Alex Haley. *The Autobiography of Malcolm X*. New York: Grove Press, 1965.

Xifra, Jordi. "Sex, Lies, and Post-Trial Publicity: The Reputation Repair Strategies of Dominique Strauss-Kahn." *Public Relations Review* 38, no. 3 (2012): 477–83.

INDEX